Today's Encouragement

Rick DeFoore

Published by Rick DeFoore, 2023.

While every precaution has been taken in the preparation of this book, the publisher assumes no responsibility for errors or omissions, or for damages resulting from the use of the information contained herein.

TODAY'S ENCOURAGEMENT

First edition. October 6, 2023.

ISBN: 979-8223700654

Written by Rick DeFoore.

Introduction

This book of daily devotional messages is designed to encourage people who believe in God, and who accept Jesus as His Son and as Savior. It can be encouraging to others, as well, but the greatest blessing is knowing Christ and accepting all that His Gift of Eternal Life can bring us.

We are incredibly blessed to live in an age when the Word of God, the Bible, is readily available to almost everyone, and when there is a wealth of Christian music as well, which supports the Word and focuses our minds and hearts on the many wonderful truths in God's word.

Each devotional is short and consists of a Bible verse, a focal point phrase, a few thoughts on this point, a prayer, and a hyperlink to a Christian song consistent with the scripture.

If you will make a daily habit of spending a few moments with God, thinking about who He is, what He has done, what He has taught us, His many wonderful gifts and blessings and promises, and How much He loves us, then your life will be blessed, and you will be changed. Not by me or the thoughts in this devotional book, but by His power at work in your life.

May God's immeasurable love and unlimited grace fill your heart and mind as you dedicate yourself to spending time with Him daily.

To receive the latest devotionals messages in your email, subscribe at
https://todays-encouragement.com/

January 1

Today's Encouragement is Philippians 4:9 NLT *Keep putting into practice all you learned and received from me—everything you heard from me and saw me doing. Then the God of peace will be with you.*

Then the Peace of God –

Philippians 4 is rich in "how-to live" wisdom. Beginning with (v4), "Be full of joy!", (v6) Don't worry! Pray instead! Ask and thank God! Then His peace! (v8) Fix your thoughts on these things! and finally, (v9) keep doing these things!

I'm a "how-to"' guy, I need a practical approach for anything I try to do... keep it simple, please! And Paul does this for us in Philippians 4. A process, a mindset, a checklist (thank you!) for moving:

From – a life of fear, worry, anxiety... To – a life of God's Perfect Peace.

He even ends the instruction with this promise...Do these things... live this way... make these choices and THEN the Peace of God will be with you!

My friend, God's Perfect Peace is not a mystery, it is not unattainable, it is not a "someday, by and by, when we all get to heaven, then things will be ok." It is NOW! God's Peace is available NOW to you and me...

Slowly read and absorb Philippians 4:4-9. Practice what it says, my brothers and sisters, and, as Paul promises... "*Then the peace of God will be with you!*"

Amen, Lord, we desperately need Your peace, help us to do our part, because we know You have already done Your part!

"He Is Our Peace"
Maranatha Singers
https://youtu.be/hrdo7e9JJTY

January 2

Today's Encouragement is John 1:4-5 ESV *In him was life, and the life was the light of men. The light shines in the darkness, and the darkness has not overcome it.*

The light of men –

Jesus is Life, and He is the Light. He is the source of everything (v3) including light. His light still shines in the darkness, my friend.

In the darkness of ignorance, of sin, of hopelessness, of depression, of illness, of poverty, of fear, of loneliness... whatever darkness we face, whatever circumstances surround and threaten... His Light will completely dispel... More than just bringing the ability to see, His Light illuminates every shadow, every darkened crevice, every sin-filled infection, His Light purifies. No darkness can remain in His Glorious Light.

Thank You, Lord Jesus, for being everything to us! You are Brilliant Light, and so much more! Illuminate the darkness within us, cleanse us with Your Perfect Light!

"Isn't He"
Natalie Grant
https://youtu.be/obVB0BB8VHo

January 3

Today's Encouragement is Matthew 14:28 NLT *Then Peter called to him, "Lord, if it's really you, tell me to come to you, walking on the water."*

Tell me –

When we sense God leading us, speaking to us, and guiding us in a direction, we often ask Him for confirmation. Here Peter was asking Jesus for confirmation that it really was Him walking on the water. (Really Peter, you needed reassurance that it was Jesus who was walking on water?)

We are such simple beings, so prone to doubt and distraction, constantly asking Him for signs, reassurance, proof of His Power, His Love, or His Word.

When do we become mature in our faith? To move from doubt to faith, from questions to belief, from testing to trust? For some, this may never come. Jesus described that the love of many will grow cold Matt. 24:12. *But, my Friends, we are not among those growing colder, but rather among those growing warmer in our faith!*

This request of Peter served to increase his faith in Christ, while also revealing the fallibility of man.

How did Peter reflect on this experience the day after? How did he relay this story to those who listened to his teaching for decades afterward?

Is it possible that this story of faith, doubt, focus, distraction, and God's power brought about by Peter's impetuous statement... has strengthened the faith of millions?

What experience of faith have you known? Whom could it encourage in their faith? Will you share it?

Father God, help us simple fumbling people to remember each time You have spoken, whispered, suggested, or confirmed Your word to us, and help us to encourage others, Father, just as You have encouraged us!

"My Story"
Big Daddy Weave
https://youtu.be/rc9IuR3ky7o

January 4

Today's Encouragement is Isaiah 38:20 ESV *The Lord will save me, and we will play my music on stringed instruments all the days of our lives, at the house of the Lord.*

All the days of our lives –

One of the greatest joys of my life is playing guitar and singing God's praises. With or without others present... He is always present, and He always enjoys my praise and worship. (Though it might not sound so great to others, my Father enjoys it!)

This scripture is the last line of King Hezekiah's prayer of gratitude after he was healed from a life-threatening condition. He gratefully praised God and then promised to praise Him... all the days of his life. But he failed to keep that promise.

We do that too – don't we? We experience God's grace and are then filled with gratitude and promise Him our faithfulness.... Only to soon fail to keep that promise...

Friend, His grace continues even when we are unfaithful. 2 Timothy 2:*13 If we are unfaithful, he remains faithful, for he cannot deny who he is.* And we can return to Him, to our promised faithfulness, at any time, by His Grace, and still strive to do as we have promised and be faithful. He is always ready to accept us!

Thank You, Father. that You keep no record of the wrongs we commit, no matter how many times we fail, Your perfect love and grace are still there for us, You are faithful!

"Faithful God"

Gateway Worship

https://youtu.be/WsiZoiqC_HQ

January 5

Today's Encouragement is Psalm 23:6 NLT Surely your goodness and unfailing love will pursue me all the days of my life, and I will live in the house of the Lord forever.

Live in the house of the Lord –

I've often had this thought when we are caring for people who are struggling so deeply: "We can help you. You, who struggle with accepting God's Grace and Love. You, who struggle with addiction, anxiety, fear, insanity. Come into our home for a while and experience God's Love here in action. No one is able to resist God's Love. By coming to live here, you leave your environment with its problems, triggers, and negative relationships, and while that old environment will not change, you can, and you will be changed" ...you will become a new creation in Christ. (2 Corinthians 5:17)

I know there are many problems with this idea... but, my friend, Is it possible that –

this is exactly God's thought for His children?... Is this His invitation, that we would come to live in His house... come to dwell, to abide, to remain, to live with Him and so become transformed into His family, his children, His likeness? Not someday by and by, but now, in spirit and in truth, you and me, dwelling with Him!

As humans, we have to acknowledge that can't transform others, as much as we might want to.

But He is able! He can and does Transform! We can come to live in His house, dwell with Him, become a part of God's family, and become reborn into a new life as His children... rebirthed from our previous life into a new nurturing, loving, relationship with our Perfect Father. And He now prepares us for the rest of our new life, now living within His family.

Help us to dwell in Your house, Lord, in spirit and in truth.

"Dwell in Your House"

Hillsong

https://youtu.be/aSqU6iLgXbk

January 6

Today's Encouragement is Philippians 4:8 NLT And now, dear brothers and sisters, one final thing. Fix your thoughts on what is true, and honorable, and right, and pure, and lovely, and admirable. Think about things that are excellent and worthy of praise.

Fix your thoughts –

Modern psychology acknowledges that our positive or negative thinking has great power over our outlook, our performance, and our direction in life. Ancient philosophers acknowledge this... as do many others. And we as Christians are advised repeatedly that we need to believe, to trust, to focus our minds and hearts on what is true and right and pure, which is Our Lord Jesus.

What we are exposed to in life usually determines what we think about, doesn't it? That TV show, that YouTube video, that Facebook post... what our "friends" have said about us, what our parents said about us... this world has every opinion, comment, suggestion, condemnation, and praise possible about you and me, and every other subject under the sun! Yet, only One opinion matters, and it's not yours or mine. It's not Facebook, your BFF, or your spouse... Only God's truth matters.

As we strive (it is work!) to think about and to fix our thoughts on things that are worthy, things that are excellent and worthy of praise... this world clamors for our thoughts! Because our thoughts control our behavior. God's best for us is that we focus on His truth, His power, His blessings, His perspective of life, of time, and of everything. By fixing our minds on Him, we rise above the din of this world, the clamoring for the attention of this "'look-at-me-selfie world"!

Help us to choose to Fix our Eyes on You, Lord, on Your world on Your plan, on Your character, Your love, and Your mercy! Only You are worthy of our praise, or our attention!

"I Fix My Eyes on You"
Tommy Walker
https://youtu.be/K_b6UnKvEF8

January 7

Today's Encouragement is Colossians 4:2 ESV *Continue steadfastly in prayer, being watchful in it with thanksgiving.*

Continue Steadfastly –

The Amplified Bible reads: *Be earnest and unwearied and steadfast in your prayer* [life], *being* [both] *alert and intent in* [*your praying*] *with thanksgiving.*

Continue Steadfastly—Don't give up, Be tenacious!

In prayer—pray continuously

Being watchful in it—Expect God's answers to your prayer

With thanksgiving—Be Grateful as you pray.

These keys to a healthy prayer life guide us to consider how we are praying, and how we approach God, Creator, and Father.

Father God, help us to continue to pray steadfastly, expectantly, and gratefully. Trusting and resting in Your power, timing, and will—alone.

"Steadfast"

Sandra McCracken

https://youtu.be/G5PGwsgYrCs

January 8

Today's Encouragement is John 6:61 NLT *Jesus was aware that his disciples were complaining, so he said to them, "Does this offend you?"*

Complaining –

In chapter 6 John relates the complaints of the Pharisees (v41), and even some of Jesus' disciple's complaints (v60).

My friend, our complaining, especially about what Jesus says, is part of our human condition and fallen nature. It is not constructive but rather indicates our doubt, our questioning, and even our distrust. Some of us have elevated it to an art form! Social media makes it so easy to air our unbridled thoughts!

Jesus had said in John 6:41 *"I am the bread that came down from heaven."* And in (v51) *"Anyone who eats this bread will live forever; and this bread, which I will offer so the world may live, is my flesh."*

Of course, it was a shocking thought, and while He was speaking metaphorically, the example was just too graphic for them to accept... and many deserted Him (v66).

When we disagree with Jesus we are on dangerous ground. So many have found and clung dearly to some issue, concept, or statement of His and said, "I just can't believe that." As these deserting disciples did... they focused on this issue, which they didn't understand, and said "No more!"

My friend, the journey of discipleship is an exploration, with new truths and new revelations occurring regularly. Our guide in this journey is His Word and His Holy Spirit. We must choose to trust Him, what He says, and where He leads, even when we cannot yet fully understand.

Father, Help us have faith to believe what You have said, even though we do not yet understand.

"Do I Trust You"
Twila Paris
https://youtu.be/GkQ1O-40BGY

January 9

Today's Encouragement is Isaiah 59:21 NLT *"And this is my covenant with them," says the Lord. "My Spirit will not leave them, and neither will these words I have given you. They will be on your lips and on the lips of your children and your children's children forever. I, the Lord, have spoken!"*

I, the Lord, have spoken –

God has spoken. Centuries ago. The same prophet, a vessel who earlier spoke with complete accuracy of the Messiah (chapter 53) now proclaims that His Spirit will not leave us, nor His words, what's more... His words will be on our lips and the lips of our children and their children and each successive generation... forever.

These are God's proclamation, His Words—not mine. We choose to believe it, or to casually set it aside with, "Ah, the Old Testament, how nice to have this history book."

Did God somehow change? Is He any different at the time of Jesus' birth, in Isaiah's day, in our day? Are the words He inspired His prophets to speak and to write, no longer filled with the power as when He first spoke to them? Malachi 3:6a NLT, *"I am the Lord, and I do not change."*

My friend, God's Word is truth. His Word, His promise is inviolate, pure, unchanging, living, and alive. (Hebrews 4:12)

And He spoke these words as a Covenant with us! He doesn't change, His Word and His covenant promises are eternal!

Lord, thank You for Your glorious promises, Your covenants, and Your Word which endures forever.

"All Flesh Is Like the Grass"
Fernando Ortega
https://youtu.be/cb4xp9XkKsk

January 10

Today's Encouragement is John 6:56-57 NLT *"Anyone who eats my flesh and drinks my blood remains in me, and I in him. I live because of the living Father who sent me; in the same way, anyone who feeds on me will live because of me."*

Feeds on me –

Jesus' words, "Anyone who eats my flesh and drinks my blood...feeds on me," are still as shocking to us today as they were 2000 years ago. These words drove people away from Him, rather than drawing them to Him. It is offensive to all of us to think of this act!

Now we know today, as perhaps a few did when hearing this for the first time, that Jesus spoke metaphorically, for when He broke bread and served wine at His last supper He proclaimed, "This is my body and my blood." Yet, at the time when He spoke these words, this extremely hard-to-accept truth was confusing and offensive!

Why, Lord? Why drive people away? Why use such an extreme symbol to teach us? Why was this necessary?

Is it possible, my friend, that Jesus knew who would be able to accept this truth and who would not? Is it possible that He had a purpose and plan as He spoke? Is it possible that He knew exactly... What. He. Was. Doing. At. All. Times? Of course, He did!

Then what possible reason for such an offensive truth? The Passover Lamb from Exodus was sacrificed and eaten, and its blood was placed on the doorposts... in order to save the people of God.

And in the same way, Jesus, the Lamb of God, was killed, sacrificed, and crucified on Passover. He had just served His disciples the bread and wine of His body at this Last Supper, the Passover meal, the very night He was arrested. They fed on Him. This was the fulfillment of the symbolism of the Exodus Passover, centuries before, now realized, and eternal!

Jesus didn't mind that some would be offended by His message, He brought the Truth, and spoke the Truth, without regard to the sensitivities of mankind.

Father, we thank You for the pure truth, without the taint of our human sensitivity, without "political correctness." It may be difficult to accept at times, Lord, yet we still choose, by faith, to follow You, and to believe You always!

"I Am the Bread of Life"

John Michael Talbot

https://youtu.be/Qys6Yh2nq7A

January 11

Today's Encouragement is Revelation 1:12-18 NLT *When I turned to see who was speaking to me, I saw seven gold lampstands. And standing in the middle of the lampstands was someone like the Son of Man. He was wearing a long robe with a gold sash across his chest. His head and his hair were white like wool, as white as snow. And his eyes were like flames of fire. His feet were like polished bronze refined in a furnace, and his voice thundered like mighty ocean waves. He held seven stars in his right hand, and a sharp two-edged sword came from his mouth. And his face was like the sun in all its brilliance. When I saw him, I fell at his feet as if I were dead. But he laid his right hand on me and said, "Don't be afraid! I am the First and the Last. I am the living one. I died, but look–I am alive forever and ever! And I hold the keys of death and the grave."*

When I saw Him –

This description of the resurrected Jesus Christ has always amazed me! Such glory! Such power! Such holiness! And of course, the King of kings and Lord of Lords is far beyond what we can ever describe or comprehend with our limited human mind and imagination.

As you listen to this worship music, will you, please – meditate on, picture in your mind, standing, kneeling, or lying before Him, this Jesus, and then – worship Him? Embrace Him in worship. Just you, worshiping Him.

Everything else is merely shadows in the light of His Presence.

Will u dare? Will you surrender to simply...

Worship Him?

Lord, help us, inadequate as we are, to worship You, to envision You in your glory, and so gain a new understanding of Your holiness.

"When I Look Into Your Holiness"
    Maranatha! Music
    https://youtu.be/jfIT3rooJWQ

January 12

Today's Encouragement is Luke 4:20 NLT *He* [Jesus] *rolled up the scroll, handed it back to the attendant, and sat down. All eyes in the synagogue looked at him intently.*

Looked at him intently –

True confession, our little Yorkie prompted this thought. She was never more alert, her ears were perked up, she stood perfectly still, and focused intently on... My wife preparing her food! Waiting expectantly in rapt attention. Every day.

My friend, could we not be so focused? Looking intently to Our Lord in eager anticipation, hanging on His every word. Could we be so focused on Him? On His Word, on His worship? Just for a few minutes each week, even every day? Could we be hungrily attentive, looking to Him intently, to be fed by His hand?

Our little dog was this way every day for the one who was feeding her.

Lord, grant us an intensity of focus on You, on Your Word. You have the Words of Life, our daily food; You are the nourishment we need!

"Your Word Awakening"

Music

https://youtu.be/dEktQ7JUdK0

January 13

Today's Encouragement is John 8:37 ESV [Jesus said,] *"I know that you are offspring of Abraham; yet you seek to kill me because my word finds no place in you."*

Finds no place –

Jesus exposed the truth to the religious leaders of His day, He pulled no punches, He laid it out clearly to them. And He bluntly explained why they were trying to kill Him.

He said you are trying to kill me because – "my word finds no place in you!"

The encouragement for us as His followers, as believers in Jesus, is just the opposite! His word, His Truth, the Word of God as revealed in this Bible we treasure... finds its place in us!

When we read or hear His Truth, His Word, it rings true! Our heart, our mind says 'Yes! This- is The Truth! This- is what I choose to believe! This is my hope! This- I want to build my life upon!"

This recognition, this acceptance, this embracing of His Truth, His word, His message, His love, grace, and mercy... this, my friend, is His Word finding a place within us!

Tragically, some hear or read His words and are unaffected... His words find no place in them, just as happened in the arrogant religious leaders Jesus so truthfully admonished. They have no eyes to see nor ears to hear. Many turn away from Him even today.

Yet for us, His Word finds a place, a home, within us, like a child nestling in its mother's embrace...

Father, fill us with Your Word, Your Truth. We accept and receive and embrace the Good News that Jesus is and which He taught and which Your Holy Spirit still teaches us today! We hide Your Word in our hearts!

"My Place Is with You"
Clay Crosse
https://youtu.be/r-0gtTQnm-4

January 14

Today's Encouragement is John 9:11 NLT *He told them, "The man they call Jesus made mud and spread it over my eyes and told me, 'Go to the pool of Siloam and wash yourself.' So, I went and washed, and now I can see!"*

So I went –

This blind man obeyed Jesus. Jesus told him to go to the pool and wash... so he did! He obeyed, and his eyes, blind from birth, now saw!

Our relationship with God is most often a two-way transaction. He speaks, suggests, or commands... and then we choose to obey or not.

I confess I've never liked the word or the idea of obedience. Something (not Him!) within me recoils at it and says 'No way! I'm the master of my own destiny! I decide how I live, and what I will or won't do! Nobody is gonna tell me what to do!!!"

On the other hand, I've also learned, through many years of hard knocks, that I sometimes don't make very good decisions, that my bullheadedness, my "I'm-my-own-man attitude" is often at its strongest right before a magnificent fail!

Friends, we have a loving Father. He has given us the gift of wisdom in His book, a treasure trove of truth. We are free to ignore it– to our great harm– or to immerse ourselves within it–to our great blessing. And each time we fail to use His wisdom, He has provided g sufficient for our every need.

Will you determine, along with me, again today, to live according to God's wisdom, His ways, and His truth? To simply choose... to obey?

Father, thank You for the wisdom You have so kindly provided for us, and the grace which removes and completely erases all our failures! Help us to obey! Help us to simply do what You say to do! We ask in Jesus' Name.

"Obey"
Soul Survivor
https://youtu.be/JtMxxE9mm9c

January 15

Today's Encouragement is 2 Corinthians 5:21 ESV *For our sake he made him to be sin who knew no sin, so that in him we might become the righteousness of God.*

We might become –

Among the many mysteries of God's plans, purposes, and provisions for His children... and as a loving Father cares for the needs of His own children, even before it is known, so has our Father prepared for us, before we know what we need...

Even so, God has prepared, set in place, arranged, and designed that we, all who believe in Jesus as Lord and Savior, ... are the Righteousness of God!

Before, we were Sin, covered in it, living in a pit of it, wallowing in it, unable to escape in any way. It was us! –And Jesus only, was the righteousness of God! He was pure and completely Right with God, as His Beloved Son, Who pleased the Father so much!

Then this perfect and obedient, Son... took our place... in Divine Exchange He changed places with us, becoming our Sin (*made Him to be sin*). He did this not merely to cleanse us, but also, my friend, He then gave us – His Righteousness!!! His perfect, right-standing relationship with the Father!

In the beautiful parable of the prodigal son, upon his repentant arrival at his father's house, the son was clothed with "the best robe" (Luke 15:22) from his father. The robe of righteousness. And we are also (Galatians 3:27) clothed with Christ.

My friend, through faith, by God's decree, by this ultimate act of Grace—We are the Righteousness of God!

Father, help us to clearly see this amazing exchange of our sin for Christ's Righteousness. The words, "Thank You" are completely inadequate, for we are amazed and humbled at Your Grace!

"Divine Exchange"
Charity Gayle
https://youtu.be/vPnjyVREIM4

January 16

Today's Encouragement is John 14:27 ESV *Peace I leave with you; my peace I give to you. Not as the world gives do I give to you. Let not your hearts be troubled, neither let them be afraid.*

Let not –

Jesus spoke these words of peace to his disciples on the last night He spent with them before His earthly death.

Focus with me on the last sentence. "Let not"—Jesus' words are not carelessly spoken, but rather perfectly chosen to communicate His truth. And this phrase "let not...neither let" clearly implies a role and responsibility that rests with us... in experiencing God's peace.

He gave us God's Perfect Peace, it is ours, it is available, and yet, we must not allow our hearts to be troubled or afraid. God does His part in making His perfect peace available to all who believe, then we must do our part.

We can live within His perfect peace by choosing to trust in Him, choosing to dwell within His presence, and choosing to worship and honor Him sincerely, but we must also 'Let Not'... by choosing to refuse to let doubt, fear, and anxiety have any place in our hearts and minds.

"Let not" implies that we would have to allow fear and worry to have a place in our hearts. It is a decision we make day by day, moment by moment.

His peace is already ours, already available. We make the choice, my friend, to live in His peace and to reject the fear and worry of this world.

Father God, help us to recognize our role in receiving Your Peace, give us strength and understanding, and the courage to refuse fear, worry, and doubt. We ask in Jesus' Name.

"Let Not Your Heart Be Troubled"
    Jillian Edwards
    https://youtu.be/khLMaoKllUA

January 17

Today's Encouragement is Leviticus 18:4-5 NLT *You must obey all my regulations and be careful to obey my decrees, for I am the Lord your God. If you obey my decrees and my regulations, you will find life through them. I am the Lord.*

You will find life –

Sadly, most new believers aren't taught obedience but rather, anything goes, and you're forgiven! Some older believers (I didn't say mature) also don't understand the personal responsibility for choosing to live in God's way. We simply haven't been taught.

My friends, of course, it is our faith in Christ that saves us. We accept and believe... And then,- we either begin to grow closer to Him through obedience, developing an ongoing relationship with Him..., or we do nothing different, we remain stagnant, making no effort to proactively grow in faith, and this approach ultimately results in sliding, gradually, quietly, away from Him.

As we grow in faith, we begin to grasp how wide, high, and deep His Love truly is, we learn to see His Commandments—from the Old Testament or New Testament— as "The Truth Taught to us by our Loving Father," Not a list of "dos and don'ts," but God's own wisdom—kindly provided to help us live wise and blessed lives in this world — Not perfectly, but intentionally.

Is it possible my friends that:

We are saved by grace... but we grow through obedience.

Now that you know these things, you will be blessed if you DO them. John 13:17 NIV

"Teach Me to Obey"

Bria Jean

https://youtu.be/F2Jt5C1qm-E

January 18

Today's Encouragement is John 6:41 NLT *Then the people began to murmur in disagreement because he had said, "I am the bread that came down from heaven."*

Disagreement –

They disagreed, strongly, with Jesus' words! Face to face with The Savior; in the presence of the Son of God... they murmured in disagreement.

Is it any wonder that today, people still disagree, find fault, nitpick, and critique His words? We may do so too from time to time. Much of Jesus' teaching is challenging, we can't understand and accept everything He said and still says based upon our limited human understanding... He never expected that we would. Rather we accept His words by faith. Faith is based upon trust that He Is who He said He is. We choose to believe... not because we have concrete proof, but because we so choose!

Demanding proof lowers faith to logical thinking... I have this proof; therefore, I believe.... Such a faith will not stand.

Friend don't fall into the trap of disagreement with the words of Jesus, nor the book which contains them, nor the Father, nor the Holy Spirit. Accept what God has caused to be written for us... by choice, by faith. And refuse to murmur in disagreement about these writings that have been gifted to us by our loving Father.

Lord, we choose to believe, we agree with Your Word, with everything You say and everything You are!

"God is in Control"
Covenant Worship
https://youtu.be/LVMU-viTHIw

January 19

Today's Encouragement is John 16:1 NLT *"I have told you these things so that you won't abandon your faith."*

Won't abandon –

He spoke to His disciples (the 11, Judas had been sent away) teaching and strengthening them for the time when He was physically no longer with them. And He spoke here... of them abandoning their faith!? He spoke to ensure that they did not turn away from Him in discouragement, begin to doubt Him, begin to question His Lordship, His kingdom, or His truth.

His words speak the same to us, my friends, wisdom, and encouragement... so that we, also, will not abandon our faith.

We are sadly quite capable of doing so. But it is His encouragement, His wisdom, and truth that helps us remain focused on Him, not turning away from Him who died for us, who prepares a place for us to be with Him, who cleanses us from all our sins, who has the Words of eternal life!

We are refreshed, renewed, and restored in faith as we hear His word preached, as we sing His praises, as we worship Him, pray to Him, and as we read His Word. So that we will not abandon our faith in Him!

Father, thank You for addressing our fallenness, our tendency to fall away, to abandon our core beliefs so frivolously. Thank You for Your grace which cleanses us from all our sin, failures, and frivolous thoughts. Help us to hold fast to You. And Thank You that even when we do fail, as we are wont to do, You still—hold us fast!

"He Will Hold Me Fast"
Keith and Kristyn Getty
https://youtu.be/936BapRFHaQ

January 20

Today's Encouragement is John 16:33 NLT *"I have told you all this so that you may have peace in me. Here on earth, you will have many trials and sorrows. But take heart, because I have overcome the world."*

Have peace in me –

We all need peace! We seek it in numerous ways, some healthy and some very unhealthy. But still, we seek peace, a calm mind, freedom from worry and anxiety, freedom from fears of tomorrow, regrets, and the shame of yesterday.... This peace is not only the absence of anxiety but, my friends, it is the fullness of God's Peace! He gives a peace beyond human comprehension! Philippians 4:7a NLT *Then you will experience God's peace, which exceeds anything we can understand.*

Then He clarified (v33) that we WILL have troubles and pain and sorrow in this world. We, too often, ask 'Why, Lord ?' when we go through the sorrows and trials of this life. Yet, my friend, although we do not know the "Why?" of our suffering... we can find peace in knowing that suffering comes to all people as Jesus states here... You will have many trials and sorrows! He did NOT say, "Now some of you might have a few trials and maybe a few sorrows." No, we will suffer trials and sorrows, all of us!

And, yet He spoke these words immediately after offering us His Perfect Peace and before His reassurance that He has overcome the world, including all our trials and sorrows!

Thank You, Jesus, for speaking so directly to our human needs as well as our spiritual needs. You know exactly what we need. You ARE exactly what we need! You ARE our peace!

"Draw Me Close"
Vineyard
https://youtu.be/CS3hMu2vkJw

January 21

Today's Encouragement is John 17:26 NLT *"I have revealed you to them, and I will continue to do so. Then your love for me will be in them, and I will be in them."*

Your love for me –

Consider with me:

Your Love for me- God's love for Jesus

will be in them – this Love will be in us...

that is, we will have the same love for Jesus as God the Father has for Jesus!

My friend, this is an indescribable love we're considering. It is God's perfect, unlimited, untainted, unqualified love for His only begotten Son! How much more could God love Jesus? There is no such measure! This love is complete and perfect. And this love unimaginably, is what Jesus prayed would be IN US!

Now, my friend, do we really love Jesus? Honestly, we answer, head hung low, "Well, probably not as much as I should." Or "I'm not really sure how to love Jesus." And both are true. Yet, my friend, this is Jesus' prayer for us! Does God answer Jesus' prayers? Of course! So, this prayer is already fulfilled, already granted!

This Love resides within every believer. It may be dormant, unacknowledged, ignored... but it is undeniably present. Is it possible that we can kindle this love to a blaze, can we nurture this latent love to its fullest potential? Can we? How? First, we must believe! Believe that – God's Love for Jesus now lives within us! And He will do the rest.

Lord, we need You to do this in us, we cannot. We trust that Your Love for Jesus lives within us now through Your Holy Spirit, bring this Love to life within us Lord. That You may dwell within us.

"Your Love is Life"

Tommy and Eileen Walker

https://youtu.be/gmJ-flMOVxM

January 22

Today's Encouragement is Galatians 3:27 ESV *For as many of you as were baptized into Christ have put on Christ.*

Put on Christ –

Let's face it folks, some of us are lots easier to love than others of us! Some seem to be born with innate beauty, external, and physical beauty as well as an internal, pleasant disposition; they make us feel good just being around them! They are somewhat rare, but most of us have known such a person at one time or another.

Now here's the encouraging part. When God looks at you, thinks of you, sees you... now, already... you are just such a beautiful person to Him!

Our flesh recoils! We say, "C'mon, how can you say that? Look at the mess I've made, the people I've hurt! God knows everything I've done! And just look at this physical body, aging, sagging, bulging... don't be lying to me! Ain't nothing lovable or beautiful about me!"

Friend, we see with our human eyes, our limited vision, and our memory of what we were or what we think we should be. But God! He sees us with His perfect eyes, unlimited vision, and an erased memory of what we were! (Hebrews 8:12b I will never again remember their sins.)

I once heard this analogy. Take a pen and put it in an open book, now close the book. Do you see the pen? No, we can only see the book which covers and encloses it. And in the same way, when God looks at, considers you and me... all He sees is Christ! His perfect, beloved, pure, and Holy child!

We are His, clothed with Christ, so that we are no longer the focus, but Christ alone remains!

Help us, Lord, to recognize that you do not see our sinfulness, our brokenness, but rather You see Christ's perfection when You look at us! Help us to believe, and to rest in the Grace of Jesus.

"In Christ Alone"
Adrienne Liesching
https://youtu.be/rn9-UNer6MQ

January 23

Today's Encouragement is John 18:8 NLT *"I told you that I AM he," Jesus said. "And since I am the one you want, let these others go."*

Let these others go –

When Jesus was arrested, the eleven disciples were with Him in the garden. He'd eaten the Passover meal with them, washed their feet, released Judas to betray Him, sung with them, and then prayed in the garden. He prayed passionately and ended His prayer in acceptance of God's will, not His.

Then, surrounded by His followers, the authorities and Judas came for Him. Like a modern-day SWAT team, they came with torches, lanterns, and weapons... after these 'dangerous criminals'... and Jesus gave them permission to arrest Him! He asked them whom they came for and He said, "I Am He!" In essence, "I'm the one you seek. Now, since you are after me, let these others go."

My friends, Jesus saves! He saves us today just as He saved His disciples from arrest 2000 years ago. He says to our enemies, addictions, shame, depression, fear, and failure... "Let them go!"

And then, the disciples fled... and so we can flee, leave the scene, get out of danger... because Jesus took the heat for us! Whatever threatens you and me, my friend, whether physically, emotionally, or spiritually, we are—already—freed! Jesus has paid the price for our freedom! It is time for us to walk away, flee, run from the scene. The SWAT team of our enemies, addictions, shame, depression, fear, and failure have arrested Jesus in our place... and we are free to go!

Father, help us to recognize that Jesus has—already—set us free, and that now we need to leave the scene, to flee from our enemies, addictions, shame, depression, fear, and failure... and live in the freedom and grace which Jesus died and rose again to provide for us! Thank You, Jesus!

"No Longer Slaves"
Zach Williams
https://youtu.be/dwLFp1weuA8

January 24

Today's Encouragement is John 18:36 NLT *Jesus answered, "My Kingdom is not an earthly kingdom. If it were, my followers would fight to keep me from being handed over to the Jewish leaders. But my Kingdom is not of this world."*

Not of this world –

Jesus was speaking to Pilate, who was interrogating Him after His arrest. And the question was, "Are You the King of the Jews?"

The Kingdom of Jesus, He explains here... "is not of this world." We see disease, oppression, hatred, and division (even in these not-so-United States...) There is some, but precious little, that is truly good in this world...

Bear with me please.... This world is fallen, diseased, corrupt with sin, and it is ultimately passing away (1 Corinthians 7:31). Our lives here are difficult, and we suffer trials of many kinds (James 1:2). We end our short span of 70-80 years on this planet and then... by faith in Christ alone, we enter Eternity, Paradise (Luke 23:43) with Him as King!

Our Hope is Jesus, our King, and His Kingdom which is a spiritual Kingdom, a realm where He is clearly recognized and honored as The King of kings and Lord of lords! Our Hope, our Home, is... not of this world.

Too often we fall into the trap of bemoaning (a very descriptive word) the bad things in this world. Some foolishly blame God for the fallen nature of humanity! It is We who have made a mess of it, my friends! Our Sin has caused the pain, suffering, and decay of this world! Jesus had provided for us another realm, another home, another Kingdom... where He reigns in righteousness and justice prevails! And His kingdom is our Home where we will one day rest and reign with Him (Romans 5:17)!

Father, help us to fix our hopes on Your Kingdom where Jesus reigns, and to live under Your Kingdom's rule here on this earth as well.

"The Kingdom of God"
Paul Baloche
https://youtu.be/lXc-4BOxt9M

January 25

Today's Encouragement is Matthew 26:39 NLT *He went on a little farther and bowed with his face to the ground, praying, "My Father! If it is possible, let this cup of suffering be taken away from me. Yet I want your will to be done, not mine."*

Your will, not mine –

This verse is overflowing with truth and meaning, but let's just focus on this last phrase as it applies to our faith. *"Your will Father, not mine."*

This is the crux of it, my friends, our struggle of faith. We all inherently and passionately desire and strive for our own way! We are born as selfish, grasping, self-willed creatures clawing our way toward whatever our hearts desire. This is our self-will in full exposure. And it's pretty hideous!

However, a life of faith is predicated, built upon, and upheld by the very painful and challenging - abandonment of our own self-will.

The world, on the other hand, idolizes self-determination, with cries of, "Be all you can be! Just Do it! Don't let anything stop you! Pursue Your Dreams!"

But God's ways, infinitely higher than our ways (Isaiah 55:8-9), are not the ways of man, of this world. And rather than exalting our own will, desires, and needs, every man... (including Jesus in this passage!) must lay aside ourselves, our dreams, desires, and will, in favor of God's Will, His perfect way, and His good plans for us.

And my friend... He has good plans for you! Jeremiah 29:11 NLT *"For I know the plans I have for you," says the Lord. "They are plans for good and not for disaster, to give you a future and a hope."*

Father, thank You for allowing us to choose Your will, Your ways, and Your plans rather than our own. You alone know what we should do, and how we should live. Give us the humility and the faith to release our will and our desires to You. Be Lord of our lives, Father, we ask in Jesus' Name.

"I Surrender"
Hillsong United
https://youtu.be/xv2KH-OIhH4

January 26

Today's Encouragement is John 21:17 NLT *A third time he asked him, "Simon son of John, do you love me?" Peter was hurt that Jesus asked the question a third time. He said, "Lord, you know everything. You know that I love you." Jesus said, "Then feed my sheep."*

Then feed my sheep –

Pretty simple, well, it's at least clear. You say you love me, then feed my sheep. The two are connected, not my thought, but Jesus' words.

So, it must be that Loving Christ is demonstrated, fulfilled, and actualized, by feeding His sheep. Notice He didn't indicate which sheep, other than Mine, so, is it possible that He was including all? The lost sheep, found sheep, dirty sheep, fat and happy sheep, lazy and dull sheep, wandering and obedient sheep, beautiful sheep, ugly sheep.... All are certainly His. Some are certainly lost (not yet found), some are certainly determined to go their own way, some make stupid decisions, (so glad I never did that!) and some stay right where they're supposed to be.

He didn't distinguish! Are we then to distinguish which sheep we are to feed?

Remember, Peter is the rock upon which Jesus built His church. What Jesus spoke to Peter 2000 years ago He still says to His church today. "Feed my sheep."

Jesus is the Bread of Life, and He is the Living Water! The Word of God is our food, and—His Word, His Mercy, Grace, Forgiveness, and Redemption, all of Him... this is what we need to 'feed' to His sheep.

And in so doing my friends... we are feeding His sheep... we then are—loving Jesus.

Father, help us to show Your love to those around us, to support, care for, and nurture our brothers and sisters in Christ, and as we feed Your sheep in this way, we are loving You.

"Loving My Jesus"
Casting Crowns
https://youtu.be/OnJFGtAXxGs

January 27

Today's Encouragement is Psalm 95:6-7a ESV *Oh come, let us worship and bow down; let us kneel before the Lord, our Maker! For he is our God, and we are the people of his pasture, and the sheep of his hand.*

Let us worship –

This isn't a command to attend church! My friend, this is an invitation to be in God's presence! At any time, in any place we are invited, encouraged, counseled... to come into the presence of our Lord, to bow down before His glory and majesty, to acknowledge His sovereignty over us and over all that is and ever will be. We will worship and bow down to no other! But to our God, Father, Savior, Master...and Friend... to Him alone... Yes, of course, we will both bow down and worship Him!

This invitation is to come before the One God who Loves us more than we can possibly ask or imagine. God so loved that He gave up His Son (John 3:16). Nothing can separate us from God's love (Romans 8:39). And before this love... for God IS love (1 John 4:8) we are invited to worship, to bow, to humble our own pride before His infinite majesty.

Because we are His people of His pasture, we live in and under His care, we are as sheep tenderly cared for by His Own Hand. His very hand sees to our needs and care.

Such a Father, perfect in every way! This is Our God! We will come to You, Lord! We will Worship You alone. We will bow down before You!

Help us, Lord, to lay aside our pride and kneel, both physically and spiritually, to You alone, to Your care and provision for us. For You are our God!

"Come, Let Us Worship "

Fernando Ortega

https://youtu.be/NpWXhEhA6RQ

January 28

Today's Encouragement is Luke 17:20-21 NLT *One day the Pharisees asked Jesus, "When will the Kingdom of God come?" Jesus replied, "'The Kingdom of God can't be detected by visible signs. You won't be able to say, 'Here it is!' or 'It's over there!' For the Kingdom of God is already among you".*

Already among you –

Jesus explained that the Kingdom of God had come, it was "already" among the people, not some far-off event, not only a Heavenly existence, not a physical place or time... but already present!

When Pilate interrogated Jesus, he was told by the Lord, *"My Kingdom is not of this world."* (John 18:36).

These two seem to conflict on the surface, first He says, "The Kingdom is already among you," then He says, It is not if this world." Let's look deeper.

We know that Jesus is the King of Kings. Is it possible that wherever the King is, this is the Kingdom of God? The realm of an earthly king extended to the borders, the limits, of that kingdom. He had no power nor authority in another realm or kingdom.

My friends, Are there any borders or limits to the Kingdom of God?

Now, we are free to ignore His Kingship and authority, and so many do sadly, or we are free to recognize, respond, embrace, and surrender to His authority as our King. We are then, already! within His Kingdom—because we acknowledge Jesus as our Lord!

Father God, help us to choose, by faith, to live within Your Kingdom, according to Your ways, Your teaching, and Your Truth, rather than the ways, teaching, and truth of the kingdom of this world. You are our God, and Jesus is our King!

"The Kingdom of God"
Paul Baloche
https://youtu.be/QSaMF6U9cbM

January 29

Today's Encouragement is Matthew 16:15-16 NLT *Then he asked them, "But who do you say I am?" Simon Peter answered, "You are the Messiah, the Son of the living God."*

Who do you say –

My friends, each person must decide who Jesus is... what they each "say" about Him, who each says Jesus is...

Many acknowledge Him as a great teacher or prophet, and some of us like Peter, as "Messiah, the Son of the Living God!"

The many names of Jesus are a great blessing to me, He is so wonderful, so great, that our language doesn't have (none does!) the vocabulary to express Who He Is!

But from His word, we know... that He Is:

Lord, Good Shepherd, Savior, King of kings and Lord of lords, Wonderful Counselor, Prince of Peace, Deliverer, Protector, Sustainer, Healer, Bread of Life, The Way, The Door, the Truth, The Living Water, The Word, The Son, Beloved Son, Holy One of Israel, Alpha and Omega, Immanuel, and much, much more... infinitely!

Lord Jesus, we acknowledge that we are unable to describe you. For you are unlimited by terminology, you are all this and infinitely more!

"You Are My King/Amazing Love"
Chris Tomlin
https://youtu.be/MA_cSFdUMqk

January 30

Today's Encouragement is Acts 3:19-20a ESV *Repent therefore, and turn back, that your sins may be blotted out, that times of refreshing may come from the presence of the Lord.*

Times of refreshing –

Doesn't that phrase bring to mind... contentment, joy, peace, relaxation, and happiness?

And this time of refreshing... comes from the Lord! We don't earn it or manufacture it... rather He gives it to us.

But... it comes after our genuine repentance, our turning from our sin and turning toward Him. And as we turn away from our sin, God blots it out, never to be seen again nor to haunt us... erased and removed and forgotten! And this occurs as we turn from and repent of our sin.

We need not dwell in a constant state of remorse and shame for our sin, because we are set free from that! Still, at the moment of our turning away from it, we then DO acknowledge our shame and remorse, because sin is shameful, we are shameful in our sin. But God! When we have repented, literally turned away from sin... turning to the only hope we have, our loving Father... we rest in this! This comes to us in return, times of refreshing!

Friends, sin brings misery. The wages it pays to us are death, rotten, and horrific decay. We may think we are "getting by ok" and that God's grace is sufficient to cover our intentional and habitual sin... but it is eating at our souls!

Turn with me, my friends, repent, and enjoy freedom from shame and guilt... and enjoy the grace and forgiveness of God — enjoy the times of refreshing from the Lord!

Lord God, we long for times of refreshing from You! Help us to turn back to You and accept the refreshing You provide to Your children.

"Lord, I Need You"
Matt Maher
https://youtu.be/LuvfMDhTyMA

January 31

Today's Encouragement is Exodus 3:10-12a ESV *"Come, I will send you to Pharaoh that you may bring my people, the children of Israel, out of Egypt." But Moses said to God, "Who am I that I should go to Pharaoh and bring the children of Israel out of Egypt?" He said, "But I will be with you."*

But I will be with you –

Moses was "all in" when God was telling him (in verses 7-9) that He's heard, seen, and is now, coming to deliver his people from their suffering... Moses was probably saying to himself, "Yeah, Lord! Come on – save your people!" Until... God said, matter-of-factly, "Come, I will send you."

"What? Wait! Me?"

"Who am I? Please send someone else. I don't speak very well..." Moses tried everything to get out of this call of God!

Friend, God works through people. His works are for people and done through people. He sends someone... just as He sent Jesus to provide salvation for all who believe... He had previously sent Moses, David, Elijah, and numerous others to do His work on this earth. God sends, works in, and through, those who love Him and honor Him.

And most of us respond just like Moses did... "Who? Me?"

And God replies ... "But I will be with you."

Lord God, we recognize our inadequacy for many of the challenges we face, we can only succeed if You are with us. Send us Lord, to do Your will, and Lord, thank You that You will be with us, always. Even to the end of the earth.

"Here I Am"

Lincoln Brewster

https://youtu.be/mpVtUgRtvgM

February 1

Today's Encouragement is Luke 6:46 NLT *So why do you keep calling me Lord, Lord !' when you don't do what I say?*

Do what I say –

Jesus asked this and then taught the parable of two men who had built their houses, that is, their entire lives, families, wealth, all they had... one built on a solid foundation, the other on sand.

The house built on a solid foundation is the man who hears and lives according to the Truth, the Word of God. The house on sand is the person who hears... but doesn't live according to Jesus' words.

Notice they both hear the truth. Yet, hearing isn't enough! It is necessary, but only 'doing' completes the process of hearing and doing -Which we call Obedience.

Is Jesus our Lord? Then we will do what He says. His wisdom and His truth are far superior to our ideas and thinking... we can trust Him, and we can follow Him. We can Do what He says!

"Yeah, but nobody's perfect!" That's very true, my friend, some are very much less than perfect, but some are trying! Now, we know it is our belief in Christ that saves us, faith alone! And yet... Doing is also a part of Believing ... we hear the Gospel and we either believe or not. Friends, we can choose to live according to God's word, doing what He says, as best we can... and trust that Christ always makes up for what we lack. (Matt. 5:17)

Father God, we thank You for giving us wisdom on how to live in this life, how to be safe, blessed, wise, and how to live according to Your truth. Give us eyes to see and ears to hear Your truth, and willing hearts to do what You say!

"Obedience"
Lindy and the Circuit Riders
https://youtu.be/fWxJwuz2jXg

February 2

Today's Encouragement is Romans 8:28 NLT *And we know that God causes everything to work together for the good of those who love God and are called according to his purpose for them.*

To work together –

As with every word of scripture, God-breathed and filled with His power... This verse is rich with wonderful truth.

You may ask, "So, are you saying that this pain I'm feeling is from God?" No, my friend. The Word does not say, God causes everything to happen to us... but that He 'causes everything to work together' – and for our good!

Little things and big things, happy things and sad things, joy and tragedy, trials and troubles, everything in the believer's life... God causes all this to "work together" for our Good!!! Because we love Him, and He has called us for His purpose for us!

So, when we are hurting physically, sick, lonely, or heartbroken by loss of any type... even in this... God IS working! Because He loves you immeasurably, my friend, He knows where you are and what is happening to you. Sometimes He intervenes and changes our circumstances... and sometimes He causes those difficult circumstances to "work together" for our Good!

Either way, my friends, we win! We are more than conquerors! We are His chosen children... and He is working everything together for your good... right now! We usually can't see it... but it is still His Truth! We choose to believe this by faith. Or not.

Father God, grant us enough faith, if only a mustard seed, to believe that, even in our darkest trials... You are working for our Good! Thank You, Father, for paying attention to us, knowing our needs... and for working all things together for our good! You are such a wonderful God!

"Your Love Never Fails"
Jesus Culture
https://youtu.be/kRtFi2Mw-c

February 3

Today's Encouragement is Philippians 4:8 NLT *And now, dear brothers and sisters, one final thing. Fix your thoughts on what is true, and honorable, and right, and pure, and lovely, and admirable. Think about things that are excellent and worthy of praise.*

Fix your thoughts –

Our thoughts... and managing those thoughts... are our responsibility! We are taught to "fix our thoughts" on things which are good, pure, and excellent.

What we think about determines our beliefs. And we are sadly, very easily deceived by people. Might not want to admit that, but virtually everyone has fallen prey to wrong thinking, which leads into wrong believing, and then finally to wrong actions. It's an inevitable spiral into failure.

We can fight this, counteract it by ensuring that our minds, our thoughts, are true, pure, and full of God's Truth, His Goodness, and His Love.... This is our response to, our defense against the lies and deception of this world and of our enemy.

As we strive (it is work!) to think, to fix our thoughts on things that are worthy, things that are excellent and worthy of praise... What does that mean to you?

Heal our minds, Lord, help us to focus on You and the beauty of Your creation, to refuse to be taken in by the lies of this world. Help us fix our minds on You and Your Holiness.

"Let's Think about Our God"
Tommy Walker
https://youtu.be/7SnjCV0b0dc

February 4

Today's Encouragement is Psalm 16:11 ESV *You make known to me the path of life; in your presence there is fullness of joy; at your right hand are pleasures forevermore.*

In Your presence –

We can only imagine what it is to be in the presence of the Lord. It's described in Revelation 1 and 4, and it is an overwhelming sight. David, in writing this Psalm, expressed his faith that... in the Presence of the Father... joy is full, complete, and pleasures which are indescribable are at His right hand! Will you allow yourself to imagine this for a moment?

Too often we are afraid, even terrified, of being in the presence of God, but my friends, fear is assigned to those who intend to harm us. We are among His chosen sons and daughters, so that when we come into our Loving Father's Presence... joy is full! The Father is full of joy, and so will we be!

In the beautiful parable of the prodigal son, God, portrayed as the father in this story, actually ran to His son, threw his arms around him, and began a celebration... the Father expressed fullness of joy! (Luke 15:20-24)

And that is the immeasurable love that God has for us, my friends... full of joy. He is always ready to welcome us into His presence. We just need to turn to Him. It is up to us.

Father, grant us humble hearts to turn to You and to admit our need for You, our failures, and our desire to become fully Yours. For in Your Presence... is complete joy!

"Fullness of Joy"
Shane and Shane
https://youtu.be/Uvf13Qjt4lg

February 5

Today's Encouragement is Psalm 101:4 NLT *A perverse heart shall be far from me; I will know nothing of evil.*

Know nothing of evil –

The people of the world often mock us believers who choose not to participate in the ways of the flesh. Sadly, when we do dabble in the world's ways, (sin) we are then held up as hypocrites, liars, deceivers, failures! The public failures of televangelists, true or not, are held up by the world as "proof" that Christians are all fakers, preachers are all after money, and we Christians are all just pretending to be different from the rest of the world.

The enemy of our souls is always accusing, and his favorite target is us, believers in Christ. We must "know nothing of evil" and ensure we are focused on God and His Ways and His Truth to avoid being taken in by the deceptive lies of this world.

Remember 1 Peter 5:8 NLT *Stay alert! Watch out for your great enemy, the devil. He prowls around like a roaring lion, looking for someone to devour.*

We are the targets of this enemy because we are the children of the Living God. So, as His children, we can choose to walk away from perversity, know nothing of evil, and watch out for the enemy who wants to devour us!

Father, we need You! Thank You for Your Grace that saves us! We need Your power and wisdom to be alert to the snares of the enemy, help us to choose You, and to know nothing of evil. You are, always, our Help (Psalm 45:1).

"Don't Tread on Me"
We The Kingdom
https://youtu.be/9dowS2k2TS4

February 6

Today's Encouragement is Isaiah 55:8-9 ESV *For my thoughts are not your thoughts, neither are your ways my ways, declares the Lord. For as the heavens are higher than the earth, so are my ways higher than your ways and my thoughts than your thoughts.*

Your thoughts –

A friend posted a scripture on social media, which prompted discussion, which elicited arguments...

One poster described how you couldn't take the Bible literally, it all must be viewed as an allegory, a parable, or a story. This fella in his "deep wisdom" even claimed that John the Baptist was the first Buddhist. Interesting... but I digress.

In our logical minds we evaluate information as believable or unbelievable, based on our own knowledge, and our own determination of what is logical or illogical. Our mind, our logic becomes the ultimate judge, the final evaluator of truth vs. fiction.

This would be a great plan if we all used the same facts and the same logical processes to determine the truth. One very wise and logical person determines that "truth A" is the absolute truth, and another equally wise and logical mind determines that "plan X" is the absolute truth.

All of man's wisdom, and our most brilliant logic, our unanswerable questions, all are quickly exposed as child-like ramblings... when we consider the words of Biblical wisdom. Such as Today's verse.

God is above all, His thinking, His logic, His power, what is easily possible for Him is quite impossible for man...

He is Truth: we either accept this or reject it. And if accepted, may I suggest that we let Him set the boundaries for truth vs lies, right vs. wrong? I'm pretty sure He is more trustworthy than the wisest person we've ever met, heard of, or read about!

Father God, help us foolish and proud people to recognize that You are God Almighty, and we are nothing without You. Our logical thinking is mere child's play compared to Your ways and Your thoughts.

"You Are The Lord"
Passion
https://youtu.be/udtq_8AqfHM

February 7

Today's Encouragement is 1 John 4:4 NLT *But you belong to God, my dear children. You have already won a victory over those people because the Spirit who lives in you is greater than the spirit who lives in the world.*

You belong to God –

Imagine that! Chew on it, meditate on it, "Selah" is a Hebrew word meaning 'pause and consider this'. So, Selah...

You belong to God, and you are His dear child; you are victorious over this world and it's evil, because—- the Spirit... who lives in you...is greater!!!

2 Kings 6:15-17 NLT *When the servant of the man of God got up early the next morning and went outside, there were troops, horses, and chariots everywhere. "Oh, sir, what will we do now?" the young man cried to Elisha. "Don't be afraid!" Elisha told him. "For there are more on our side than on theirs!" Then Elisha prayed, "O Lord, open his eyes and let him see!" The* Lord *opened the young man's eyes, and when he looked up, he saw that the hillside around Elisha was filled with horses and chariots of fire.*

Father, thank You for choosing us as Your sons and daughters. For making us Yours! Open our eyes too, Lord, to the truth that You surround us with Your unlimited love and power because... We belong to You!

"Surrounded"
Bethel Music & Kari Jobe
https://youtu.be/Pz7578ZNwNU

February 8

Today's Encouragement is Malachi 3:10 NLT *"Bring all the tithes into the storehouse so there will be enough food in my Temple. If you do," says the Lord of Heaven's Armies, "I will open the windows of heaven for you. I will pour out a blessing so great you won't have enough room to take it in! Try it! Put me to the test!"*

The windows of Heaven –

'The tithe' is as old as mankind. Even the sons of Adam and Eve, though known for other reasons, brought a tithe to God, an offering of their efforts, some of the "fruits of their labor" we call it. Without any commandment, all through history, people recognized that God is the giver of every good and perfect gift (James 1:17) and so, some tangible acknowledgment of God's goodness is only appropriate.

This tangible acknowledgment we call 'tithe," and it is defined as one-tenth of all the blessings we are granted by God. This tithe is returned to Him as an acknowledgment that everything we have has come from Him.

God's math is not the world's math, my friends; Everything I have, minus one-tenth, is NOT only 90 percent. No, in God's math... it's far more than I can calculate! Because God promises us in this verse, when we honor Him with a tithe, He "will open the windows of heaven for you!" Imagine that...

We are even assured with the closing words, "Just try it!"

This isn't a winning slot machine: put in my tithe today and win the jackpot tomorrow. Rather by consistently, sacrificially, and worshipfully giving the tithe to Him, God opens the windows of heaven to us and pours out blessings... perhaps financially, but is it not possible that these windows might also pour out blessings that matter so much more... blessings such as good health, peace, joy, and contentment?

Try it! Put God to the Test!

God grant us enough faith to trust You in this, help us completely surrender our finances to Your control.

"Better"
Pat Barrett
https://youtu.be/cgpvCVkrV6M

February 9

Today's Encouragement is Matthew 7:24 NLT [Jesus said,] *Anyone who listens to my teaching and follows it is wise, like a person who builds a house on solid rock.*

Solid Rock –

Years ago, a wise friend pointed out that, although we went to different denominational churches, we had many essential beliefs in common, he described it this way. "There's really only a few things worth falling on your sword for!"

As I recalled his words, I asked myself, what are the key principles which comprise the foundation, this solid rock, of our faith?

Here's a start on that:

Jesus—He was and is the only begotten Son of God, born of a virgin, lived a pure life, died a sacrificial death, was raised to life, ascended, still lives today, and will return!

Salvation- we are saved by acceptance of Christ as our Savior, by grace alone.

Lordship- we surrender our will to Christ as our Lord. We surrender our whole lives, and our possessions, demonstrated by tithes, offerings, and service.

We were **created to:**

-Obey,
-Worship,
-Love God,
-Love others,
-Have a relationship with God, our Father as His adopted children
-Pray.

Father, help us be aware of, and confident in, these solid rock principles and truths of our lives as Your children, as Christians.

"We Believe"
Steve Green
https://youtu.be/6-U4z-_mxb8

February 10

Today's Encouragement is John 11:25-26 ESV *Jesus said to her, "I am the resurrection and the life. Whoever believes in me, though he die, yet shall he live, and everyone who lives and believes in me shall never die. Do you believe this?"*

Shall never die –

We need to change our terminology, friends. Jesus said, you will never die, yet we consistently say, "My friend is dead" or "He has passed away."

Do we truly believe the words of Christ? Was He right about most things but not quite correct on this? Of course, we believe that Jesus always was, and always is, The Truth. Then why do we speak the opposite of what Jesus reveals to us as if it were true?

Those who believe in Jesus, are alive eternally. We will all cease to breathe on this earth, but our next breath, our next heartbeat, our next nanosecond of thought... is with Him, in eternity, in Paradise. We believe this, it is truth. And isn't this the exact opposite of the world's limited perspective of reality? How can we believe this, and still say, "He is dead"?

As Billy Graham famously said, 'Some day you will read or hear that Billy Graham is dead. Don't you believe a word of it. I shall be more alive than I am now. I will just have changed my address. I will have gone into the presence of God."

My friend, the end of this life, for the believer, is the most wonderful, beautiful, peaceful, joyful moment, so far... because when we are with Christ, though we do not have words to describe it, Eternal Life is unimaginably greater than this earthly life.

Lord, we confess that it is difficult to believe in the idea of Eternal Life. We need Your help to accept this Truth. Give us the gift of faith in Your perfect gift of Eternal Life.

"No More Night"

Glen Campbell

https://youtu.be/PKFnf2_qIQo

February 11

Today's Encouragement is Philippians 2:9-11 NLT *Therefore, God elevated him to the place of highest honor and gave him the name above all other names, that at the name of Jesus every knee should bow, in heaven and on earth and under the earth, and every tongue declare that Jesus Christ is Lord to the glory of God the Father.*

At the Name –

I invite you to use your imagination, and immerse yourself, for just this brief moment, in the Word.

At the Name of Jesus—

Every knee will bow. Can you imagine this? Everyone in the world bowing on their knees to Jesus! Everyone who has ever lived... from Adam to you, and the yet unborn... bowing before the majesty, glory, power, and love of God fully and perfectly expressed in the Name, the Being, the God-Man whose name is... Jesus...

And —

Stay with me... At His Name...

Every tongue confesses, proclaims, and speaks aloud in reverent worship... "Jesus is Lord!" Over every other voice, every other thought, or utterance! Jesus is Lord. What must that sound like? Deafening? Like a mighty rushing wind? A still small voice!... Every tongue, every place, every language, every era of time, all proclaiming 'Jesus is Lord!"

This is worship, my friends, this is surrender, this is acknowledging and glorifying our Lord our Savior, our Jesus! Do not wait for "someday."

Bow and Confess Jesus is Lord!

Father, grant us the privilege of considering the Power of the Name of Jesus, His Name above all names, our Savior, Redeemer, and our Friend. Thank You, Father, for Jesus whose Name is above all!

"Your Great Name"

Natalie Grant

https://youtu.be/PasbQx0VilQ

February 12

Today's Encouragement is Ephesians 2:8-9 NLT *God saved you by his grace when you believed. And you can't take credit for this; it is a gift from God. Salvation is not a reward for the good things we have done, so none of us can boast about it.*

By His Grace –

God saved you. We say things like, "When I decided to come to Christ," or "When I accepted Jesus," as if it was something we did, our own efforts. Truth is my friends... God chose us and gave us this Gift of Salvation. Not our efforts, not even... bear with me... not even our decision.

Consider with me, ...Who are your parents? ... It wasn't your decision to be born to them, where were you born, what nation... again, not your call. How tall are you? Not your call. Hair color? You get the idea. Some things in this life are our decisions, but many things are not... and thankfully, we can change some things too, by our decisions.

But salvation?... This is God's work. He saved us! "God saved you by his grace" ... when you believed... we do have that role to play! We either believe or we don't. If you've ever known anyone who chose NOT to believe... you can see for yourselves the tragic results of that decision.

My friends, God's Grace has saved us, rescued us from ourselves, from this world, from a life controlled by and known by our sin... He alone calls, invites, prepares, encourages, motivates, and guides us... to Himself.

Father, You are so good to us, so patient, so kind, and so full of Love for us. Thank You for this immeasurable gift of Salvation, by Your Grace.

"What Grace Is Mine"
Keith and Kristyn Getty
https://youtu.be/yazxxkbSkZE

February 13

Today's Encouragement is Jeremiah 31:34b ESV *For I will forgive their iniquity, and I will remember their sin no more.*

Remember no more –

Does this amaze you as it does me? That God, who can do anything, would choose to remove from His perfect, complete, and limitless memory... all our sin!

We often struggle with forgiveness, first from God, but also from ourselves.

We think, "I need to hold on to this guilt and shame over this sin because it was really terrible and I want God to know that I really regret it, and if I forget it then I might do it again."

Let me ask you, "So, how's that working for you?"

Friends, it is the freedom from guilt and shame, bought for us by the blood of Jesus, which sets us free from the power of sin. This freedom results from accepting, even embracing the grace, love, forgiveness, and this "merciful forgetfulness" of our Perfect Father.

Erased, blotted out, removed, remembered no more... these are some of the words used throughout the Bible to describe what God has done (already, through the blood of Jesus) with our sin!

Now, the next question is what will we "do" with the memory of our sin?

Father God, in Your infinite power, please help us also to "remember no more" and to forget completely our own sin. Erase its memory and scars, guilt, and shame, from our lives, and also from the lives of those we've hurt by our sin. You alone can heal all this.

"He Forgives and He Forgets"

Share McKee

https://youtu.be/ZrTL5DrlqVM

February 14

Today's Encouragement is Philippians 3:8 NLT *Yes, everything else is worthless when compared with the infinite value of knowing Christ Jesus, my Lord. For his sake I have discarded everything else, counting it all as garbage, so that I could gain Christ.*

The infinite value –

This infinite value is knowing Christ. Everything else, Paul says, is worthless.

What do we hold as valuable, my friends? Family, wealth, friendships, our health, property, our own treasures – all the special things we accumulate in life... how valuable are these? You may think, "Wait, you can't include things like family and health in this list!"

Paul means everything, and he calls it worthless, compared to knowing Christ. Remember Paul never met Jesus during his days on the earth, he wasn't one of the twelve disciples. So, when he speaks of knowing Jesus, it is the same type of relationship that you and I can have with Him. It isn't knowing "about" Jesus...Rather it is knowing Him as you know your best friend, even more... as well as you know yourself!

Knowing Jesus, my friend... nothing else matters. No valuable possessions or even our most treasured relationships... can compare to the relationship we can have with Him... knowing Him! And this relationship is an infinite journey, process, experience, because... He is Infinite!

Father God, help us to know Christ, to enter into and remain in a growing personal, honest, and even intimate relationship with Jesus.

"Knowing You"
Graham Kendrick
https://youtu.be/4r8XfE_VNb0

February 15

Today's Encouragement is Hebrews 8:13 ESV *In speaking of a new covenant, he makes the first one obsolete. And what is becoming obsolete and growing old is ready to vanish away.*

New Covenant –

Hebrews 8:6-7 ESV *But as it is, Christ has obtained a ministry that is as much more excellent than the old as the covenant he mediates is better, since it is enacted on better promises. For if that first covenant had been faultless, there would have been no occasion to look for a second.*

The old covenant (of laws, perfect obedience, sacrifice) has grown old and vanished. We live under and within the New Covenant of Grace.

Jeremiah 31:31 ESV *Behold, the days are coming, declares the* Lord, *when I will make a new covenant with the house of Israel and the house of Judah.*

And just what is the New Covenant?

Jesus Himself told us – in Luke 22:20 ESV *And likewise, the cup after they had eaten, saying, "This cup that is poured out for you is the new covenant in my blood.*

This new covenant has replaced the old covenant of obeying all the law, priests as intermediaries, and animal sacrifices for redemption, etc.

With the new covenant of Christ our Lord as high priest, our intermediary, and His shed blood, the supreme sacrifice once for all sin, for all time, for all who believe and trust Him as Savior. The new covenant is this: we are one with Him through His blood. We are the Righteousness of God, through Christ! (2 Cor. 5:21)

Thank You, Lord, for a new covenant, a covenant of Love between You and Your people. Thank You for making us right with You through the blood of Jesus.

"New Covenant –Yeshua"

Joshua Aaron

https://youtu.be/QhHGzTCouQA

February 16

Today's Encouragement is Galatians 2:20 NLT *My old self has been crucified with Christ. It is no longer I who live, but Christ lives in me. So, I live in this earthly body by trusting in the Son of God, who loved me and gave himself for me.*

No longer I –

The rebirth, becoming a new person, is a mystery, a unique attribute of our Christian faith. As believers in Jesus, we don't just follow an ancient teacher who taught the path to enlightenment, we don't only adhere to an ideal set of principles, rather... we become totally new creatures! We are spiritually reborn from our old life of sin into a new life in Him! It is no longer we who live—now Christ lives in and through us!!!

2 Corinthians 5:17 NLT *This means that anyone who belongs to Christ has become a new person. The old life is gone; a new life has begun!*

No longer I... The old life is gone! A New life has begun! In this New life, we may still carry the memories of the old life... we may carry some of its scars, wounds of the past, some healed, some still needing healing, some still "open" wounds. My friends, did Jesus partially recreate you? Did He say, "I'm giving you a new life, but you still need to hold on to the pains and hurts and wounds of your past life?" And, oh yeah, be sure to remember how bad you were, and keep carrying that shame with you... yes, that'll be good for you to keep carrying that pain and shame." Is that why Jesus died? To give us that kind of new life? Honestly, my friends, that wouldn't be much of a new life, would it?

We choose, my friends, to either hold on to our old self, old life, old memories, old hurts, old shame... or to choose a complete Rebirth! —living in the freedom of—A New Life with Christ!

Father God, help us to release our old life completely, and by embracing the cross of Christ, to be completely reborn—New creations in Christ.

"Embrace the Cross"
Steve Green
https://youtu.be/CWec-lHOQtk

February 17

Today's Encouragement is Matthew 6:12,14-15 NLT ... *and forgive us our sins, as we have forgiven those who sin against us. If you forgive those who sin against you, your heavenly Father will forgive you. But if you refuse to forgive others, your Father will not forgive your sins.*

If you forgive –

Some biblical truth is "hard truth." It goes against our human nature to the point of irritation, grating, even pain. This is one such truth. "God forgives us—only if we forgive!"

I admit, I don't like this! It's not how I want it to be! I want it to read differently... like "God forgives us completely and purely, regardless of how we treat others." But that is not what Jesus said!

My friends, the truth is—We must forgive others for what they have done before God will forgive us for what we have done! Read the verse again, there's no way around this "hard truth."

Forgiveness is not an option for the believer! We don't have the luxury of forgiving some things but holding on to the "unforgivable" that each of us has suffered at one time or another.

Perhaps this explains the awe we experience when we hear about someone who sincerely forgave the horrific criminal who hurt them so deeply. We see the harmed one experience the joy of forgiveness, regardless of how the criminal responds. This forgiveness is setting free the forgiving one!

Father, help us to see that we are set free when we forgive others! Help us to forgive, Father, every wrong done to us and be forgiven by Your Grace, completely set free!

"Forgiveness"
Matthew West
https://youtu.be/uyGbb18wUts

February 18

Today's Encouragement is Psalm 91:14-15 ESV *Because he holds fast to me in love, I will deliver him; I will protect him, because he knows my name. When he calls to me, I will answer him; I will be with him in trouble; I will rescue him and honor him.*

I will rescue –

My friends, throughout His written word, God speaks of saving, rescuing, delivering, protecting, helping, showing mercy, blessing, caring for, watching over, singing over, reassuring, encouraging, and gathering to Himself – His people, you, and me!

His promises are born from His immeasurable Love for us!

As in this passage, notice among these promises of God... "I will rescue." God does it—"I will"

We need it—only those in serious trouble need rescue. Because—he holds fast to me in love - God delivers, protects, answers, and He rescues those who love Him.

We will have trouble and we will need His rescue! But He promises to be with us in our troubles, to never leave us, as we—hold fast to Him in love.

When we realize how truly, purely, and completely God loves us, then we are inevitably drawn to and enabled to... love Him, to hold fast to Him in love. It may be that we don't "know how" to love Him, yet—is this love for God a learned behavior, like driving a car? Or is it possible that loving Him is a spiritual response, inherent, and instinctual in our spiritual nature? Surely this must be awakened, by Him alone. No decision of man, nothing of our self-will, can create or work through mentally the steps of "loving God."

Father, awaken within us this love for You, which clings to You, which holds fast to You. Help us to love You because You have first loved us. (1 John 4:19)

"Rescuer"

Rend Collective

https://youtu.be/leh-4fCc5MI

February 19

Today's Encouragement is 1 John 4:19 NLT We love each other because he loved us first.

He loved us first –

God boldly proclaims His Love for you and me, First! While we were yet sinners Christ died for us. God initiates; we respond.

God – First – loves us. We can choose to believe, to trust, to rely on His love... filthy sinners though we are... we realize we cannot save, or even help ourselves... we need a Savior, One who can save us... and only Jesus can. Or sadly we can also choose to doubt His love...

Yet His word clearly explains that He first loved us, He sent Jesus to teach, live among us, die in our place, return to life in victory over death, and ascend to heaven... and as He promised, He will return!

Friends, all this is God's work, His hand—directing, arranging, and designing.

We may only observe glimpses, tidbits, and whispers of His handiwork from time to time, yet He is always creating, still. He has arranged and designed a new life for each of us! A life which He directs! A life of love.

We are only able to love others and to love Him, as we have accepted and embraced the love which He has poured out upon us in the gift of Jesus.

And once our acceptance of His gift occurs... we cannot be unchanged, we are truly transformed into new creations! (2 Corinthians 5:17)

Accept His love (again) today! Allow Him to fill (refill) you with Himself. Then, my friend, we can live a new Life, by accepting His love, then loving Him, loving others, accepting His grace, and extending it, forgiving others, forgiving ourselves, now and forever free.

Father, we now fully accept your love and mercy. Transform us Father, as You will.

"First Loved Me"
Covenant Worship
https://youtu.be/fg7wwyz63Aw

February 20

Today's Encouragement is Numbers 13:27-28a NLT *This was their report to Moses: "We entered the land you sent us to explore, and it is indeed a bountiful country – a land flowing with milk and honey. Here is the kind of fruit it produces. But—the people living there are powerful, and their towns are large and fortified."*

But –

God promised the nation of Israel that He would bring them out of Egypt and slavery, into their own land, flowing with milk and honey.

And He Did! But – the people complained, grumbled, and cried because there were already others living in this promised land!

Was God true to His word? Did He bring them? Was the land fruitful and remarkable? Did He provide for them food, water, protection, and guidance during their entire journey? Did He deliver them from Egypt? Did the Egyptians shower them with gifts as they left? Yes! And abundantly! Yet they did not focus on what God had said, now what He had already done, rather they focused on what He Did Not say. He kept His promise!

Friends, like the people of Israel, we are also too often distracted by the obstacles in our way (which are not insignificant!) and don't recognize that God's Sovereign Hand has already made the way for us. It is our faith that is tested by these obstacles. We can either trust Him and focus on His promises, remembering what He has already done... or we focus on the obstacles and falter.

What obstacle has your attention right now? Is it possible that God is inviting you to see beyond this obstacle, to recall His promises and His all-powerful hand of mercy on your behalf?

Philippians 4:13 NLT *For I can do everything through Christ, who gives me strength.*

Father, grant us sincere faith and vision that is clearly focused on You and Your promises to us. Strengthen our faith, Lord!

"Give Me Faith"
Elevation Worship
https://youtu.be/SjFIhTNDyz0

February 21

Today's Encouragement is Proverbs 19:11 ESV *Good sense makes one slow to anger, and it is his glory to overlook an offense.*

Overlook an offense –

It's pretty needed today don't you think? The ability, the humility, the grace... to overlook an offense.

Seems that we are all offended these days! By this or that, what is said, not said, by a cap, a slogan, a chant, an idea, how another thinks, their political leanings, how they drive, a pronoun, a face mask or lack thereof... we have become... highly offended to the point of the ridiculous!

We are now offended by the very life of another person; every aspect of their existence is offensive to us! Because... we have chosen to do the opposite of this verse of wisdom! We have instead chosen this "perverted proverb" for today's world: "Store up offenses, accumulate resentment, and fill your heart and mind with bitterness. It is your right to detest the choices, the foolishness, the very existence of others who disagree with you!"

Yet, Jesus taught us wisdom, my friends, (and so much more!) as He revealed to all—that loving God and loving others as we love ourselves... is the greatest instruction of God!

We find what we look for, don't we? It's difficult to change our focus from finding fault and offensiveness in this world (there's certainly plenty of both!) to finding ways to Love God and love others. But we can choose, each day, to seek, to try, to focus on, exhibiting love for God and man, or sadly, we can continue to store up offenses, bitterness, and resentment. We choose.

Father, cleanse us of our pettiness and being offended by every behavior of others. Help us to recognize the desperate need within each of them for—Your Perfect Love.

"For the One"

Jenn Johnson

https://youtu.be/e_bj6mjUj7k

February 22

Today's Encouragement is James 1:27 NLT *Pure and genuine religion in the sight of God the Father means caring for orphans and widows in their distress and refusing to let the world corrupt you.*

In their distress –

So many times, we ask ourselves, and others, and finally, we rightly ask God... "What am I to do? What really matters? How am I to spend my time? Where do I go next?"

Friends, God has already answered these questions. We just haven't listened or perhaps we didn't like His answer...

Caring for others, like widows and orphans – in their distress. These are those without family. Some may have a biological family yet have no relationship and need help of some kind... they're in distress!

We too often look around for the Great Opportunities of service! Where we can achieve great things in our sight and within the sight of others, some great spiritual accomplishment, some great success, "I did this!" we proclaim, or "I built this!" "Look at ME!"

Friends, God's ways are not our ways... He encourages us to serve Him by caring for others... In their distress... Through poverty, illness, in the prison of incarceration, drugs, or mental illness! We are His ambassadors of hope and salvation for this life and for eternity!

Father, cause us to be moved to compassion by the needs of those around us, the least of these, the poor, the widows, and orphans... anyone in distress... and to love them with Your immeasurable mercy and grace.

"For the One" (yes, it's the same as yesterday)

Jenn Johnson

https://youtu.be/e_bj6mjUj7k

February 23

Today's Encouragement is Romans 6:4 NLT *For we died and were buried with Christ by baptism. And just as Christ was raised from the dead by the glorious power of the Father, now we also may live new lives.*

Live new lives –

We will often discuss the idea that we are exposed to The Truth in the Bible. It may not be logical to us, it may not "feel right," or "seem reasonable." Yet, many miracles in the Bible also are "not logical." The question then, my friends, is it Truth or is it as some say, allegory; stories told for a purpose, to teach a lesson?

We can choose to accept God's Word as the ultimate truth, whether it seems "reasonable" to us or not. And this new life which we are given is Truth, it is not a "maybe God will do this for us," or "if we are good," or "if we are worthy" ... it is a truth!

I confess it is rare to meet someone who truly lives a new life, but then, how common is a new creation? And yet, you and I are that – new creations. But what does it mean to live new lives? One aspect would be that all the sins, errors, scars, and pain of our old life would be gone! Another thought would be that our future is completely unencumbered by our past! In essence, we are new every morning! (Lamentations 3:23)

Father, thank You for Your amazing gifts, this new life You have given us has such amazing meaning!

"All Things New"
Big Daddy Weave
https://youtu.be/4_2aX_i4qpM

February 24

Today's Encouragement is Numbers 17:12-13 NLT *Then the people of Israel said to Moses, "Look, we are doomed! We are dead! We are ruined! Everyone who even comes close to the Tabernacle of the Lord dies. Are we all doomed to die?"*

Doomed –

"Ok now, exactly how is this encouraging," you may ask... Consider with me, my friends, the context of this complete panic among God's chosen people:

They had been enslaved in Egypt. God miraculously delivered them from that slavery.

The powerful Egyptian army pursued them, a nation of former slaves, they were delivered by a miracle, through the Red Sea, and Egypt's army was devastated.

They were thirsty, and God miraculously provided water.

They were hungry, He gave them manna.

They wanted meat, He surrounded them with quail.

Some rebelled against Moses, God's representative, and died.

They grumbled and complained and now panicked, "We're all going to die!"

Repeatedly, these people, God's chosen, showed clearly how unfaithful, cowardly, ungrateful, and unworthy they were! Repeatedly and miraculously saved... yet repeatedly and inexplicably fearful and blind to God's provision. And this is who WE are! We are the same as Israel! We are like them, sheep without a shepherd.

But God!—Romans 5:8 NLT *But God showed his great love for us* [by sending Christ to die for us] *while we were still sinners.*

We were a foolish, fearful, and faithless people. But God's mercy provided Jesus our Savior. And now, through Christ, we are...Completely, Perfectly, Eternally, Right, With God!

Father, thank You for Your mercy, for Your great love, for our Savior! We recognize we are nothing without Jesus.

"How Great Is the Love"
Paul Baloche
https://youtu.be/huGSh3sUyBE

February 25

Today's Encouragement is Romans 4:18 NLT *Even when there was no reason for hope, Abraham kept hoping-believing that he would become the father of many nations. For God had said to him, "That's how many descendants you will have!"*

No reason for hope –

God's promise to Abraham was that he would become the father of many nations; and that even in his advanced years he and Sarah would have a child. It wasn't logical, it wasn't even biologically possible, yet Abraham believed God. He did not weaken in faith (v19). It was Abraham's faith which was considered as right standing before God; made him right with God. And it is our faith in Christ that gives us this same right standing (v 24).

Friends, our faith is totally inconsistent with the logic and wisdom of this world. The wisdom of man does not line up with the wisdom of God. Man's greatest intelligence, accomplishments, achievements, abilities, capabilities, and philosophies... is foolishness before God!

Just Faith my friends; Hope when there is no tangible reason for Hope.

Father, help us to continue to place all our hope, our faith, and our confidence in You alone! You are God – and we are the people of your pasture, the flock under Your perfect and loving care.... We trust in You alone!

"Give Me Faith"
Elevation Worship
https://youtu.be/SjFIhTNDyz0

February 26

Today's Encouragement is Isaiah 6:5 NLT *Then I said, "It's all over! I am doomed, for I am a sinful man. I have filthy lips, and I live among a people with filthy lips. Yet I have seen the King, the Lord of Heaven's Armies."*

I have filthy lips –

This was Isaiah's response to God's call. There are many stories of "reluctant leaders" in the Bible. Saul hid among baggage (1 Samuel 10:22). Moses offered God a series of excuses and he finally whined but "I am slow of speech and tongue" (Exodus 4:10). Jonah ran away (Jonah 1:3). Even the disciples all hid behind locked doors after Jesus' death! (John 20:19).

But notice—God still used these ordinary, fearful, even reluctant people to do His work. These were all transformed into heroes of the faith… AFTER they were called by God to do what He had planned for them.

Is He calling you? Are you offering excuses, hiding, or running away? Well, my friend, you're in really good company! Remember these people all finally did say "Yes", despite their concerns, doubts, and limitations. And what a difference they made!

Lord, help us recognize that we are woefully inadequate, yet You will always provide everything we need as we say "Yes" to You.

"Wherever He Leads"

Alan Jackson

https://youtu.be/mRJY7SlujNw

February 27

Today's Encouragement is 1 Samuel 17:45 NLT *David replied to the Philistine, "You come to me with sword, spear, and javelin, but I come to you in the name of the Lord of Heaven's Armies – the God of the armies of Israel, whom you have defied.*

In the Name of the Lord –

The record of David's encounter with Goliath the giant is one we all remember, an inspiring battle of good vs evil, faith vs brute strength.

Notice what David, probably a teenager at the time, did not say, "I come against you with stones and a sling!" He didn't say, "My skill in battle is greater than yours!" nor, "I am smarter and quicker than you are!" There was no reference to David's own ability nor his own strength (which was considerable!) but only to the "Name of the Lord of Heaven's armies"!

Friends, we face many types of battles and struggles in our lives; there are many types of "giants" that threaten to destroy us. These giants clearly have the power; the odds are on their side. These same giants have destroyed others before... the giants of gossip, addiction, shame, depression, fear, illness, and even physical enemies, to name a few.

But God! We are always victorious—when we face these giants in our lives as we come face to face with them – in the Name of the Lord! Not in our strength but His. Whatever battle we face, emotional, physical, or spiritual... our victory is found in His name!

Father, help us to respect, honor, and call upon Your name, the name of Jesus, in all situations, all struggles, and all our need. You alone are our strength, power, and hope!

"In the Name of the Lord"

Sandi Patty

https://youtu.be/CD-6nv43Bs4

February 28

Today's Encouragement is Lamentations 3:22-23 ESV *The steadfast love of the Lord never ceases; his mercies never come to an end; they are new every morning; great is your faithfulness.*

New every morning –

These beautiful words of assurance, so uplifting, so faith-filled... emerge from the heart of Jeremiah in his book of Laments. He pours out his broken heart to God in this book, weeping as he writes to express his inexpressible grief and sorrow for the sin of his people and the suffering they experienced as the direct result of their sinful choices.

Friends, God loves us so much that He tells us clearly to avoid the sin which will destroy us. He sums this up in Ten Commandments, a list of ten things that will corrode our character, and eat at our souls and our society like a cancer. We ignore God's counsel and advice to our own peril, and so had the nation of God's people done. And Jeremiah mourned for his people.

And out of this great mourning, comes this pinnacle of praise...

Your love never ceases,

Your mercies never end,

They are renewed every morning,

And Your faithfulness, Father God, is great!

It is immeasurable!

Lord, help us to see clearly how desperately we need You to save us, for we all have sinned. We rely only on Your steadfast love, Your mercy, Your faithfulness. Thank You, Lord.

"The Steadfast Love of the Lord"

The Island Sing

https://youtu.be/EnOFh9WFe6k

February 29

Today's Encouragement is John 1:16 ESV *For from his fullness we have all received, grace upon grace.*

Grace Upon Grace -

- From His fullness (God is the source of everything, and has unlimited power to do, create, cause, limit, anything!) and from His unlimited abundance of Grace, Love, and Mercy... from this eternal supply...
- We have (now, already)
- All (everyone who accepts God's invitation to become His)
- Received (this gift, God's doing - not our effort)
- Grace upon Grace.

We are given this gift of Grace, often described as undeserved favor, in unlimited abundance! Grace upon Grace... we aren't given, just a little grace, sometimes, if we are really good and deserve it... No! His Grace is without limits! More Grace heaped upon the Grace we have already been given.

(The Amplified Bible expounds upon the scriptures with many expressions of the original language, here is this verse with that added perspective.) John 1:16 AMP "For out of His fullness [the superabundance of His grace and truth] we have all received grace upon grace [spiritual blessing upon spiritual blessing, favor upon favor, and gift heaped upon gift]."

Father God, we cannot fully understand, much less deserve Your Grace upon Grace... but help us to accept it by Faith, as Your immeasurable gift to Your dearly loved people. Thank You for Your Grace!

"Grace upon Grace"
Brooke and Boggs
https://youtu.be/fCR93GIRMGU?si=J4UL1Hce1diloGP6

March 1

Today's Encouragement is James 4:14b ESV *What is your life? For you are a mist that appears for a little time and then vanishes.*

You are a mist –

We all too often focus on our daily earthly life, as if this life was "all there is", Now, certainly, we need to make the most of the days we have here – being productive, helpful, working while it is day, resting and loving God and others to the best of our ability. He alone enables us to live and enjoy this life! Yet if only for this life we have hope... we are to be pitied! (1 Cor. 15:19)

This earthly life is a mist, my friend, a nanosecond of the eternity which we, as eternal beings, will enjoy with God. And we have now, already, this eternal life, it isn't something we "get" when we leave this world... our eternity has already begun! (John 5:24)

And one day, those of us who believe, who trust in Jesus as our Savior... will see Him face to face... and then, my friends. Nothing. Else. Will. Matter.

Father, open our eyes to the brevity of this life, and to the magnitude of eternity with You. Grant us a clear perspective, Lord.

"Face to Face"
Zach Williams
https://youtu.be/XXzgQmnCQZk

March 2

Today's Encouragement is Romans 8:1 ESV *There is therefore now no condemnation for those who are in Christ Jesus.*

No condemnation –

No one can condemn you, because you are under the protection and the grace, the undeserved favor, and blessing of Jesus.

Now this world is full of people, and our minds can be full of thoughts... which will TRY to condemn you. They accuse, us (both people and our own thoughts) they point out our failures, focus on our sins, and whisper (or scream), "You don't deserve to be forgiven for that!"

And we don't! The lies and accusations of our enemy are usually based on a truth, but with a tiny bit of poison included. The truth is we don't deserve the grace of God, but... it is given to all who accept Jesus as Lord! The poison is the implied "So, shame on you!" which goes along with every accusation.

Friends, the enemy always accuses us—any time anyone or any thought brings you shame... it is the work of the enemy.

Refuse the Shame, my friend! There is NO condemnation for you—because you belong to Jesus! He has saved us from all condemnation!

While it is true that we are guilty and need to refuse sin, turn away from evil, and turn to God's Grace... We are forever. Free. of Shame! Condemnation! Guilt!

Father God, grant us the discernment, clarity of mind, and spiritual eyes to see the condemnation that seeks to slink into our hearts. Help us to accept instead, the amazing Grace of the freedom which Jesus died to bring to all Your children.

"My Chains Are Gone/Amazing Grace"
Chris Tomlin
https://youtu.be/Jbe7OruLk8I

March 3

Today's Encouragement is Romans 8:2 ESV *For the law of the Spirit of life has set you free in Christ Jesus from the law of sin and death.*

Has set you free –

Not maybe, not later on, not depending on how you behave, not contingent upon anything... except God! We are., Already. Set Free!

When the law of sin and death was in power over us, before we belonged to Christ... we had no hope, we were victims; our lives were the enslaved subjects of the evil, relentless rule of sin and death!

But now! By faith in Christ Jesus alone! Now, my friends, we are Free! Free from the power, control, domination, of Sin and Death.

Sin certainly still exists, we see its effects everywhere around us, and it still tries to creep into our lives at every opportunity, but sin is never free, never without cost, never separated from its master, Death. Oh, but my friends, His grace is sufficient (2 Corinthians 12:9) and has already, and is continually, setting us Free!

We now live under the law, rule, and control of the Spirit of Life! The world, sadly, still lives under the law of sin and death. We do not have a "free pass" to sin, but rather, we have the freedom to pass up the sin that wants to destroy us!

Remember sin shall no longer be your master (Romans 6:24)! Because, my friends, we are (already) Free! Set Free by Jesus Christ!

Father, help us to embrace, dwell in, rejoice in, and rest in the freedom You have given us through Christ!

"No Longer Slaves"
Zach Williams
https://youtu.be/dwLFp1weuA8

March 4

Today's Encouragement is Romans 8:5 ESV *For those who live according to the flesh set their minds on the things of the flesh, but those who live according to the Spirit set their minds on the things of the Spirit.*

Set their minds –

We can choose what we think, and where we set our minds.

Many of us allow someone or something else to decide where we set our minds. For some, it is the latest news report, or their health issues, stress at work, family issues, finances, arguments, or an unlimited list of other useless subjects. And this is all, my friends, setting our minds on the things of the flesh!

Setting our minds on the things of the Spirit is a very different "mindset." We have all heard the "glass is either half-full or half-empty" messages. And there is truth in this idea. But God's truth is the ultimate source of all truth for us as believers! And for us as believers, we are able, if we do choose, to set our minds on the things of God's Spirit and reject setting our minds on the things of this life, of the flesh.

Where is your mindset today? You can redirect it, you can decide to set your mind on God's truth, His promises, His blessings, and protection and provision for you.

Or we can choose the flesh, this world. One is life, and one is death.

This choice, my friends, determines the direction of your life... toward God, or away from God.

Father, help us choose to set our minds on the things of Your Spirit, and so live according to Your Spirit. We ask in Jesus' Name.

"Set Your Mind on Things Above"

Dallas Holm

https://youtu.be/YfCyj7xpqXg

March 5

Today's Encouragement is Romans 8:9 ESV *You, however, are not in the flesh but in the Spirit, if in fact the Spirit of God dwells in you. Anyone who does not have the Spirit of Christ does not belong to him.*

In the Spirit –

If in fact, the Spirit of God dwells in you...

Sadly, many of us who believe in Christ, choose to harden our hearts and minds to the idea of any spiritual matters. As if buying a book... we made an exchange and consider that it is complete... we bought the book, gave something for it and now we have it, it belongs to us. We may never read it, but we perceive it is still ours.

So, it may be compared to our belief in Christ. I heard the message, that Jesus will save me and forgive me if I accept Him as Lord, so I choose, with my will and my mind, to do so. Transaction complete, or so many consider. We are saved by our faith, and our decision to honor Him as Lord and Savior... but this is the beginning point of our relationship with Him, far from the end.

Now, the Spirit of God comes to our lives to dwell, to live, and remain, to fill, to guide, to bring eternal life, and eternal perspective, and to bring light to our darkness. We, however, can choose, as in the analogy, to leave the book closed, many say, "No I won't go there, I don't believe in that stuff, It's too strange for me."

Yet my friend, the spiritual world is eternal, even more "real" than this world. This world of earthly things (the flesh) is fleeting, a mist. It is only the unseen spiritual world that lasts, and the unseen spirit of God which lives within us, who guides and provides for us a life "above" the flesh.

Will you acknowledge His Spirit, which is already living within you? Accepting God's Spirit as already residing within you? Laying aside the flesh of this fleeting world for the eternal world of His Spirit... and so grow in relationship with Him more fully. Will you?

Father God, we need Your guidance as we accept and acknowledge and begin to relate to Your Holy Spirit living within us.

"Spirit of the Living God"

FFH

https://youtu.be/BagH-zTfnsQ

March 6

Today's Encouragement is Romans 8:15 NLT *So you have not received a spirit that makes you fearful slaves. Instead, you received God's Spirit when he adopted you as his own children. Now we call him, "Abba, Father."*

He adopted you –

As adopted children, we are (already) specifically chosen by God. Imagine that for a moment... He looks around this world, and as He does, He selects people for adoption as His very own children! We were chosen before our birth, before we knew Him, before we were even conceived! How is this possible? Remember, He is God... unlimited by time, space, or especially our extremely limited human understanding, knowledge, and logical thinking.

You and I, my brothers and sisters, my friends, were hand-selected, we might say, by God to be members, forever, of His own family.

And we are permitted the incredible privilege, we are so close to Him, His beloved children sitting in His presence... to call Him "Abba," which means "Daddy."

We've often seen TV shows where the adoptive parents anticipate the beautiful moment of acceptance when the child first calls them Mom or Dad... how gratifying, how powerful, how wonderful, this recognition of their love and care for the child! Now, isn't God's heart for us, His love, immeasurably stronger than our human love could ever be, even for our adopted or biological children? How then would God the Father respond to us when we look to Him, run to Him, lift our arms to Him, and speak the word, Daddy!

His love for us is immeasurable. He is our Daddy.

Father God, help us to run to You, arms upraised, and cry out to You, "Daddy"!

"Run to the Father"

Cody Carnes

https://youtu.be/HcpeLDp0Foo

March 7

Today's Encouragement is Romans 8:18 ESV *For I consider that the sufferings of this present time are not worth comparing with the glory that is to be revealed to us.*

Not worth comparing –

The horrible suffering of some people in this life, the abuse, persecution, discrimination, genocide, physical or mental illness and disease, heartbreaking loss of loved ones, the list seems endless... this most terrible and relentless suffering, unimaginable to those of us who haven't experienced it...

Even this...

Is not worth comparing...

to the glory that is to be revealed to us.

As painful as it is even to imagine this most horrific human suffering... such as Jesus' agonizing death on the cross, from which comes the word "excruciating," even this... isn't worth comparing.

There is no downplaying of our human sufferings intended here, these life-threatening and life-taking sufferings are real!

Yet the Truth says... as horrible as these sufferings truly are... they aren't even worth comparing to the Glory that will be revealed to us.

Certainly, this Glory is reserved for us when we see Christ face-to-face, as is recounted in Revelation 1:12-16 or standing before the Throne in Revelation 4. And even these amazing descriptions are but a glimpse of the "Glory that is to be revealed"!

My friends, the wonderful joys, and the immeasurable sorrows of this life... are but a mist, all this will pass away... as will our earthly lives.

Yet, you and I will one day witness this! It will be revealed to us one day... The Glory of God! And on that day, the suffering of this life will vanish from our memory as insignificant.

Father God, help us to realize that our lives here, our sufferings, our pain, are not worth comparing to Your Glory which we will one day experience. Help us keep our eyes on You, and not on ourselves.

"We Shall Behold Him "

Sandy Patti

https://youtu.be/ZVza89G8Sbw

March 8

Today's Encouragement is Romans 8:22-23 NLT *For we know that all creation has been groaning as in the pains of childbirth right up to the present time. And we believers also groan, even though we have the Holy Spirit within us as a foretaste of future glory, for we long for our bodies to be released from sin and suffering. We, too, wait with eager hope for the day when God will give us our full rights as his adopted children, including the new bodies he has promised us.*

We wait with eager hope –

Creation groans—for the day when Christ restores its Eden status. Untainted by sin, by sin's abuse and disregard... restored to the Perfection of God's original Creation.

And so, we too, groan, longing for the day when Righteousness is restored, when sin and sorrow are removed from our lives and from all creation.

Because, my friends, we have the Holy Spirit within us, now, as a foretaste of the future glory! And because we now have this foretaste, we are able to recognize that something is lacking. This lack we sense, this incompleteness, is this the "full rights as His adopted children"?

My friends, it is good and right to recognize that we have the Spirit, and to realize that He is only a foretaste of future glory. And because we have this foretaste, we long, we groan, for things to be made Right—which is the Righteousness of God.

This also makes clear to us that we belong to that realm, the kingdom, where Jesus rules as King, it is His kingship that we long for and groan for, along with all creation! This spiritual kingdom is already ours, guaranteed by the Holy Spirit's presence in our lives... a mere foretaste of God's Glory!

Father God, we thank You for this foretaste which strengthens our hope, our confidence, our blessed assurance that "Jesus is mine."

"Blessed Assurance"

Randy Travis

https://youtu.be/rbXjpC9fhC8

March 9

Today's Encouragement is Romans 8:24 NLT *We were given this hope when we were saved. (If we already have something, we don't need to hope for it.)*

Given this hope –

Hope is often recognized as an essential element of human life. It is tragically clear that a person who becomes Hope-less is not functioning well at all and may not live very long in that state of mind.

Hope is a unique and essential component of our faith also, and as today's verse explains... "we were given (already!) this Hope". It is a gift from God, "when we were saved."

Our God-given type of Hope may not be rational or logical according to the world's standards, but it is not those standards that determine our lives as believers! We are set apart as His deeply loved children, to have Hope!

As Paul begins to conclude his letter to the Romans, he sums up in 15:13 NLT *I pray that God, the source of hope, will fill you completely with joy and peace because you trust in him. Then you will overflow with confident hope through the power of the Holy Spirit.*

The source of Hope is our God! As we continually, consciously choose to trust in Him—we overflow with confident hope!

Father, thank You for the Hope You have already given us, and please strengthen our hope to become overflowing, confident Hope.

"My Hope"
Paul Baloche
https://youtu.be/5wslWBp0Tm4

March 10

Today's Encouragement is Romans 8:26-27 NLT *And the Holy Spirit helps us in our weakness. For example, we don't know what God wants us to pray for. But the Holy Spirit prays for us with groanings that cannot be expressed in words. And the Father who knows all hearts knows what the Spirit is saying, for the Spirit pleads for us believers in harmony with God's own will.*

The Holy Spirit prays for us –

Like me, you might need to re-read this verse.... We all appreciate when someone prays for us, along with us, for our needs, for healing in sickness, for peace in grief, for God's blessings we seek... How much more my friends, are we blessed when the Holy Spirit of God, who Himself resides, dwells, and makes His home in our lives, THIS Holy Spirit, God's Spirit—is praying for us!

Remember the precious prayer for all believers which Jesus prayed? It was close to the end of His earthly life, John 17:20-21 NLT *"I am praying not only for these disciples but also for all who will ever believe in me through their message. I pray that they will all be one, just as you and I are one - as you are in me, Father, and I am in you. And may they be in us so that the world will believe you sent me."*

So, my friends, Jesus has prayed for us, and the Holy Spirit is now, still, actively praying for us... and according to, and "in harmony with God's own will"!

What should we fear? What can stand against us? We are more than conquerors... we have God's Spirit living within us and praying for us!

Thank You, Father, for the incredible blessings You have already given us! Awaken us to Your blessings, Lord, especially to the presence of Your Holy Spirit residing within us and praying for us! We truly have nothing to dread, nothing to fear, with You, Lord—so near!

"Everlasting Arms"
Alan Jackson
https://youtu.be/ah8y1wYIRQI

March 11

Today's Encouragement is Romans 8:28 NIV *And we know that in all things God works for the good of those who love him, who have been called according to his purpose.*

(a wonderful verse to memorize!)

For the good –

Read it slowly please, phrase by phrase...

And we know—This is what we are confident of! This is Truth we can rely upon! We can know and believe this—deep in our hearts.

In all things—in every circumstance and situation, no matter how desperate or hopeless, God **works**—It's His doing, not ours! He is in control!

For the good—to our ultimate betterment, His wisest outcome for our benefit.

Of those who Love Him, called according to His purpose—That's US, we love Him because He **first loved us**, (1 John 4:19) We love God and our neighbor, not perfectly—but sincerely.

My Friends, in every situation, every trial, every blessing, every challenge... even in THIS—God is working for YOUR GOOD! What a good God we have!

As this beautiful song says "When I cannot see it, God, I still believe it. You are working all things for my good!"

Father God, we thank and praise You for this amazing promise! That we can have Your peace and even joy, knowing that You are using all things together for the good of Your children! All praise and thanks to You, Lord!

All Things (please don't skip this wonderful worship song!)

"Covenant Worship"

https://youtu.be/dR-WF7J6Sf8

March 12

Today's Encouragement is Romans 8:31 NLT *What shall we say about such wonderful things as these? If God is for us, who can ever be against us?*

God is for us –

Despite this truth, it often seems to us that "everyone is against me", "nobody cares", and "I'm all on my own."

In today's social media world, we too often see folks living in this 'poor-pitiful-me' state of mind. Expressing their loneliness and pain to the digital world... My friends, it is true that the world often turns on us, against us and we are often isolated, even abandoned, by those who live by the standards of this world.

But!

We have a friend, closer than a brother, stronger than any other, and more perfectly loving than any person could ever be to us!

Our God is FOR us! This whole world might be against us, the world certainly was against Jesus Himself! But God was FOR Him just as God is FOR you and me!

Remember Jesus' words- John 16:33 *NLT "I have told you all this so that you may have peace in me. Here on earth, you will have many trials and sorrows. But take heart, because I have overcome the world."*

The world may be or seem to be against you... but, my friend, God is FOR you!

Father God, Help us to recognize, today and always... that You are FOR us!

"The Blessing"

Kari Jobe and Cody Carnes

https://y outu.be/tNk_xCa7zaQ

March 13

Today's Encouragement is Romans 8:32 NLT Since *he did not spare even his own Son but gave him up for us all, won't he also give us everything else?*

Give us everything –

Even in human terms, if you were my child, and I have given you a priceless gift, a new house let's say, (don't hold your breath!) because of my overwhelming love for you… would I later say "No" if you asked me to buy your lunch, or to provide for you so that your bills were paid, or to take care of you in any other way? Everything else, every other need we have… pales in comparison to the overwhelming gift — of Jesus.

Yet we often strive exhaustively to get what we need, our own desires, on our own, without ever asking our perfect loving Father for what we need! In His model prayer, Jesus instructed us, invited us, to ask – even for our food, our daily bread!

The blessings we have as the deeply loved children of God, the Almighty Creator of All, are unlimited! Now, He is far too loving to grant us our every selfish whim, and yet He is also far too loving to ignore our prayers for actual needs!

He provides exactly, precisely, perfectly everything we need. And He begins… with the Savior!

Lord God, Your immeasurable goodness to us…what You have already given and what You plan to provide for us… is overwhelming! Salvation through Christ! Eternal Life with You! Treasures in Heaven! Forgiveness for Sin! Freedom to Worship You! The Bread of Life and Living Water! Truthfully, You have already provided all that we need, and infinitely more than we could ever deserve! Help us to have appropriately thankful hearts!

"Do It Again"
Elevation Worship
https://youtu.be/0B_lnQIITxU

March 14

Today's Encouragement is Romans 8:33-34 NLT *Who dares accuse us whom God has chosen for his own? No one – for God himself has given us the right standing with himself. Who then will condemn us? No one – or Christ Jesus died for us and was* raised to life for us, and he is sitting in the place of honor at God's right hand, *pleading for us."*

No one –

Who could dare to accuse or condemn us? No one – because we have been, we are now, we ever will be—His chosen ones!

Friends, we are not the teacher's pet, spoiled brat, type of "chosen" ones. These are tainted by the immature, selfish needs of their teachers and parents.

Rather my friends... we are the highly favored and deeply loved children of the Most High God, the all-wise one, the creator, all-powerful, and All in All! No words can describe Him! And we are selected by Him! And Christ Himself has bought our eternal lives for Himself!

Now in earthly terms, some other child or adult would be very foolish to accuse the teacher's pet or the spoiled brat of something... everyone clearly recognizes they 'can do no wrong' in the eyes of their protector.

In the same way, but to an infinitely greater degree, and in complete purity and holiness, without any hint of self-serving... Our Father sees us with eyes of love, with mercy and compassion and favor, and as cleansed completely by the blood sacrifice of Jesus our Lord! And this my friends, is the right-standing (v33) the righteousness, which "God Himself has given us"!

Thank You, Father, for giving us right standing with You! Thank You, Jesus, for dying and rising for us and pleading for us! Thank You, our God, that no one can accuse nor condemn us because—we are Yours!

"Rooftops"
Jesus Culture
https://youtu.be/4-gLdIO5G-Q

March 15

Today's Encouragement is Romans 8:35 NLT *Can anything ever separate us from Christ's love? Does it mean he no longer loves us if we have trouble or calamity, or are persecuted, or hungry, or destitute, or in danger, or threatened with death?*

Can anything ever separate us –

I invite you to ask yourself—"What is it that threatens to pull me away from God's love?" What thoughts, sins, temptations, problems, worries, fears, doubts, diseases, disappointments, disabilities, discouragements, questions, memories, relationships... what is it that most threatens to erode, decay, or slip in between you and Jesus?

Now whatever that is for you, (and it may be different things from time to time, or a recurring issue) grab it (figuratively), and set that thing, whatever you perceive it to be, on a table (as if an altar) before you, look at it carefully, and then recognize... "This Issue, this beast, will never separate me from the love of Jesus! Never! I am victorious over this thing and everything like it!"

This passage confidently assures us... that Nothing can ever be successful in separating us from the love of Christ! Nothing!

We can rest in this truth, that God Himself has called us to be His, adopted, chosen, and selected each of us before we were conceived... as His! And nothing can separate us from His love! We are eternally His!

Thank You, Father, for this assurance, this promise, this Truth... that we are always Yours, and always within, covered by, immersed, surrounded... by the love of Christ!

"What Can Separate"
Vineyard Worship
https://youtu.be/-jCRmvvDFnE

March 16

Today's Encouragement is Romans 8:37 NLT *No, despite all these things, overwhelming victory is ours through Christ, who loved us.*

Overwhelming Victory is ours –

(Other translations read: we are *more than conquerors through Christ.*) In several instances in the history of the nation of Israel, when they were going into battle with other nations, all of which were sin-filled, idol-worshipping people, and also when those nations were attacking Israel, God Himself would intervene in miraculous and amazing ways! He is unlimited in power and creativity, and at times Israel walked into a victory without lifting a finger in battle! That's overwhelming victory! That's more than conquerors!

My friends, this victorious position, is ours through Christ, because of His love for us, because we are His. It is a spiritual blessing, a spiritual position, a spiritual truth that overrides time and this world. That is, we may look at our circumstances, and ask "This is victory?" Yet, it is not the circumstances, our debt, our failures, our troubles, or our battles that determine who we are in Christ... it is God's Word, His Truth, which is the authority, the Truth. Our earthly lives, our earthly realities are "but a mist"... transient and dissipating in a moment.

The eternal beings we are, as the Children of God, are not limited to this earthly life. We are, in Truth, though it may not be apparent to anyone, including ourselves, the chosen children of God, and because He is always victorious... overwhelming victory is ours... because we are His! He is victorious (of course) over every enemy, Sin, Fear, Doubt, Depression, Poverty, Hunger, and earthly or spiritual enemies, and therefore... so are we! (see the verse) Despite all these things, these enemies which persistently strive to defeat us... we are, now, already, through The Love of Jesus Christ... Overwhelmingly Victorious!

Lord, Your goodness, Your blessings for us, Your chosen children, are truly overwhelming. Thank You, Lord! Give us grateful hearts, as we choose to believe Your promises and truth.

"Victory Is Yours"
Bethel
https://youtu.be/rZatAFGvD_Q

March 17

Today's Encouragement is Romans 8:38-39 NLT *And I am convinced that nothing can ever separate us from God's love. Neither death nor life, neither angels nor demons, neither our fears for today nor our worries about tomorrow – not even the powers of hell can separate us from God's love. No power in the sky above or in the earth below – indeed, nothing in all creation will ever be able to separate us from the love of God that is revealed in Christ Jesus our Lord.*

Nothing can ever –

God's used chosen words, as He inspired them to be written, centuries ago, through people like you and me, in ancient languages... His words are Truth, selected specifically to clearly communicate His intended purposes. Hebrews 4:12a NLT *For the word of God is alive and powerful.*

I am completely convinced! I believe - I have concluded - it is my decision

That nothing! Including these things which threaten to separate

Can Ever! Never means never! Throughout all time, including Eternity

Separate Us from God's Love! God's love is revealed, perfectly through Jesus!

Selah (means pause and consider this)

My friends, we are now His! We always will be in His Love! Nothing can ever separate us from His Love! A list of those things which seemingly might threaten our relationship with God's Love is provided, but not limited. Whatever you may be facing, the giant in your path, perhaps unknown to anyone else, can Never! separate you from the immeasurable Love of Your Father.

Nothing. Never. Period.

Father God, thank You for providing us with this assurance, for creating this concrete, absolute, immovable, and immortal relationship with You. You are so good to us.

"Nothing Ever Could Separate Us"

Citizen Way

https://youtu.be/pxx0vPDfv0Q

March 18

Today's Encouragement is Romans 8:28,32,37 ESV *And we know that for those who love God all things work together for good, for those who are called according to his purpose. He who did not spare his own Son but gave him up for us all, how will he not also with him graciously give us all things? No, in all these things we are more than conquerors through him who loved us.*

All things –

We might miss a key point here. Let's consider the term "all things." It's mentioned in each of these remarkable and powerful verses in Romans 8, which is one of the most glorious chapters of the entire Bible. This chapter defines our life in the Holy Spirit, our status as God's children, the future Glory we shall know on that day, and finally God's everlasting love! Truly a wonderful, powerful chapter.

And "all things"—the original Greek term is "pas," and it means all things, everything, the whole, whoever, whatever.

28 **God works all things** — everything, the whole, whoever, whatever... for our Good!

32 **God gave us Christ** — so wouldn't He also, because He is full of Grace, give us all things—everything, the whole, whoever, whatever!

37 **We are more than conquerors**, overwhelmingly victorious in all things—everything, the whole, whoever, whatever!

God's word often repeats key truths, ideas, concepts, and promises in order to plant these seeds deeply within our spirits, hearts, and minds, to assure us of His intended message.

And so beautifully here, "All Things" is used to plant deeply these truths within us.

Lord, we thank You for emphasizing, repeating, patiently teaching, and guiding us to know You more, to know Your Truth and Your Love. You are so very patient and good to us.

"All Things"
Covenant Worship
https://youtu.be/dR-WF7J6Sf8

March 19

Today's Encouragement is Psalm 18:1-3 NLT *I love you, Lord; you are my strength. The Lord is my rock, my fortress, and my savior; my God is my rock, in whom I find protection. He is my shield, the power that saves me, and my place of safety. I called on the Lord, who is worthy of praise, and he saved me from my enemies.*

My place of safety –

David was king when he wrote this song, he finally had victory over all his enemies, and he was completely victorious! Most people would celebrate by congratulating themselves, recounting their glorious battles, and focusing on what their own great strength had accomplished.

Not David, not this "man after God's own heart." In true wisdom, David gave all the praise to God, because David knew that only God could have given him these great victories! So, David thanked God and praised Him with this song.

He mentions that God is his strength, rock, fortress, savior, protection, shield, power, and safety. And next, David says, "I called upon the Lord... and He saved me!"

No matter what battles we face, how incredible our enemies may seem, whether they are physical, emotional, or spiritual enemies, and there are many types of enemies set on destroying every one of God's children, He saves us! The enemy you're facing today may seem invincible — depression, hopelessness, fear, doubt, rage, sin, cancer, illness, people after you, debts, your past, your present or future, relationship failure. Whatever enemy it is for you at this moment... God can bring you through to victory... not because you deserve it, but because you are His own! He is the source of our strength, our hope, and confidence. We can trust Him to save us from all enemies!

Father God, thank You for protecting and strengthening us. You are always victorious! Please help us always to call out to You for help, to stay near to You, and so to remain safely in Your Presence, in Your Victory.

"Came to My Rescue"
Hillsong United
https://youtu.be/xhiRLb5Tvjg

March 20

Today's Encouragement is Psalm 57:1 NLT *Have mercy on me, O God, have mercy! I look to you for protection. I will hide beneath the shadow of your wings until the danger passes by.*

I will hide –

We are overwhelmingly victorious, as Romans 8:37 explains. And at times, as we face our battles, the giants in our lives head on; we are courageous through the strength He gives us (Philippians 4:13). And still at other times, we need a place to hide; we need God's mercy and His divine protection.

We are not, on our own accord, invincible warriors all the time. We are all, at some times, in need of rest, in need of protection, in need of a hiding place! Remember that *For everything there is a season.* (Ecclesiastes. 3:1), and at times, we just need to rest, even to hide, in His Presence.

My friends, He is just as willing to be our hiding place, as He is willing to be our courage and strength for the battle. Because—Philippians 4:19 NLT *And this same God who takes care of me will supply all your needs from his glorious riches, which have been given to us in Christ Jesus.* He will supply all our needs!

Father God, we thank You and praise You that You always provide all our needs, whether it is strengthening or safety in hiding. You are unlimited in every way, Father. Help us to wisely turn to you for our every need.

"You Are My Hiding Place"
Selah
https://youtu.be/xHr7Dy6sTqc

March 21

Today's Encouragement is Romans 10:10 NLT *For it is by believing in your heart that you are made right with God, and it is by openly declaring your faith that you are saved.*

Believe and declare –

It's clear, it's simple, it's possible for anyone who is willing, it's available, it's free, it's "almost too easy" we're tempted to think. We are saved by simply believing and declaring.

Salvation is often referred to as rebirth, we die to our old life and are reborn as new creations. Jesus said we must be born again (John 3:3) and Paul says if anyone is in Christ, they are a new creation (2 Cor. 5:17).

Now just consider this for a moment. We are born again, new creations, ok, right... so what do newborns do? What do they know? What do they need? They can't do much of anything! They don't know anything, and they need to be fed, changed, and cared for intensely! My friends we begin our Christian life by salvation... it is the beginning point. It's real and it's sure, yet it is not fully matured. We can begin to grow as Christians in our relationship with the Father, the Son, and the Spirit! This growing and maturing is our lifelong blessing, obligation, and privilege!

Galatians 5:22-23a NLT *But the Holy Spirit produces this kind of fruit in our lives: love, joy, peace, patience, kindness, goodness, faithfulness, gentleness, and self-control.*

Mature plants produce fruit; immature plants don't! These fruits are the clear marks of a mature Christian, someone who has experienced a growing, vibrant, sincere relationship with God! They are spiritually mature!

Salvation is the essential beginning of a Christian life, but, my friends, it is far from the end of this wonderful journey! Don't miss the rest of this blessing by stopping at salvation!

Lord, help us to grow in faith as Your loved, chosen, and adopted children. Help us to grow in relationship with you now that we are Yours.

"For Your Splendor"
Christy Nockels
https://youtu.be/DC_QCKCuAM8

March 22

Today's Encouragement is Psalm 25:5 NLT *Lead me by your truth and teach me, for you are the God who saves me. All day long I put my hope in you.*

Lead me –

David asks God to lead him, by the Truth, and teach him. He is recognizing, and acknowledging that God, alone, is the One who guides, teaches us truth, and who saves! He, alone, is our source of hope!

This psalm begins, (v1) *O Lord, I give my life to you.* Such clear dedication and devotion to God... a wonderful way to begin a prayer. Total surrender; no conditions. Just – Surrender.

Next, David asks God to lead him. Friends, we need God! We need Him to lead us through the day, the night, at all times, through workdays and rest times, through happy times and sorrows, through success or failures, always!

Today's song offers a wonderful way to pray these truths, to offer ourselves totally to Him, to ask for His guidance, and to surrender to His will and His ways. To learn from Him and live within His protection, and His defense. There is no better life, my friends!

I invite you to join me and sing, pray, and worship along with this song, the lyrics are provided, and let this be your prayer today.

Father God, we need You! ...and we surrender to whatever You choose for us.

"To You, Oh Lord"

Graham Kendrick

https://youtu.be/OthK0qvRx5w

March 23

Today's Encouragement is John 13:17 NLT *Now that you know these things, God will bless you for doing them.*

Knowing and doing –

Imagine with me please, you are a 6-year-old child about to go ice skating on a frozen pond. Dad is there to assure you that the ice is several inches thick, and you can see others skating, yet you still are uncertain that this is safe.

You have knowledge of the thickness of the ice from your Dad's reassurance, and from the other skaters, you have faith in your Dad and what your eyes can see - yet, you haven't skated, you haven't done it... what you believe can be done. It is not until you do skate... then you have done it! And then you experience the blessing. The joy and fun of skating! This blessing comes because you did what you knew and have chosen to believe.

The same is true with our faith. We read God's Word, hear it preached, sing of His power, glory, mercy, and love.... All of which are not "on the ice" but rather standing on the shore. These are passive functions, hearing, choosing, believing... and yet "doing" is the active function... acting and living according to our faith!

And this, my friends, the *doing*...this is where blessings are poured out!

What is it that God is inviting, encouraging, and equipping you to do? What has He been teaching you, granting you knowledge of, increasing your faith for?

Whatever this may be, my friend... You will be blessed if/when you *do it*!

Father. Please help your children to act on the faith and knowledge which You have given us, so that we may be blessed by You!

"Give Me Faith"
Elevation Worship
https://youtu.be/bBfhfV9WcNI

March 25

Today's Encouragement is Romans 12:3 ESV *For by the grace given to me I say to everyone among you not to think of himself more highly than he ought to think, but to think with sober judgment, each according to the measure of faith that God has assigned.*

The measure of Faith –

God has given differing measures, degrees, or depths of faith to each believer. We now have the privilege and choice to grow our Faith and to exercise what Faith we have.

This "differing measures" thought is supported by the following verses. Jesus explained that some may have a tiny faith, like a "mustard seed"' measure (Matthew 17:20). Some have "little faith" (Matt. 6:30); some have "great faith," like the centurion. (Matthew 8:10 NIV) So, it's clear that there are different measures of Faith!

And, we have the opportunity and privilege to nurture that faith to its greatest fullness! Jude 1:20 *But you, beloved, building yourselves up in your most holy faith and praying in the Holy Spirit... Build yourselves up in faith!*

Friends, we grow in faith by prayer and by living in, exercising, and "practicing" the measure of Faith we do have... as we live in Faith, trusting Him, then our Faith grows, strengthens, and matures.

Father, increase our faith, help us to become the godly men and women you have designed us to be, that you desire us to be! And may Faith become the primary characteristic of our lives. We pray in Jesus' Name.

"Increase My Faith"
Buddy Davis
https://youtu.be/6Bd4-jQRyFY

March 25

Today's Encouragement is Matthew 6:14-15 NLT *If you forgive those who sin against you, your heavenly Father will forgive you. But if you refuse to forgive others, your Father will not forgive your sins.*

If you forgive –

Jesus was – still is – unequivocal—(leaving no doubt, without variance)

He was careful in His choice of words and fully aware of the power of His teaching. He never spoke carelessly or without purpose.

With this perspective, do you notice the word "if"?

This verse amazes and perplexes me. Since we know we are saved by faith in Christ, how is it that we must also forgive others (v14) in order to be forgiven by our Father?

Is it possible that IF we refuse to (I just can't!) forgive others... we also haven't truly recognized the immeasurable, incomparable Forgiveness that we ourselves have already received from God? As the parable in Matthew 18 explains, we do not fully understand God's forgiveness until we ourselves can forgive others. Matt. 18:33 NLT *"Shouldn't you have had mercy on your fellow servant, just as I had mercy on you?"*

Do you and I deserve God's forgiveness? Of course not!

My Friend, choose to Forgive! Forgive all, Now, choose forgiveness for those who have hurt you, and be set free to experience God's immeasurable grace and His Forgiveness—by releasing the unforgivable harm that has been done to you!

Father, remind us of the immeasurable love and mercy that You've already shown to us by forgiving us for everything, and open our hearts to likewise forgive everyone who has harmed us! Help us to forgive now and every time the hurtful memory returns.

"Forgiveness"

Matthew West

https://youtu.be/h1Lu5udXEZI

March 26

Today's Encouragement is Philippians 4:6-7 NLT *Don't worry about anything; instead, pray about everything. Tell God what you need and thank him for all he has done. Then you will experience God's peace, which exceeds anything we can understand. His peace will guard your hearts and minds as you live in Christ Jesus.*

God's Peace –

We'll focus on this powerful, encouraging, hope-filled, promise-filled passage for the next several days. It's a great one to memorize; it provides wisdom and guidance as to how to stop worrying, how to pray, and how to have God's Peace! It's a how-to verse for dealing with the stress of this life, our chronic propensity to worry, fret, and obsess. I've been 'an expert' on worry most of my life, but I'm finally gaining some freedom, and this passage is the key to that freedom!

Psalms 119:11 *I have hidden your word in my heart, that I might not sin against you.* When we hide the Word of God in our hearts (through memorizing and thinking about it, we have the strength to resist Sin!

So, read and re-read this passage in Philippians, and break it down into bite-sized phrases to help you remember and hide it in your heart.

Don't worry about *anything*.

instead, pray about *everything*.

Tell God what you need,

and thank him for all he has done.

Then you will experience God's Peace,

which exceeds anything we can understand.

His Peace will guard your hearts and minds

as you live in Christ Jesus.

Father, help us to hide Your word in our hearts, beginning with this passage, and please Lord, fill us with Your perfect Peace as we strive to apply the truths of this passage to our lives!

"Be Anxious for Nothing"

Sherri Youngward

https://youtu.be/UPzKtlJW6Tw

March 27

Today's Encouragement is Philippians 4:6-7 NLT *Don't worry about anything; instead, pray about everything. Tell God what you need and thank him for all he has done. Then you will experience God's peace, which exceeds anything we can understand. His peace will guard your hearts and minds as you live in Christ Jesus.*

Don't worry about anything! –

(I pray you aren't growing tired of this amazing passage. This repetition is helpful to memorize, or just remember God's Truths.)

This idea isn't new! We tend to think that we have a much harder life than folks who came before us, that we carry the weight of the world with today's stresses and bad news and the constant noise of life, input from TV, social media, and the seemingly, always negative news... There's so much 'good material to feed our worry!' But 2000 years ago, Jesus gave us the solution to a life of worry!

As He always does, Jesus calls us away from the cares of this world, to focus on the Real World of the Kingdom of Heaven... the Spiritual Truths of the Spiritual, Everlasting World which we have inherited as His people.

He calls us away, from fears, anxieties, and worries... into Faith, Hope, and Trust in Him... totally contrary to the ways of this earth... and we can only walk in His ways as we focus on Him, turn our eyes, and hearts to Him. We can do this amid the clamor of this life, at any time... by turning to Him!

Matthew 6:31-33 *"So don't worry about these things, saying, 'What will we eat? What will we drink? What will we wear?' These things dominate the thoughts of unbelievers, but your heavenly Father already knows all your needs. Seek the Kingdom of God above all else, and live righteously, and he will give you everything you need."*

My friends, we choose to worry, or not to worry. The only successful plan of "not worrying" is Trust. Turn to Jesus in Trust!

Father, Help us to choose to Trust You, to seek Your Kingdom, and leave worry to those who choose not to trust You!

"We Turn Our Eyes"
Adrienne and Jeremy Camp
https://youtu.be/KzEQP9-kkck

March 28

Today's Encouragement is Philippians 4:6-7 NLT *Don't worry about anything; instead, pray about everything. Tell God what you need and thank him for all he has done. Then you will experience God's peace, which exceeds anything we can understand. His peace will guard your hearts and minds as you live in Christ Jesus.*

Instead, pray about everything –

Can you see the choice being made here? Turning away from worry to prayer, from our world to His, from our problems, fears, our self-focus... to Him and His power, to His ways, and to His Truth! It is so clear, so simple! Yet, breaking the old patterns, habits, and even addiction to fear, worry, and anxiety is far from easy... still, the Truth is simple.

Focus on God's power. Pray about everything! Let God handle it!

We sometimes think we shouldn't pray for this or that, we shouldn't 'bother God' with this or that, or we want to "pray correctly" so that our prayers will be answered. My friends, God loves you and He wants to hear your heart. He's our loving Father, a Good, Good Father, perfect in every way, and He hears what we're praying- with His loving heart... as through the filter of Jesus, He "sifts" our prayers to comply with His will, purifying the focus of our prayer to be consistent with His Will.

In everything, my friends, every situation, every tragedy, every fear, and every worry... In everything, our answer, our response, our plan, our best choice is Prayer! Take everything to Him! The blessings that await us when we turn from worry to prayer are pretty unbelievable!

Lord, help us to let go of all our worries, fears, and anxieties and turn to You in prayer, to surrender our burdens through prayer to You.

"I Get on My Knees"
Jaci Velasquez
https://youtu.be/caAb-rMTiRI

March 29

Today's Encouragement is Philippians 4:6-7 NLT *Don't worry about anything; instead, pray about everything. Tell God what you need, and thank him for all he has done. Then you will experience God's peace, which exceeds anything we can understand. His peace will guard your hearts and minds as you live in Christ Jesus.*

Tell God what you need –

What? Does God need me to tell Him what I need? Well, no, He doesn't... but we do! We have a need to express our desires, and our needs to God. When we do, we begin to hear ourselves asking Him, we pause and say, "Is this wise, is this a good thing to ask Him for, am I being petty or selfish, am I praying for blessings for myself and others or for harm?"

We have just been invited to pray about *everything*, now we are invited to pour out our needs, not a Christmas wish list of selfish wants, but our *needs*.

As you do, consider Jesus' fervent, agonizing prayer in the Garden the very night he would be arrested, He prayed, *"Father, if you are willing, remove this cup from me. Nevertheless, not my will, but yours, be done."* (Luke 22:42)

The perfect ending statement to every prayer. "Your will be done!" Yet, we are still free to pour out our every need to Our Loving Father! So freely ask, and then surrender your request to God's Perfect Will, His will that brings all things around for our Good! (Romans 8:28)

Father, Thank You for the privilege of bringing our every need to You. Thank You for the comforting truth that Your will is always for our good! We are amazed at Your love and kindness for us. Help us to take our needs to You in prayer.

"What a Friend We Have in Jesus"
unknown artist
https://youtu.be/YTpUQO0aryw

March 30

Today's Encouragement is Philippians 4:6-7 NLT *Don't worry about anything; instead, pray about everything. Tell God what you need and thank him for all he has done. Then you will experience God's peace, which exceeds anything we can understand. His peace will guard your hearts and minds as you live in Christ Jesus.*

Thank Him for all He has done –

A thankful, grateful prayer is so much more powerful than a doubtful, uncertain prayer. God doesn't reject our prayers... ever, He hears and understands and responds, always. He can do this because He is God, we cannot understand how He could... because we are not God!

And because we are not God, it is helpful for our own spirits, hearts, and minds to pray from an attitude, from a position of, thankful, grateful Trust. That is, as we pray, we can say, Father Thank You for listening to me, Thank You for the privilege of coming to You with this need, thank You for all You have done and that You are going to do... (whatever is on your heart at the time to pray about).

When we pray with thankful, grateful hearts, we are expressing Faith that God will hear, will act, and will Himself take on the burden and cares we have—so that we don't continue to carry them.

1 Peter 5:7 NLT *Give all your worries and cares to God, for he cares about you.*

Father, we thank You that You care about us, help us to bring all our cares and worries to You, and to trust You, to leave our burdens with You, and to live in sincere gratitude and thankfulness for who You Are, and all you've done for us! We pray in Jesus' Name.

"Cares Chorus"
Kelly Willard
https://youtu.be/pZVwTwkvu7Q

March 31

Today's Encouragement is Philippians 4:6-7 NLT *Don't worry about anything; instead, pray about everything. Tell God what you need and thank him for all he has done. Then you will experience God's peace, which exceeds anything we can understand. His peace will guard your hearts and minds as you live in Christ Jesus.*

Experience God's Peace –

Notice that Paul says, confidently... "*Then you WILL experience God's Peace! When*"? As a result of, choosing prayer instead of worry, telling God everything you need with a heart of gratitude and thankfulness... the result of this is God's Peace!

We cannot know the Peace of God and also choose to worry. Worry is a common form of fear, as is anxiety. When we ask someone why they are so worried or anxious the answer is often "I'm afraid that...."

Repeatedly God speaks to us through the Bible – "Do Not Fear," He says this in so many ways! "I am always with you," "I have prepared a place for you," "I am your protection," "your fortress," "your shade," "your deliverer," "your Father", "I am your Savior," and "I am everything that you need"!

My friend, what more can God say, or do, to assure us that He is our Peace and that He longs for us to know His Peace! His Peace is confident faith in the face of trouble.

Daniel-in-the-lion's-den type of Peace.

And now, we know how!—He has told us in this passage—We can and will experience His Peace!

Help us, Lord, to turn from fear to faith, prayerfully, thankfully bringing our every need to You in confident prayer; and so, to truly experience Your Peace.

"He Is Our Peace"

Maranatha Singers

https://youtu.be/hrdo7e9JJTY

April 1

Today's Encouragement is Philippians 4:6-7 NLT *Don't worry about anything; instead, pray about everything. Tell God what you need, and thank him for all he has done. Then you will experience God's peace, which exceeds anything we can understand. His peace will guard your hearts and minds as you live in Christ Jesus.*

Exceeds anything we can understand –

Other translations read, the peace which ...

- "is beyond our understanding,"
- "passes all understanding,"
- "surpasses understanding," and
- "transcends all understanding."'

God's Peace doesn't make sense, given the circumstances! Those who don't know Him will think we are crazy to be at Peace in this situation, it doesn't make any logical sense in this predicament! Because it is not our circumstances which provide our Peace... rather it is Him!

Because we have prayed about everything, given God our needs, in thankfulness and gratitude to Him, and have chosen faith over worry, —- then His Peace arrives... a Peace which isn't logical in this situation.

(God is not limited by man's determination of what is logical or not. Who decided that God must meet our human definition of 'logic'?)

Thank you, Father God, that You and Your Peace are far greater than anything that we, in our limited human capacity, can understand. Help us believe, trust, and seek Your Peace.

"It Passes All My Understanding"
Cherie Call
https://youtu.be/_6vUXhQMAig

April 2

Today's Encouragement is (still, and this is the last day) Philippians 4:6-7 NLT *Don't worry about anything; instead, pray about everything. Tell God what you need, and thank him for all he has done. Then you will experience God's peace, which exceeds anything we can understand. His peace will guard your hearts and minds as you live in Christ Jesus.*

His peace will guard –

When we experience God's Peace, then His Peace guards our hearts and minds... as we continue to live in Jesus.

The fruit borne by following the instruction/wisdom/guidance of this passage... is God's Peace, which is beyond our ability to understand, guarding our hearts and minds.

Most of us already have enough battle scars, some still open wounds, in this life to know that we need all the guarding of our hearts and minds that we can get! God's Peace is what provides this protection! Jesus is our Shepherd, and the shepherd guards his sheep, protects them from the attacks of all enemies; He feeds, and cares for them... This is the image of Christ which we are provided in Scripture. And this loving, caring Shepherd, provides for us a peace-filled life... with our entire lives, hearts, and minds under His Divine All-Powerful Protection.

Yet, we can choose to live outside of this protection, when we choose – to worry and not to pray, when we choose not to bring our needs to God or to thank Him for all He has done for us... then we have no peace. The choice is ours, as God's beloved, chosen sons and daughters... we can live within His Peace, with our minds and hearts guarded by Him... OR we can live a life of worry, with our hearts and minds unprotected, harassed by the cares of this life.

Father, help us to choose Your Peace as You have taught us in the passage. Thank You, Lord, for the freedom to choose Your Way! And for the Peace You provide us when we do!

"Peace"

We the Kingdom

https://youtu.be/_UREG0ZRhlY

April 3

Today's Encouragement is Psalm 100:4 NLT *Enter his gates with thanksgiving; go into his courts with praise. Give thanks to him and praise his name.*

With Thanksgiving –

We may think at times, "I don't really have anything to be thankful for!" My friends, it may seem that way sometimes... but the Truth isn't subject to our feelings! God's Truth is eternal, never changing!

This prayer of thanksgiving has helped me every day to gratefully remember all He has done and will do for me. It contains just a few of His promises and reminders of His already-provided blessings. It always lifts our hearts when we come to Him with thanks!

Father God, I thank You that:

I am Your son (or daughter) (John 1:12), blood-bought (1 Cor. 6:20), sanctified (Hebrews 10:10), and justified (Romans 5:1), made Righteous by the Blood of Jesus (Romans 5:9) and filled with Your Holy Spirit (John 14:16)

No weapon formed against me will prevail (Isaiah 54:17); You are my Ever-Present Help in time of trouble (Psalm 45:1) You will never leave us nor forsake us (Heb. 13:5)

You have Good Plans for me, plans to bless me, to give me a hope and a future. (Jeremiah 29:11)

I am more than a Conqueror (Romans 8:37). I have been given a spirit of power, love, and self-control, and not of fear! (2 Timothy 1:7). I have the Mind of Christ (1 Cor. 2:16). I am the righteousness of God. (2 Corinthians 5:21)

Without You, I can do nothing (John 15:5), but I can do all things through Christ who gives me Strength (Philippians 4:13)

You have called me to feed Your sheep (John 21:17); to be Your ambassador (2 Corinthians 5:20).

Father, grant us grateful hearts as we remember all that you have done for us. Thank You for Your goodness to us...

"Lord You've Been Good to Me"
Graham Kendrick
https://youtu.be/fnbQF8rb9Q8

April 4

Today's Encouragement is Psalm 34:1 NLT *I will praise the Lord at all times. I will constantly speak his praises.*

Constantly speak His praises –

The songwriter David is rejoicing over God's goodness to him, grateful for God's deliverance (v4) and His salvation (v6).

What would our lives be like if we actually did this? Imagine if we praised God at all times, constantly speaking His praises. Could we consider this just for a moment? Selah—(means pause and consider this)

The car breaks down – "I Praise You, Lord, I trust that You're going to help me deal with this and You will work this for my good." (Romans 8:28)

A bad medical diagnosis – 'I Praise You, Lord, You are my healer, should this end in my death, I will live in glorious joy eternally with You!' (John 3:15)

Good news comes – '" Praise You, Lord, Every good and perfect gift comes from You!' (James 1:17)

So, is it possible, my friends, to constantly speak His Praises, at all times, and in all circumstances?

In our hearts and minds and spirits, we can praise Him always. When we forget to praise Him, we can, at that moment, choose to praise Him because we have remembered! Nothing we do is perfect, we're terribly inconsistent, aren't we? Maybe consistently imperfect! Yet God finds our perfection in Jesus! But we are most blessed... when we praise Him at all times, singing and speaking His praise!

Thank You, Father, for Jesus, for eternal life, for forgiveness, for Your amazing promises to us, for choosing us to be Your own family... Your goodness to us, Your Love for us, is overwhelming, immeasurable!

Help Us to Always Praise You!

"Stones"

Kim Walker-Smith

https://youtu.be/vtyoJX-2uig

April 5

Today's Encouragement is 2 Corinthians 12:8-9 NLT *Three different times I begged the Lord to take it away. Each time he said, "My grace is all you need."*

All you need –

It's difficult for us humans to conceive this concept of Grace. It's often described as "unmerited favor," the approval of God, undeserved, unearned, freely given from Him to us—simply because He Loves us. It goes against our inherent understanding of fairness and justice because we know – we don't deserve His mercy and grace! In truth, we deserve punishment, for all have sinned (Romans 3:23). But God is not bound by our human conventions, our concepts of fairness or justice. He created these moral principles, and He can bend them or redefine them to use as He chooses.

In this passage, God tells Paul that He will not remove the painful "thorn in his flesh." Something I'm sure that we'd all like removed, too, whatever it was! But God in His wisdom says, "No, My Grace is enough, it's all you need." We never are very satisfied when God says, "No," but we must acknowledge that He knows what He is doing.

Friends, His Grace truly is all we need! Give that a few moments of thought.

Father, thank You for the incredible gift of Your Amazing Grace, which is truly all we need!

"Your Grace is Enough"
Matt Maher
https://youtu.be/LISbMRp0Y64

April 6

Today's Encouragement is Matthew 5:9 NLT *God blesses those who work for peace, for they will be called the children of God.*

Work for Peace –

Ever notice how much fighting and arguing goes on each day? Talking heads on TV, Radio talk, social media, even in our homes.... We fight! We proudly proclaim, "A" is best, it's right, it's the way, it's the answer! I support 'A'!" ("A" can be whatever you wish, sports team, political position, candidate, climate issue, vaccination, the list is nauseatingly endless!)

And others proclaim "No, you are wrong! 'A' is wrong! 'B' is right, it's the answer! I believe in 'B'!" Or C or D... take your pick, because in the end... none of it matters! And this battle is endless. And as Ecclesiastes wisely explains, "All is meaningless!"

The voice of reason, the one who works for peace, recognizes that people have differing opinions, but these opinions should not, do not have to, drive a wedge of animosity, and when fully mature, hatred between us.

Consider the underlying source of all this arguing – James 4:1 NLT *What is causing the quarrels and fights among you? Don't they come from the evil desires at war within you?*

And the solution to this endless "war"? True peace only comes from God! Jesus is the Prince of Peace. One of His many but significant titles.

Peace within, from Jesus, the Prince of Peace, leads to peace without, peace between us.

Father, help us to work for peace, to find a way to live together in Your Peace, with no more screaming, yelling, arguing, and fighting with each other. We ask in Jesus' Name.

"Peace"

Josh Baldwin

https://youtu.be/mO9NNVoyO3k

April 7

Today's Encouragement is Job 2:9-10 NLT *His wife said to him, "Are you still trying to maintain your integrity? Curse God and die." But Job replied, "You talk like a foolish woman. Should we accept only good things from the hand of God and never anything bad?" So, in all this, Job said nothing wrong.*

Accept only good and never bad –

Job lost everything, his possessions, his children, his wealth, and even his own health. His wife told him to just give up, "Curse God and die!" (What a joy she was!) But Job held strong. He recognized that God gives, and God takes away (Job 1:21); that life involves both joy and pain, peace and suffering. So, in the inevitable times of pain... when suffering seems so overwhelming... put all your Hope in God...

Friends, we may never understand why... but we can be assured that He does. We don't have to know everything... because He does... It's almost supremely arrogant to demand that we understand everything... folks, that is God's business... Let Him handle it. We just trust Him... HOPE in Him...

Lord God, please grant us such faith, that we might trust You enough to accept both good and trouble. And when trouble does come, as it does to all, help us to continually look to You. You are our Hope. You are the Only Hope. And You are always Faithful!

"Our Hope Endures"
Natalie Grant
https://youtu.be/unD8w1lZ4yU

April 8

Today's Encouragement is Hebrews 13:15 NLT *Therefore, let us offer through Jesus a continual sacrifice of praise to God, proclaiming our allegiance to his name.*

Sacrifice of Praise –

Praise as a Sacrifice? Might that mean it's not convenient? Or that we just don't really feel like praising God? Or that we think we don't really have anything to be grateful for?

Friends, we believers have all received the greatest gift any person could ever receive... eternal life! We have life today, our breath, His Perfect Love, and His mercy which are new every morning! We can always, always (continually) thank Him and Praise Him for that!

Your mind might be saying, "Yeah but my life stinks!" I won't argue that sometimes life seems more than we can bear, but we still have the choice, every day... to choose—life or death, faith or doubt, hope or despair.

This life is filled with problems and pain. He never promised we'd live free of these, but that He would be with us through it all.

Choose Life, my friend... Choose Hope and Faith and Praise Him for all He is.

Lord, Help us to choose to trust You and to Praise You continually this day, regardless of our circumstances.

"Ever Be"
Bethel Music
https://youtu.be/BhasSpSBdEE

April 9

Today's Encouragement is 2 Thessalonians 2:16-17 NLV *Now may our Lord Jesus Christ himself and God our Father, who loved us and by his grace gave us eternal comfort and a wonderful hope, comfort you and strengthen you in every good thing you do and say.*

Eternal comfort –

Isn't it interesting how the writer puts this prayer? He states that God loved us and by His grace – gave us these gifts! Then, He prays that God will strengthen and encourage our hearts in every good thing we do and say. These gifts are eternal comfort and wonderful hope! Friends, these blessings are already given to us because of His love and by His grace.

So, consider what amazing blessings we have received. Already! Not someday in some uncertain future, but an accomplished act... Eternal Comfort and Encouragement! And Wonderful Hope! Already ours?

"But", we admit, "I often don't feel comforted, encouraged, or hopeful... much less eternally... so can this be true?" Friends, our true standing is from God and is not limited by how we feel, or what we think, nor any other limitation. We are adopted sons and daughters of the Living God, given amazing blessings like Eternal Comfort and Wonderful Hope! Whether we fully recognize it or not, whether we act upon our position as His children or not, doesn't change the reality.

Just as if we were financially broke, but suddenly inherited a million dollars which is in a bank account in our name. If we never are told about it, never believe it, never draw upon it, never use it... we remain impoverished, and we feel poor... but in our minds only... in Reality—we are rich. We just don't believe or "feel" it, so it isn't real to us. In the same way, we are blessed unimaginably as the sons and daughters of the Living God, in reality, whether we feel like it or not!

Eternal comfort and Wonderful Hope... are just the tip of the iceberg!

Lord, open our eyes, hearts, and minds to the incredible, even limitless blessings we have from You. Help us to believe and rejoice in Your amazing kindness and generosity. Help us to accept Your Eternal Comfort and Wonderful Hope today, Your gifts to your beloved children. Please Encourage our hearts Lord and strengthen us for every good thing we do and say!

"Lord, You've Been Good to Me"
Graham Kendrick
https://youtu.be/fnbQF8rb9Q8

April 10

Today's Encouragement is Romans 8:14-15 NLT *For all who are led by the Spirit of God are children of God. So you have not received a spirit that makes you fearful slaves. Instead, you received God's Spirit when he adopted you as his own children. Now we call him, "Abba, Father."*

Children of God -

We too often think to ourselves, "Yeah, God loves me, but He loves everybody... so it's no big deal." Our minds are tricky things (deceitful) and the lies we believe keep us broken, weak, and alone. How often do we say "Yes, but..." when we read God's promises and His love? As in, "Yes, but that's for good people, who really love God, who live good lives, But not for people like me, who have had the past or problems that I have."

Friend, God's love is specific... He chose YOU to adopt as His beloved child. He makes no mistakes; he chooses His children carefully. We are among those who are privileged to call him Daddy (Abba). This is not adoption into an institution filled with lost and lonely children... this is the embrace of a Loving, Personal, Close, and Perfect Father. And You are chosen (by one who knows everything about you, past and future) to be HIS!

This is the Good News... we just believe, and He does this (and even much more) for us... What loving father doesn't want to bless his kids with everything? And God is so much greater than any loving father we can imagine.

Lord, open our hearts to accept Your Love and embrace the truth that we are Your very deeply loved sons and daughters. Because of Jesus!

"Who You Say I Am"

Hillsong

https://youtu.be/IcC1Bp13n_4

April 11

Today's Encouragement is Psalm 91:1-2 NLT *He who dwells in the shelter of the Most High will abide in the shadow of the Almighty. I will say to the Lord, "My refuge and my fortress, my God, in whom I trust."*

Dwell in the shelter –

This is my very favorite Psalm. It is filled with His blessings, protection, love, mercy, kindness, compassion, security, rest, comfort and so much more.

And all these promises and blessings are ours when we dwell in His shelter. Dwelling in Him is our choice, my friends. We can "dwell on" or "dwell in" anything else, we have lots of options. Bills to be paid, our health, our weight, what to eat, what to wear, how to please another person, how to avoid another person, how to raise the kids, how to deal with this or that, the national debt, world politics, you name it – we have lots of options...

And my friends, dwelling on, or in, anything other than The Shelter of The Most High, yields nothing! Only in God's Shelter, His Presence, His Truth, His Peace, Grace, and Love... only here do we find His promises fulfilled, our protection, peace, and blessings far beyond all this world has to offer. To dwell in His shelter, to abide in His shadow, we must be near to Him. Like standing under His umbrella of protection, we have to be NEAR to Him!

Father, help us choose to "Dwell in Your shelter," today and always; to stay near to You. You are always true to Your promises. We trust in You.

"Jesus Draw Me Close"
Lenny LeBlanc
https://youtu.be/kvKQZBH5rZU

April 12

Today's Encouragement is Hebrews 12:15a NLT *Look after each other so that none of you fails to receive the grace of God.*

Look after each other –

We know it's a good idea, we think about it from time to time, and we even watch Hallmark movies about it (well, some of us do!) Looking after each other is a gift we can give to others that blesses us, a gift that gives.

Friends, when, as believers in Christ, we care for each other, pray for each other, and do any kindness for another person, we are sharing God's Love. We are even, and this blows my mind... expressing Love to God! We demonstrate and act out, our Love for God when we love others. Hebrews 6:10 NLT *For God is not unjust. He will not forget how hard you have worked for him and how you have shown your love to him by caring for other believers, as you still do.*

And notice the context... "so that... none of you fails to receive the Grace of God"! We experience the grace of God when others look after us! After a terrible car wreck years ago, I was very well cared for by hospital staff, my precious wife, and several others... it was very humbling and yet such a blessing to be "looked after." I certainly saw God's Grace and Love in action from these caring people.

And now, Lord, it is our turn, to look after others... especially believers, but also those who have not yet believed... so that no one fails to receive Your Grace!

"Living Hope"
Phil Wickham
https://youtu.be/9f2FXxDVO6w

April 13

Today's Encouragement is Hebrews 12:15b NLT *Watch out that no poisonous root of bitterness grows up to trouble you, corrupting many.*

Bitterness –

It's described here as a poisonous root. Consider that analogy with me, a root grows plants, it is the source of nourishment and produces a flower, bush, or tree many times its size, if the root dies, so does its plant. So it is with bitterness... it starts as a seed, a thought of resentment, anger, hatred even, planted within the soil of our heart, our soul our emotions... and it begins to grow, silently, quietly, until it begins to break the surface, and we then have this growth to deal with, having almost a life of its own ... it drives us into separation from others, even from God! It is bent on only destruction; no good ever comes from this root!

My friends, the alternative, the antidote to this bitterness root... is the Grace of God. Once we see how great our own sin is, and how immeasurably great His Grace is for our sins... we can recognize that there is no room in our lives for bitterness, resentment, or unforgiveness (all have this same root)! When we live under and within the Grace of God, then we can share, and extend that Grace with others... and those who have hurt us, no matter how deeply, even our disappointment with God Himself... can never overcome the Grace and Love and Mercy of God for us.

When a root is dug up, and exposed to the direct sunlight, it withers and dies. The only way a root lives is when it is buried in the soil. When we recognize and confess our bitterness, resentment, and unforgiveness... the root is exposed to the direct sunlight of God's Truth, His Grace, and Love!

In the Light of His Love... the root of bitterness withers and dies!

Lord, please expose to us the root of bitterness, resentment, shame, or unforgiveness that lives within us, uproot it, and remove it from us, Lord. Thank You for giving us freedom from this poisonous root!

"Let Me Live"

Charley Pride

https://youtu.be/BKuBP7dNug0

April 15

Today's Encouragement is 2 Peter 1:2-3 NLT. *May God give you more and more grace and peace as you grow in your knowledge of God and Jesus our Lord. By his divine power, God has given us everything we need for living a godly life. We have received all of this by coming to know him, the one who called us to himself by means of his marvelous glory and excellence.*

Given us everything we need –

Imagine having everything you need. Not only physical needs but emotional and spiritual needs, all satisfied. It's rather surprising to learn... we already do! We have everything that "we need for living a godly life," and, please explain to me... what else really matters?

We may not "feel" like we have everything, at least not yet!

But our feelings aren't our true reality. Being unaware of our blessings doesn't make us impoverished. But rejection of the blessings God has provided us, refusing to search for, to trust in His Hand at work in our lives... this makes us destitute.

Lord God, open our eyes and hearts to the amazing blessings You have given to us, Your loved children.

"Blessings"
Laura Story
https://youtu.be/XQan9L3yXjc

April 16

Today's Encouragement is Luke 23:48-49 NLT *And when all the crowd that came to see the crucifixion saw what had happened, they went home in deep sorrow. But Jesus' friends, including the women who had followed him from Galilee, stood at a distance watching.*

Stood at a distance –

Perhaps this group of "Jesus' friends" included the disciples. Certainly Mary Magdalene, maybe Nicodemus, or the centurion whose daughter was restored to life, perhaps Lazarus too was there with his sisters Mary and Martha, all these unnamed... standing, watching... in silence... from a distance.

For a moment, allow your imagination to take you to that day, to that very place, you're among them, standing with his disciples around, the people who loved Him, respected Him, knew Him... and now the sun has blackened, the earth quaked... he's been killed, brutally, viciously beaten, and crucified... and it's over, it's all over. His life is gone, his wisdom which He shared with everyone, His Love, His caring attention to each person's need... he seemed to look directly into our hearts.... and now, this wonderful man, this Son of God.... is dead.

Such a sobering, heartbreaking thought... but my friends...

we know the rest of the story... We know that... Sunday's Coming!

Father Help us remember, no matter how dark today may seem, this is not the end, You are still in control, You have a plan, and You can do anything!

"It's Friday, But Sunday's Coming!" (please don't miss this message!)

SM Lockridge

https://youtu.be/e_sgheKJH4g

April 17

Today's Encouragement is Mark 16:6 NLT *But the angel said, "Don't be alarmed. You are looking for Jesus of Nazareth, who was crucified. He isn't here! He is risen from the dead! Look, this is where they laid his body."*

He has Risen –

Friends, He isn't in the grave. He isn't walking around the multiple "holy places" in Israel. He doesn't "haunt" the cathedrals or hang out in our church buildings. No, He is Risen! He lives today in His perfected form, ruling all of Heaven and ruling the Kingdom of God – which is within us!

The following magnificent description of Him, the Resurrected Christ, only begins to describe Him! Revelation 1:13-16 NLT *And standing in the middle of the lampstands was someone like the Son of Man. He was wearing a long robe with a gold sash across his chest. His head and his hair were white like wool, as white as snow. And his eyes were like flames of fire. His feet were like polished bronze refined in a furnace, and his voice thundered like mighty ocean waves. He held seven stars in his right hand, and a sharp two-edged sword came from his mouth. And his face was like the sun in all its brilliance.*

Jesus—Then, was a seemingly ordinary person,

Jesus—Now, is a completely Extraordinary Being!

Jesus—Forever, Lord of lords, King of kings, our Savior, our Master, our Friend!

Father, help us to recognize that Jesus is truly risen and glorified as described above, King of Heaven, and yet, still our friend.

"King of Heaven"

Paul Baloche

https://youtu.be/VO76W9Zw0cs

April 18

Today's Encouragement is John 14:13 NLT *You can ask for anything in my name, and I will do it so that the Son can bring glory to the Father.*

In my name –

Once upon a time... a young man walked into a bank and asked to withdraw $10,000. The teller skeptically asked, "And what account number?" The young man replied with his account number and was told, "I'm sorry sir there is only $26.15 in your name."

The man said, "OK, how about my Father's Name? His account number is 1234567." The teller straightened up and said "Of course sir! How would you like your money?"

Asking, praying In Jesus' Name is drawing from His unlimited Wealth, Power, and Strength. Not limited to money or the wealth of this world, but more importantly to the immeasurable power which God has. We have access, through prayer, to ask Him for whatever we need... because He already owns, controls, and manages everything!

We pray in Jesus' Name and so approach God, the Father, as one of Jesus' people, His disciples, His chosen ones. When we ask in Jesus' Name, God's ear is attuned to our request. God is still sovereign, He still knows what is best for us, and for His plans for us (Jeremiah 29:11), so, He still decides!

My friends, we have been given permission – by Jesus – to ask for anything – in His Name! This is the Power of the Name of Jesus!

Thank You Father for the amazing gift of speaking to you directly, asking You for anything in the Name of Jesus. Help us to come to You in sincere faith, trusting in You and in the Name of Jesus, our Savior, Redeemer, and Lord.

"In Jesus' Name"

Katy Nicole

https://youtu.be/YqHjjZz1Syg

April 19

Today's Encouragement is 2 Corinthians 1:3 NLT *All praise to God, the Father of our Lord Jesus Christ. God is our merciful Father and the source of all comfort.*

The source of all comfort –

God our Father is The Source of everything good. And Comfort is certainly a good thing! We seek it naturally. It's inherent to us and even to animals to seek our own comfort.

Yet, we can and often do, reach for something else, anything else, and so often, the wrong things for our comfort. The list of these things is endless, whatever comes to your mind first is probably your own most-often-chosen source of comfort. And, my friend, if our most-often-chosen comfort is not God Himself, we are fooling ourselves, we're accepting a cheap, temporary substitute for the Comfort of God. He designed us to only be truly satisfied, only be truly comfortable in Him!

This is a decision, my friend, a choice we make at a point in time when we choose to follow Christ, but also a daily choice, to seek Him, to be close to Him, to find in Him—our every need! James 1:17a *Whatever is good and perfect is a gift coming down to us from God our Father...* He is the Source of Comfort, and every good thing! The wise look to Him, and we are foolish to look elsewhere!

Father God, thank You for providing for our every need, and for providing every good gift for us! You are so good to us! Help us always to choose wisely, to seek You for our Comfort, and every other need also.

"Not for a Moment"
Meredith Andrews
https://youtu.be/qoh26pC2RT8

April 20

Today's Encouragement is 2 Corinthians 1:4 NLT *He comforts us in all our troubles so that we can comfort others. When they are troubled, we will be able to give them the same comfort God has given us.*

In all our troubles –

Seems like there ought to be an easier way... but that's just me... God is saying that we suffer trouble in this life, and He comforts us... in all our troubles. Jesus told us in John 16:33 NLT *"I have told you all this so that you may have peace in me. Here on earth, you will have many trials and sorrows. But take heart because I have overcome the world."* Many trials and sorrows, troubles, pain, suffering...we think, "Why Lord! Shouldn't we be sheltered from all this and not have to experience such pain in this life? We're Your own chosen, adopted children! We should get a pass!"

God is too wise to shelter us from the pain and suffering of this life,— He didn't shelter Jesus! Instead, He shelters us THROUGH the pain and suffering, "He comforts us IN all our troubles"! And He does this with a purpose! SO THAT... we can comfort others with the comfort He has given to us! If we don't suffer troubles, we wouldn't be able to comfort others.

"My thoughts are nothing like your thoughts," says the Lord. "And my ways are far beyond anything you could imagine". Isaiah 55:8 NLT. He knows what He is doing! We just need to accept His ways, His plan... and seek Him in our troubles, and not blame Him for them. And as we do... we will clearly find, His Comfort!

Father, thank you for Your wisdom, and Your Comfort!

"Through it All"

Andre Crouch and CeCe Winans

https://youtu.be/mNbspjDX4IY?t=32

April 21

Today's Encouragement is 2 Corinthians 1:5 NLT *For the more we suffer for Christ, the more God will shower us with his comfort through Christ.*

Shower us with his comfort –

Here's another "hard truth" in the Gospel. We are comforted according to the suffering for Christ which we experience. We all just want the comforting part, don't we? But the comfort described here is provided... through Christ... to those who suffer... for Christ.

Christ is the center, the reason for suffering and the source for comforting. Those who suffer greatly for Him need great comfort from Him.

My friends, are we willing to suffer for Christ? It could be any type of suffering, emotional, physical, mental, spiritual... but it is the suffering FOR Christ which matters... and when we suffer anything for Him, God will – He Promises here – shower us abundantly with His own comfort (the best type of comfort there is!) through Jesus!

Father God, may we have the courage to suffer for Christ, as we are assured of You showering us with Your Comfort through Him!

"He Knows"

Jeremy Camp

https://youtu.be/OsccUg4TDd8

April 22

Today's Encouragement is 2 Corinthians 4:7 NLT *We now have this light shining in our hearts, but we ourselves are like fragile clay jars containing this great treasure. This makes it clear that our great power is from God, not from ourselves.*

Not from ourselves –

When we live, as best we can, a life led by God's grace and love, we are transformed into the image of Christ, and we begin to exhibit Christ-like behaviors. We don't ever fully become like Him in this life, but we do change, growing in the direction of His life and His character. (See Romans 12:2).

And yet, my friends, we are still in this world and our character is still, and always will be far from perfect. We grow toward Him, but in this life, we still fall short in every way... and this shortfall, Jesus fulfills!

We are like fragile, ordinary, clay jars or pots containing His Glory! Every person, including the most devout believer, is still just an ordinary clay jar— even Billy Graham! Mother Teresa described herself as "only God's pencil."

Yet, within these clay jars of human frailty, the treasure of God's presence, His Holy Spirit living within us, is shining forth in, through, and from our hearts and lives! The light of His Love and Grace cannot be contained!

If you see any good in other believers, remember it is Christ! Please do not expect perfection from pastors, teachers, leaders, or anyone... you will always be disappointed. Instead, look for the work of His Spirit in them, the Light within, and that Light resides within all who believe, including you! Look to the Light! He is present and He is available!

Thank You, Lord, that in Your perfect wisdom, you allow the light of Christ to shine in and through us, imperfect, ordinary human beings.

"I See the Light"
Bethel Music and Kalley
https://youtu.be/iOqt85lLq4U

April 23

Today's Encouragement is 2 Corinthians 4:18 NLT *So we don't look at the troubles we can see now; rather, we fix our gaze on things that cannot be seen. For the things we see now will soon be gone, but the things we cannot see will last forever.*

Don't look at the troubles –

Recently we were talking with dear friends who were in the midst of great troubles. They didn't bring it on themselves, it just came on them. We discussed many possible responses with them, do this, don't do that, try this... and we finally agreed that prayer was the best solution. Not our efforts, not our plans, but God's plan.

We also, finally, when it should have been our first consideration, recognized that this trouble was spiritual in nature. Not all troubles are, but for us, God's adopted children, many of our problems are spiritual because we are spiritual beings... we are not of this world... we belong to God's family.

This verse rang true with our discussion with our friends... and our recognition (finally) that we were focused on the troubles, the things we saw, rather than focusing on what we could not see, the spiritual matters that were influencing the physical troubles.

Look beyond, my friends, all the light momentary troubles of this world... and fix your gaze on things which cannot be seen, the eternal truths which God has revealed to us in His Word! This is reality, He is Reality. This world and its troubles and its pleasures will soon be gone.

Father, help us to recognize that as Your children, as eternal beings of Your own choosing, the unseen world is our true reality, lasting forever... and this "seen world" and all its troubles will soon be gone!

"I Fix My Eyes on You"
Tommy Walker
https://youtu.be/K_b6UnKvEF8

April 24

Today's Encouragement is Psalm 57:8-10 NLT *Wake up, my heart! Wake up, O lyre and harp! I will wake the dawn with my song. I will thank you, Lord, among all the people. I will sing your praises among the nations. For your unfailing love is as high as the heavens. Your faithfulness reaches to the clouds.*

Wake the dawn –

What a beautiful idea, waking up the dawn with a song of praise to our God!

We can choose that: our first waking thought is "Thank You God!"... For another day, for sleep (a little or a lot), for what health we have, for the gift of His salvation... simply because He is Good, He is worthy of our praises! We always have this choice, regardless of our circumstances.

Such praise doesn't only come when life is easy... just look back to verse 4 of Psalm 57: *I am surrounded by fierce lions who greedily devour human prey— whose teeth pierce like spears and arrows, and whose tongues cut like swords.* The writer wasn't exactly leading a charmed life! Surrounded by lions, yet He choose to get up before dawn to sing God's praises! Selah (pause and consider this). Give it some thought.

Is it possible that beginning the day with a song of praise to the One who saves you... might create within us a thankful heart, hope, and encouragement?

Help us, Lord, to look to You for our every need, and to do so First, daily, and during the day when challenges arise. Help us to praise You even when surrounded by lions.

"Praise You in This Storm"

Natalie Grant

https://youtu.be/DJdd5OXZNZE

April 25

Today's Encouragement is John 15:5 NLT *"Yes, I am the vine; you are the branches. Those who remain in me, and I in them, will produce much fruit. For apart from me you can do nothing."*

Produce much fruit –

Jesus told us that He is the vine and that we are branches of His vine. Only by our contact with Him, through our vital connection with Him, only by recognizing our relationship with Him, do we ever have "fruit," or any real success, or do we have any lasting value! The analogy goes on to be even more critical because without the Vine, our life-giving connection to Him, we can do Nothing!

Nothing? Nothing of any real value, nothing that lasts, nothing that truly matters.

But by remaining IN Him, attached to His Vine, then my friends, we will bear much fruit.

Lord, draw us nearer, help us remain in You. Make us more fully aware of this life-giving and life-sustaining relationship with You. So that we can produce the fruit of Your love for this lost and dying world.

"Without Him"

Josh Turner

https://youtu.be/qgxVMFQZWxM

April 26

Today's Encouragement is Daniel 6:16 NLT *So at last the king gave orders for Daniel to be arrested and thrown into the den of lions. The king said to him, "May your God, whom you serve so faithfully, rescue you."*

Rescue –

We know the story: the king is manipulated into passing a law that no one can pray to anyone except him, Daniel remains faithful to God, the accusers "catch him" and report him to the king who is now trapped into executing his trusted and closest advisor.

Consider this king, rather than focusing on Daniel for a moment. He was trapped by the cunning of some of his jealous, conniving "friends," and he struggled to find a way out of this mess (v14). He prayed, (v16) May your God rescue you! And he even fasted all night long.

God did! Daniel was miraculously rescued, but so was the king! He was rescued from the snare his associates had set for him! Even though he wasn't a believer himself... God rescued him also, perhaps because he respected Daniel so much.

God is like that... He blesses even those who care for His children... His love is broad and wide and deep!

Friends, if God can rescue this pagan king from the trap set by his own associates... will He not rescue His own children? Maybe not in our preferred time or in our preferred manner (Daniel spent all night with these hungry lions!) but His rescue was certain!

Lord, help us to have this "Daniel-depth" of faith, that we would honor You above our very lives. First, because You deserve our honor and our lives, but also so that others may see Your power!

"Rescuer"
Rend Collective
https://youtu.be/OjmAuphVpuQ

April 27

Today's Encouragement is 2 Corinthians 6:11-13 NLT *Oh, dear Corinthian friends! We have spoken honestly with you, and our hearts are open to you. There is no lack of love on our part, but you have withheld your love from us. I am asking you to respond as if you were my own children. Open your hearts to us!*

Open your hearts –

Paul writes his friends describing in previous verses the sufferings he has endured for the gospel so that he can bring the message of Jesus to them and summarizes this sacrifice as *"our hearts are open to you"* (v11).

What more could he do for them, what more could anyone ask of the one delivering the message, at the repeated risk of his own life... certainly he had opened his heart to these people!

And in turn, he asks them to open their hearts to him. The manner of this openness is undefined, possibly so that God can guide their response to him.

And for us, the call is still... open your hearts! To God's Love, to the Good News of Jesus, to the needs of others around us – for His love, an act of kindness, a gift of mercy, a word of encouragement, a prayer, whatever this might mean to you today – Open your heart!

Father, guide us to open our hearts to You today, to allow You to do and say whatever You desire, whatever is helpful to others, whatever brings You glory! Open our hearts, Lord!

"We Open Our Hearts"
TFH Worship
https://youtu.be/eyy2-zLn1ak

April 28

Today's Encouragement is 2 Corinthians 9:8 NLT *And God will generously provide all you need. Then you will always have everything you need and plenty left over to share with others.*

Plenty left over –

What kind of a friend would I be... if I knew something, with complete confidence, which would be a great blessing to you, but I was afraid to tell you, because it might offend you, even harm our friendship? Not a true friend at all, right?

Here's a sensitive subject, yet God's truth is unquestionable! He will provide, ...generously!!!... All we need! Even enough so there is plenty left over to share with others!

"Wait! How do I deserve that? How do I get to that place with Him—that I have everything I need, and plenty left over to share with others? I want to be there!!" Don't we all?

Consider the context. This chapter is clearly focused on giving, helping others, supporting the church, and God's abundant blessings for those who do this!

Verse 6: *Remember this- a farmer who plants only a few seeds will get a small crop. But the one who plants generously will get a generous crop.* It might make us uncomfortable to talk about money and giving... but it's God's Truth, not man's! And it begins with faith: plant the seed in faith, and God supplies the abundant harvest.

The Old Testament clearly taught that tithing, bringing a tenth of our earnings... and the first and the best of what we've earned, brought great blessings, as does all our obedience to God's wisdom. Men distort God's truth all the time... but the Truth is still untainted! When we honor God, in any way, including giving, He will bless us!

My friends, let's honor Him! Plant the seed, the tithe, the first and best gift... in faith, and see this verse become true in your life.

Thank You Father that You provide for us abundance, not scarcity. Help us to trust You with everything we have, all that we hold dear, including our money.

"Amazing Love"
Chris Tomlin
https://youtu.be/EwoCbcSXlSM

April 29

Today's Encouragement is 2 Corinthians 1:10 NLT *And he did rescue us from mortal danger, and he will rescue us again. We have placed our confidence in him, and he will continue to rescue us.*

He did and He will –

What a clear revelation of one of the purposes of our Bible!

Of course, the reason for the book we call the Bible, is Jesus! He is revealed throughout the OT in prophecy and in the examples of the leadership of God's chosen men — Moses, Joshua, and many others.

Yet here we see a second purpose, assurance to us that God has done great things, for His people, and through His people... and He will again do great things for and through His people!

Our understanding of what those great things might be is often limited, or even obscured by our own thoughts... but God isn't limited by our misunderstandings! His purpose remains and will be fulfilled!

He has rescued us, and He will rescue us again! He has done great things for, in, and through His people, and He Will. Do. It. Again!

Father, grant us patient hearts, faith-filled hearts, and confident hearts as we wait for You to rescue us from our difficulties of this day. You have delivered us from death into Life through Christ, help us to be confident that You will continue to deliver us from the trials of this life... through our faith in Him! We pray in Jesus' Name.

"Do It Again"
Elevation Worship
https://youtu.be/0B_lnQIITxU

April 30

Today's Encouragement is Matthew 13:22 NLT *The seed that fell among the thorns represents those who hear God's word, but all too quickly the message is crowded out by the worries of this life and the lure of wealth, so no fruit is produced.*

The worries of this life –

Worry crowds out, the ESV says it *"chokes the word,"* the truth of God. Imagine putting your hands around the neck (forgive me for this graphic example but they're His words, not mine) of the one bringing you the Word of God and choking him. Horrifying! But that is what He said that we do... when we allow worry into our hearts...

You see His Word is crowded out, choked out when we allow worry and the cares of this world, the lure of wealth to dominate our thoughts and hearts, rather than trusting His Word... trusting Him. We cannot do both, my friends. We either Trust in Him or we can worry.

Lord, help us depend upon Your Word so that it is fruitful in our lives and help us reject the temptation to fall into the self-destructive sin of worry.

"Trust In You"
Lauren Daigle
https://youtu.be/qv-SXz_exKE

May 1

Today's Encouragement is John 14:1 ESV *"Let not your hearts be troubled. Believe in God; believe also in me."*

Let not –

Jesus instructed us to believe in Him just as we believe in God. And notice the way He puts it... "Let not..."

He could have said, "When you believe in me you will never worry." He could have said, "I will take away all your worries and problems, and when you believe in me, life will be happy and wonderful all the time." Or "Just say a quick prayer every morning and I will make sure you have a wonderful day, I'm a great good-luck charm!" But thank God He didn't say these things, although we often act like, believe as if, He did!

Instead, my friends, Jesus told us to "Let not your hearts be troubled." As believers we now have the choice of a troubled heart or a heart at peace... we Choose! By faith, we can trust in Him as our Savior, day by day, and choose trust and peace. Or we can "Let" our hearts be troubled, anxious, worried, or fearful by focusing on the problems and fears that may come our way.

The point is- we CHOOSE- to "Let" our hearts be at peace, believing Him and His promises, or we CHOOSE to "Let" fear, worry, and anxiety rule in our hearts.

The choice is ours...

Father God, help us, give us the ability, to choose faith, hope, and love, to fix our minds on You, and to choose to reject fear, worry, and the many cares of this life.

"Because He Lives"

Matt Maher

https://youtu.be/PBvU7arNhQs

May 2

Today's Encouragement is Psalm 119:105 NLT *Your word is a lamp to guide my feet and a light for my path.*

A light for my path –

I took a walk late one night just after sunset and it was getting darker with each step. My mind (fearfully) envisioned snakes warming on the hot pavement waiting for me to get close enough to spring at me, fangs glistening, in the moonlight. (Isn't the mind amazing, how quickly it jumps from peace to fear to fantasy?) So, to combat my irrational fear, I began to pray.

Then, it suddenly dawned on me, "Hey, I need some light!... light would make a difference... need to 'shed some light' on this situation." Took out my phone (such handy things) and turned on the flashlight app and voila! There was light! A few steps more and this verse came to mind.

With this light, just like an ancient lamp, only a few feet were visible. Yet, what a difference it made in my circumstances! Peace returned, and I enjoyed the walk again. All because Light was present in the surrounding darkness!

My friends, God's Word shows us the way, a light in the darkness. Jesus is the Word and He is the Light and... He shows us the WAY!

Lord, help us walk in Your Light, relying on You to dispel and remove whatever darkness we face.

"Marvelous Light"
Ellie Holcomb
https://youtu.be/_md12ROLpvQ

May 3

Today's Encouragement is Psalm 69:13 ESV *But as for me, my prayer is to you, O Lord. At an acceptable time, O God, in the abundance of your steadfast love answer me in your saving faithfulness.*

At an acceptable time –

David was in great distress (v17), despair (v20) and he was weary (v3) from crying out to God! He acknowledged his own sin (v5), and his own responsibility for being in this very bad situation. His enemies were powerful, a huge number, and they hated him (v4)!

And yet – his faith is so loudly proclaimed in this song... trusting in, waiting on, and asking God to deliver him from this painful trial.

And David's response to this waiting? *I will praise the name of God with a song; I will magnify him with thanksgiving* (v30).

He sang! He sang God's praises while still waiting for God to act! He praised God even while he was in despair and worn out from asking God to rescue him. And why does he trust God to rescue him? Because of the abundance of God's steadfast love!

Father, grant us this depth of faith, this measure of confident hope in You, Your Love, and Your deliverance... at the time acceptable to You, in Your time and in Your way... We trust in You for our help! Always. Your way is best!

"Even When It Hurts"
Hillsong
https://youtu.be/3Sv_876eqxg

May 4

Today's Encouragement is 1 John 3:8b ESV *The reason the Son of God appeared was to destroy the works of the devil.*

The reason –

Christ came for many reasons, He fulfilled the law (Matt. 5:17), He saved the lost (Luke 19:10), and He revealed to us the Father (Matt .11:27) and there are other reasons, too many to list here. But one of His purposes for coming to us was to destroy the works of the devil.

Now I ask you, did Jesus fail?... At any time?... At anything He set about to accomplish? Pretty sure He didn't... so, since we know that He succeeded, then the works of the devil must be already destroyed... and through Jesus, we are on the victorious team!

Please know I don't claim to understand or have all the answers, I'm just trying to deal with what the Word is saying...

Jesus has already(!) destroyed the work of the devil, the enemy of our hearts.

Maybe this isn't "news" to you, but to me... that's some pretty good news, my friends!

Lord God, Help us to live victoriously today; to refuse to listen to the lies of our enemy, who is already defeated. Instead, help us listen to the promises and blessings of our Lord and Savior, who is victorious!

"The Victory Is Yours"
Bethel Music
https://youtu.be/rgTavMhgn00

May 5

Today's Encouragement is Romans 8:15 NLT *So, you have not received a spirit that makes you fearful slaves. Instead, you received God's Spirit when he adopted you as his own children. Now we call him, "Abba, Father."*

His own children –

God's love for us, our relationship with Him, doesn't change with our feelings, emotions, or life circumstances. The truth is we are chosen by Him, adopted as His sons and daughters, and as brothers and sisters of Jesus Christ. We have such a close relationship with God our Father, that we can call Him Dad!

And all relationships need to be nurtured. How? At least with time, communication, and attitude. Are we spending time with God, communicating with Him (reading the Bible to listen to Him, praying to speak with Him) and what is our attitude toward Him? Are we trusting—or doubting His love for us? Remember there is no condemnation from God towards us, so no guilt or shame is appropriate here, only recognition that He is available and waiting on us.

Consider that our Dad, our Father God, loves you immeasurably; He is always, always, always waiting with open loving arms for us to turn to Him. He never has and never will turn away from us!

We may turn away, but He never will!

Father God, please give us the courage to turn to You, to spend time communicating with You, in an attitude of confident trust that You are always our Loving and Perfect Dad.

"I've Always Loved You"
Third Day
https://youtu.be/bnc5thfP-qY

May 6

Today's Encouragement is 1 Peter 5:10 NLT *In his kindness God called you to share in his eternal glory by means of Christ Jesus. So, after you have suffered a little while, he will restore, support, and strengthen you, and he will place you on a firm foundation.*

A little while –

The suffering we endure in this life is only "a little while"! That's Good News!

And after that suffering, look what awaits us! More Good News! We will be Restored, Supported, Strengthened, and placed on a firm foundation.

The troubles and considerable, painful, sometimes paralyzing suffering of this life can threaten to overwhelm us, and even cause us to doubt God's love or power or concern for us. But friends, is it possible that God can use every experience of our lives, including our suffering (Lord, please make it just a little while!), to bring us to the finished product, the person He created us to be?

Father God, thank you for allowing us to suffer for only a little while, it too often seems like forever... so that we can be complete, as You designed each of us to be. Give us patience, strength, and hope as we wait for You to complete what You've begun in each of us. We trust in You.

"There's a Rainbow At the End of Every Storm"
Marty Stuart
https://youtu.be/zWIfMKUvpUQ

May 7

Today's Encouragement is Lamentations 3:22-23 ESV *The steadfast love of the Lord never ceases; his mercies never come to an end; they are new every morning; great is your faithfulness.*

Never ceases –

His love never ceases... His mercy never ends, His love and mercy are new every morning!

Every morning we can begin our lives with a new, overwhelming, outpouring of His love, kindness, and compassion! Every morning we are showered with, no... completely immersed in, no... completely cleansed by, (can't think of a better way to say it...) His Grace and Mercy and Love... Of course, we are cleansed by the blood of Christ eternally! But this speaks of daily renewal... a fresh start each day with a fresh abundance and outpouring of His kindness to each of His children.

We might not feel like it. but our feelings don't determine what is true. God's Word determines and establishes the Truth... Our part is to accept, believe, adopt, agree, and live this Truth...

Thank you, Father God, for this daily blessing, this "waterfall" of Your renewed Love and Mercy for us. Help us to recognize that we walk in, live within, are immersed in – Your love all the days of our lives!

"Redeemed"
Big Daddy Weave
https://youtu.be/vSyLqbP8Z4I

May 8

Today's Encouragement is Galatians 2:20 NLT *My old self has been crucified with Christ. It is no longer I who live, but Christ lives in me. So, I live in this earthly body by trusting in the Son of God, who loved me and gave himself for me.*

Christ Lives in Me –

Like so many passages in the Bible, this is one of those mysteries... *It is no longer I who live...* Wait a minute... I'm still here, I'm still alive, still have the same name, same face... what does this mean? Is it possible that this is a Spiritual truth, not a Natural truth? That it is, it is supernatural, above, beyond, and outside of the natural world.

Now, I no longer live... but instead... Christ lives within me. Christ guides, speaks, hears, thinks within this body... because I trust in Him, the One who loved me and gave Himself for me.... Because I trust Him, He lives within me. Still blows your mind, doesn't it?

Father, we have such limited understanding. We hear Your truth, we see the words, we choose to believe, yet our depth of understanding is so shallow. Open our hearts and eyes and minds to grasp the amazing spiritual truths, like this one... so that we may truly experience Christ living within us! Every moment, every day. We pray this in Jesus' Name!

"Alive in You"
Kim Walker-Smith
https://youtu.be/xIZI8Q4VUZQ

May 9

Today's Encouragement is Psalm 73:28 NLT *But as for me, how good it is to be near God! I have made the Sovereign Lord my shelter, and I will tell everyone about the wonderful things you do.*

I have made –

The songwriter chooses to make God his shelter, refuge, his "safe place." Many folks are continuously looking for their own "safe place"! What shelter have you chosen?

The Bible is full of references to the shelter that God alone provides, and everything else, that the world seeks so desperately, just isn't!

Psalm 91:1 NLT *Those who live in the shelter of the Most High will find rest in the shadow of the Almighty.*

John 15:4 NLT " [Jesus said,] *Remain in me, and I will remain in you. For a branch cannot produce fruit if it is severed from the vine, and you cannot be fruitful unless you remain in me.*

One important distinction to consider, we often think of shelter as a place we go when we're in trouble, the hiding place we run to when we need protection. But the clear idea in both John 15 and Psalm 91 is relationship – remaining, dwelling, living in, abiding in His Presence. He is our shelter and safe place. He is with us always; we can choose to live within and abide in Him, we can "remain" in Him. Always.

Father, help us to choose You alone as our shelter and to remain, abide, dwell, and live in Your sheltering presence always. Help us to abide with You.

"Abide with Me"

Amy Grant

https://youtu.be/6l9N-QVuigs

May 10

Today's Encouragement is Ephesians 2:8 NLT *God saved you by his grace when you believed. And you can't take credit for this; it is a gift from God.*

It is a gift –

Isn't it nice to receive a gift? Especially from someone who knows you well! Sometimes we get (and give) gifts to others whom we don't know very well, and the gift isn't a very good fit. Good for re-gifting! And then once in a while, usually from someone who knows us very well, we get the 'ideal' gift... and when this happens, we are delighted with it, and express sincere gratitude to the giver!

We take the gift home, set it in a special place where we can see it often, and when we do so, we remember the giver... and we continue to be grateful for their thoughtfulness, their knowledge that this is just what we wanted, their generosity, their love expressed through this gift.

And isn't God's saving grace such a gift, the perfect gift, the ideal gift? One we can never hope to repay, nor to deserve, but the perfect gift from the One who knows us completely... knows exactly what we need and want and desire... and has the kindness and love for us to give us such a gift!

And my friends, what is our proper response to any such ideal gift? Gratitude, a grateful heart, affection for the Giver, and each time we consider this gift, we remember.

Communion is such a remembering moment, but we have other reminders daily, of the immeasurable, perfect, free gift of salvation...

Lord, open our hearts to see the many reminders You provide us to cause us to remember Your Perfect gift of salvation through Jesus. We are grateful Lord, please help us always to remember and always to remain... sincerely grateful. You are so good.

"Lord, You've Been Good to Me"
Graham Kendrick
https://youtu.be/fnbQF8rb9Q8

May 11

Today's Encouragement is Ephesians 3:20 NLT *Now all glory to God, who is able, through his mighty power at work within us, to accomplish infinitely more than we might ask or think.*

Infinitely more –

Paul ends this glorious prayer (v16-21) with these thoughts:

- Glory to God. It's all about Him, because of Him and through Him!

- His power—at work—through us

- He is unlimited in power. He can do anything. He can choose to work in us and even through us...

- Accomplish infinitely more!

And He can do infinitely more, working in and through us, than we could ever ask or even conceive!

Just for a moment, think about what God could possibly do through you...

And yes, He can do infinitely more than that! Whatever you and I are capable of imagining, dreaming, hoping for... God can do immeasurably more! And He can do this through us!

The key is our availability, willingness, and surrender. He will not use us against our own will to accomplish these things. He will do as He chooses, in His way, in His time, through US! With our availability... He is more than able!

Lord God, please help us to fully surrender to Your leadership, Your Lordship, in our lives today. What You choose, Lord; not what we choose.

"He is Able!"

Maranatha Singers

https://youtu.be/uhJlCJ8jkec

May 12

Today's Encouragement is Psalm 27:13-14 AMP *I would have despaired had I not believed that I would see the goodness of the Lord in the land of the Living. Wait for and confidently expect the Lord; Be strong and let your heart take courage; Yes, wait for and confidently expect the Lord.*

I would have despaired –

The writer of the Psalm admits that, if he didn't have faith, if he didn't believe that God would show him His Goodness while living on this earth... he would have despaired!

But, he does have this faith! He does believe! So, he speaks to himself, and to you and me thousands of years later (and to the millions who have read his words) ... "Be patient! Wait for Him! Expect Him! Be strong, Take courage in your heart!"

Friends, like the writer of this Psalm, we also must tell our emotions, our feelings, what the Truth is. The Truth, whether it feels like it or not, is that God is going to act on behalf of His people. He always has and always will! It's rarely on our schedule. (After all, He is God and we ain't!)

Father God, please help us to cause our minds, and our faith, to rule over our emotions. To choose faith rather than despair, to trust You rather than doubt. We ask in Jesus' Name.

"Take Courage"
Bethel Music
https://youtu.be/z6itgjC2IlY

May 13

Today's Encouragement is Ruth 2:12 NLT *May the Lord, the God of Israel, under whose wings you have come to take refuge, reward you fully for what you have done.*

To take refuge –

The story of Ruth is so very beautiful. Read it and be blessed! In this passage, Boaz, the owner of the barley field where she has come to gather the leftovers from the harvest, meets her and blesses her. He does this because he has heard about her and her kindness and loyalty to her mother-in-law Naomi.

Now, the book of Ruth is a "type" of the story of Jesus' redemption. A type is a person or thing in the Old Testament that foreshadows (an indication beforehand) a person or thing in the New Testament. In this "type," Boaz represents Jesus, the redeemer, deliverer, protector, and husband. Ruth represents you and me.

Ruth sought refuge and help and provision for herself and Naomi by coming to this particular area of the harvest... and God guided her there, to the one place where she would find all that she needed!

My friends, this is how God guides us, very often unknowingly, to the place of His refuge. Because He is Love (1 John 4:16) – He brings us to the best place and there He provides all that we need. He is that Good!

Father God, please help us always to come to You, to find refuge and everything we need, under Your wings, and to remain there with You!

"Sheltered in the Arms of God"

Hillary Scott

https://youtu.be/udSnfL-F7dg

May 14

Today's Encouragement is Ephesians 6:10 NLT *A final word: Be strong in the Lord and in his mighty power.*

Be strong –

How are we to be strong? In the Lord! And His mighty power! This isn't a coach yelling at us, "Get up and get back in there and fight!" This isn't, "You can do it, just keep on trying!" This isn't, "Call upon your inner strength and keep going!"

What is it? This is "Call on God for your help, ask Him to be your strength, rely on Him – not on yourself." Friends, we need to recognize that most battles worth fighting are far greater than our own strength can handle. We need God's strength for the battles we face. As God's children we have, will, and do face great battles! But we are already victorious when we rely on God's strength!

And – This is a choice we make! We choose to fight the battle with our own strength, or we read on and choose to wear the full armor of God, including our great weapon, (v 17) *the sword of the spirit, which is the word of God!*

Father, help us to choose Your way, the plan You clearly laid out for us—being Strong in Your Strength. Help us choose to wear Your armor and carry the sword of Your Spirit—Your Word, so that we can be victorious in every fight.

"Surrounded"
Bethel Music
https://youtu.be/Pz7578ZNwNU

May 15

Today's Encouragement is Joel 2:32a ESV *And it shall come to pass that everyone who calls on the name of the Lord shall be saved.*

Everyone who calls –

On the Name of the Lord—Will be saved -

The Old Testament prophecies of the Messiah, Jesus, are everywhere, and they're extremely accurate. Like this prophetic verse, written centuries before Jesus' birth, and which is not limited only to Israel, not limited only to those who comply with God's Law, but for Everyone! This verse is quoted directly in both Acts and Romans, as proof of God's Salvation Plan through faith in the Name of Jesus... for Everyone who calls upon His Name, Everyone who believes! Will be Saved!

My friends, God's saving grace and mercy and His Love are available to all... all who will call on His Name!

All our Lord asks of us... is this: Call on my Name.

And then... because you call on His Name... you will be Saved...

Certainly, this saving includes eternal salvation, saved from death, granted eternal life with Him, a place He has prepared for us... all the beautiful promises of rest and peace in eternity... yet is it limited to—one day out there, after this earthly life is over for us?

Is it possible that "will be saved" applies to our needs for "saving" today? We all need some type of "saving" regularly, don't we? What saving – what salvation do you need today? Will you call on His Name today for that salvation?

My friends, read it again, and choose to believe it!

Everyone...

Who calls...

on the Name of the Lord... Will be Saved!

Father, help us to believe, and to call on Your Name for our salvation, and every time we need saving! We ask in Jesus' Name.

"Call on Your Name"

Planetshakers

https://youtu.be/3Pdzk9q81CM

May 16

Today's Encouragement is Philippians 2:13 NLT *For God is working in you, giving you the desire and the power to do what pleases him.*

Working in you –

It's all God's doing! He has called you and is guiding, creating, and working... In You!

Because He has already acted—to choose you, to adopt you, to claim you, to transform you, and to Love you... it is all His Work! And it is His Work... within You and me!

Read it again... God is working in you!

He is even the Source of our desire to do what pleases Him! Plus, He is the Source of our strength and power to do what pleases Him! Every good and perfect gift (James 1:17) my friends, comes from Him, including the desire to honor Him, to Love Him!

It's all Him!

Father, help us to recognize that You are the Source of everything, including our love for You, and our desire to honor and worship You. It is... it's always been, and it will always be... You, Lord! And You alone!

"It's Always Been You"
Phil Wickham
https://youtu.be/58pBvQa0XSM

May 17

Today's Encouragement is Philippians 3:13b NLT *But I focus on this one thing: Forgetting the past and looking forward to what lies ahead.*

Forgetting the past –

We can get very tied down to the past, can't we? A painful experience, a loss, a trauma, or even a better life in previous years... The past has the power, if we allow it, to dominate our present and even our future, or even our current situation. We can be so focused on what's going on right now, that we don't see the blessings which await us!

Looking back, or even looking at our circumstances today, causes us to stumble today. It's good to remember lessons learned from our past experiences, of course, but dwelling on, living in, the past, whether it's good memories or painful ones, leads to failure today.

God even does this for us my friends, in Hebrews 10:17 NLT *He says, "I will never again remember their sins and lawless deeds."* God forgets our sins! So, we are free! Free from the past, from all sins, from the experiences that want to overtake and control us today!

Will we embrace this freedom today and live in the present which He has granted us? Or will we wallow in our past? We make this choice my friends! He has provided a clean, fresh new day... what do you choose?

Lamentations 3:23 NLT *Great is his faithfulness; his mercies begin afresh each morning.*

Help us Lord to forget the past, to rest in Your Grace and forgiveness, and live in the present, in your new mercies!

"The Steadfast Love of the Lord"
Dave Hunt
https://youtu.be/0NWJOYUxwcI

May 18

Today's Encouragement is Philippians 4:8 NLT *And now, dear brothers and sisters, one final thing. Fix your thoughts on what is true, and honorable, and right, and pure, and lovely, and admirable. Think about things that are excellent and worthy of praise.*

Think about –

How many times every day do we hear or say something like this? "What do you think?" "What was I thinking!" "I just wasn't thinking!" "I think that..." "He doesn't think before he acts...." "There's something very wrong with his thinking...." "That was thoughtless!" and dozens of other common phrases relating to our thinking and thoughts. Why?

Is it possible that—our thoughts direct our actions and so, our very lives?

We readily acknowledge that someone who loses the ability to control their thinking, and their minds, will become completely unstable, unable to function at all. The mind is the director of our lives! Our thinking directs, determines, and essentially rules over our actions and so, our lives.

Hopefully, you find all this fairly obvious... why focus so deeply on it? Because our thinking, my friends, determines our reality.

In this passage for example, we're advised to think first... about what is True! For us as believers, we readily respond...Jesus is the Truth (the way and the life).

Whatever else we are thinking about—our problems, the suffering we or others face, the decline of civilization, the horrors of this life, or worse, when we focus our minds on our own depraved thinking, our fears, worries, and the darkness.... This "thinking" leads us in the direction of that thinking.

So, what are you thinking, my friend? May I suggest we focus our thinking on ... Who God is, what He has done, what He can do, and His wonderful promises to us? He can change our thinking! Romans 12:2b NLT *...but let God transform you into a new person by changing the way you think.*

Lord, help us to consider what we are thinking about. Help us to recognize that You will help us to refocus from the negative thoughts onto Your beautiful Truth.

"Let's Think about Our God"
Tommy Walker
https://youtu.be/7SnjCV0b0dc

May 19

Today's Encouragement is Psalm 118:24 NLT *This is the day the Lord has made. We will rejoice and be glad in it.*

We will rejoice –

Is it possible that we have a choice; that we aren't the victims of our circumstances? That regardless of the troubles and challenges and even overwhelming obstacles we are facing... we still can choose... To rejoice...?

Even when we don't feel like it.

Even when we can't see any reason for joy...

Is it possible?

Did God send Jesus to live and die and return from death, and in doing this, set us free from death... in order that we could live in misery, depression, and addiction; in resentful, anxious, and sorrowful lives?

When we focus on this world around us, our own problems, the crime, war, suffering, and heartbreak that we see everywhere... we can easily lose our focus and even forget... the Truth! The Truth that – we have been, and now are – set free from all of this! – From all the decay of society, the death of life as we know it... we are not of this world!

We are only here for a tiny portion of our eternal lives, my friend! The Truth is... all of this shall pass away and we, who are of eternity... can choose, today, now, regardless of our circumstances... to Rejoice in Our Father, the Lord! He has set us free from death and all the forms of dying that surround us in this life!

Father God, help us choose to Rejoice!—as we focus on You and all You have done, are now doing, and will do!

"Joy"

For King and Country

https://youtu.be/E-r7ogDaaEQ

May 20

Today's Encouragement is Philippians 4:19 NLT *And this same God who takes care of me will supply all your needs from his glorious riches, which have been given to us in Christ Jesus.*

All your needs –

Sometimes a verse, a sentence, or a thought can stand alone. It is a truth with no need of further explanation. And yet, almost always, we can learn more about this truth, clarify the intent, and grow in our spiritual understanding, as we consider the context of the message. This is an example.

The preceding sentence adds great depth to this statement, that God will supply all! Paul explains... Philippians 4:18 NLT At *the moment I have all I need and more! I am generously supplied with the gifts you sent me with Epaphroditus. They are a sweet- smelling sacrifice that is acceptable and pleasing to God.*

The Philippian church had just made a generous gift to him, which Paul described as pleasing to God. And Paul now responds, "God will supply all your needs."

My friends, God is pleased when we are genuinely generous to others. Why is this? Is it possible that our generosity reflects our understanding of His generosity towards us? We can give generously because He has already, first, given so generously to us. In the same manner as His Love, in 1 John 4:19 NLT *We love each other because he loved us first.*

Similarly, 2 Corinthians 9:6 NLT *Remember this — a farmer who plants only a few seeds will get a small crop. But the one who plants generously will get a generous crop.*

Father God, please grant us the faith to give generously, with gratitude in our hearts, because we realize that You have already given so generously to us, and because we know that You will supply all our needs.

"My God Shall Supply All My Needs"
Reba Rambo
https://youtu.be/e5V0MrKtQCk

May 21

Today's Encouragement is John 14:6 NLT *Jesus told him, "I am the way, the truth, and the life. No one can come to the Father except through me."*

The way –

Jesus didn't quibble; He didn't dance around the issue. He simply stated Truth. He is The Way, The Truth, and The Life!

Got a problem? Jesus is the answer! Pray in His Name, in faith, trusting in His Way.

Got a question? Jesus is the answer! Ask Him, trust Him, and wait for His response.

Got doubts, fears, anxiety? Jesus is the answer! He is the Prince of Peace. We can place all our cares on Him because He cares for us. (1 Peter 5:7)

Whatever the question—The answer is Jesus.

Father God, help your children to recognize that You have already given us the answer to every question. Thank You, God, that Jesus is the Answer!

"Jesus Is the Answer"

Michael W Smith

https://youtu.be/7uZJiHb2ENU

May 22

Today's Encouragement is John 14:14 NLT *Yes, ask me for anything in my name, and I will do it!*

In my name –

Friends this is not some "magic formula," not a genie-in-a-bottle. But recognize– Jesus said this!

Do we believe—that He is who He says He is and that He will do what He says He will do? (Heb. 10:23)

Sometimes (often) it just doesn't happen soon enough for us. We're so impatient! So, we begin to doubt... and when we doubt, we don't receive! (James 1:6-7)

Jesus acts in His own Name is His authority, His strength—not ours; His bank account—not mine, His reputation—not mine. His is the Name above all names!

This idea of "in His name" is somewhat like a power of attorney. The use of His Name must be in full respect of His reputation, His character. It must be respected, not used in vain, for our silly, selfish wants and desires, but for those things which bring Him glory!

Lord God, give us faith to trust fully, and accept completely, the Truth, You have given us in Christ! Give us both patience and strength as we wait for You to act.

"In Jesus' Name"

Katy Nichole

https://youtu.be/R84PqRdZ7_Y

May 23

Today's Encouragement is Psalm 81:13 NLT *Oh, that my people would listen to me! Oh, that Israel would follow me, walking in my paths!*

Listen to me –

God speaks to His children. He speaks in unlimited ways, for He has no limits. Primarily through the Holy Spirit living within us, and also through His written Word, He speaks!

When we claim we cannot hear Him and say we don't know what to do, which way to go, what is God's will for us, we do not speak the truth... He has spoken and He still speaks! We must train our ears, our minds, our own spirit, our own will... to "hear" His Voice. The problem is our hearing, our listening, not His speaking.

When we understand that Jesus has restored us to right standing, to righteousness before God, we are now, already, as close to God as Jesus is, as close as Adam was in Eden. We now, already have the mind of Christ! (1 Corinthians 2:16)

My friends, God's voice, what He speaks to His deeply loved children, will always, always, always line up with His Word, the Truth reflected in the Bible. Because... He does not change.

So, we can "hear' His Voice! We can know His will, we can walk in His paths... and in doing so, we remain under His blessing. We can do all things through Christ (Phil. 4:13)

God wants us to hear Him and walk in His ways. Because He loves us, He wants what is best for His children, just as we earthly parents do.

The choice is ours.

Father God, help us to hear and listen to You and walk in Your paths.

"Speak to Me"

Tommy Walker

https://youtu.be/y1k30qOnK9M

May 24

Today's Encouragement is Colossians 1:3-4 NLT *We always pray for you, and we give thanks to God, the Father of our Lord Jesus Christ. For we have heard of your faith in Christ Jesus and your love for all of God's people,*

And we give thanks –

Paul was praying his thanks to God for the Colossians' faith and their love. This is a prayer of gratitude, not of petition. He prayed with joy, thanking God for the faith and love of the believers in this area.

We too often approach our Father, the God of all creation, with our pleas for this or that, our anguish, our needs, our wants, or even our demands. And we are welcomed by Him, at all times! We are invited to pray about everything, without ceasing! (Eph. 6:18) Yet my friends, would it not be a good idea, occasionally, if not regularly, to Thank Him, for Who He Is, for His unfailing Love, for what He has done for us, and for others? Just expressing sincere thanks, just gratitude, just acknowledging Him for His great mercy and kindness.

Friends, God doesn't "need" this... but we do! We need to express our gratitude, in order to bring it to the forefront of our thoughts! We can live in an attitude of gratitude when we remember to pray and sincerely thank God for what He has done for us, and for all His children.

Help us, Lord, to give You the proper thankfulness that You deserve, for the people You've placed in our lives, for Your kindness, for forgiveness, and for eternal life in Christ. We thank You for all this Lord.

"Thank You, Lord"
Paul Baloche
https://youtu.be/wwjBCn2GcK0

May 25

Today's Encouragement is Colossians 2:6-7 NLT *And now, just as you accepted Christ Jesus as your Lord, you must continue to follow him. Let your roots grow down into him, and let your lives be built on him. Then your faith will grow strong in the truth you were taught, and you will overflow with thankfulness.*

Let your roots grow down –

We are saved when God calls us to Himself through the grace and mercy of Jesus Christ and we respond with "Yes, Lord."

And that is Salvation!

Now we can continue to follow, to "let our roots grow down" deeper into Him, into His Truth, into relationship with Jesus, and even so that our lives are built upon Jesus!

And as we do so, our faith will grow, and we will overflow... with gratitude!

We'll have so much gratitude to God that it will overflow and spill onto those around us!

Is this our desire, to be strong in the Truth, and to overflow with gratitude? Then, my friends, build your life on Jesus, grow deeper and deeper roots in Him; into relationship with Him and His truth, mercy, grace, and compassion...all that He is!

It's all about Jesus! Build your life on Him! Renew this commitment now, along with me.

Father God, thank You for the salvation You have provided us through faith in Christ! Help us now – to grow in faith, in relationship with Jesus, so deep that our lives are built upon Him, the Solid Rock.

"For Your Splendor"
Christy Nockels
https://youtu.be/4BQDrgFMu4Q

May 26

Today's Encouragement is Philippians 2:20-21 NLT *I have no one else like Timothy, who genuinely cares about your welfare. All the others care only for themselves and not for what matters to Jesus Christ.*

What matters –

Paul honors Timothy as being unique because he cares about what matters to Jesus, unlike all the others – who care only for themselves.

Ever think about that? What it is—that matters to Jesus? Paul did, and Timothy also did, he cared about the welfare of the church in Philippi, the people, their spiritual condition, and growth... he cared about what matters to Jesus.

So, in your world, your sphere of influence, what is it that matters to Jesus? Is it possible that His focus hasn't changed? That the thing that matters to Jesus... is still, and always will be... the spiritual well-being of people... their souls.

Friends, there is an unlimited number of other things to be concerned about, to focus our attention on – making a living, paying bills, hobbies, raising kids, friends, enemies, even church activities... but what is it that Truly Matters to Jesus? Note, it's not about what matters to you and me, but what matters to Him!

If we believe the biblical truths that, this life is just a mist, that we have an eternal soul, that we can be born again, that God will dwell within us through His Holy Spirit, that God loves all people, that He has called us to be free, then perhaps we can see – just a glimpse of – what matters to Jesus.

Father, help us to see and focus on What Matters to Jesus. We ask in His name.

"If All I Had Was Christ"

We the Kingdom

https://youtu.be/j_jDTuO4vXM

May 27

Today's Encouragement is Colossians 4:2 NLT *Devote yourselves to prayer with an alert mind and a thankful heart.*

Devote yourselves –

To Devote means to commit, dedicate, or focus. This is a choice we make; we choose what we devote ourselves to. Is it family, fishing, or financial gain? Is it accumulating stuff? We have so much "stuff" that we rent storage buildings because our homes can't contain all our stuff! (We have one too...)

But what is it that we are truly devoted to?

For some sadly, it is our addiction: food, fear, worry, gossip, drama, drugs, alcohol, our illnesses, lust, or self-pity; the list is endless.

The wisdom of God suggests, instead of these things, that we instead choose (we still get to decide) to devote ourselves to Prayer! With an alert mind, considering what we are praying—with wisdom, and with a thankful heart.

This is praying from our position as a beloved son or daughter of God. We begin with the truth of God as Our Father, our relationship with Him, and gratitude for Who He is and all He has already done, and for His very great promises for us all!

Notice my friend, that anyone, rich or poor, healthy or ill, wise or slow, anyone can do this. No special skill or ability is required. Just a willing heart.

Father, please help us, for we can do nothing without You, to devote ourselves to prayer, recognizing that You can do immeasurably more than we could ever do, or ask, or even imagine. We rely on You.

"Knees to the Earth"

Watermark

https://youtu.be/-AQL8Zk2sOk

May 28

Today's Encouragement is Colossians 3:9b-10 NLT *...for you have stripped off your old sinful nature and all its wicked deeds. Put on your new nature and be renewed as you learn to know your Creator and become like him.*

Put on –

There are several references in Chapter 3 to "putting on" and "taking off." The NLT reads, "You have [already] stripped off your old sinful nature," now it is time to "put on" our new nature! (v10) says, put on Christ, the ESV says, clothe yourselves (Galatians. 3:27) with Christ!

This happens at salvation doesn't it, a one-time rebirth? Yes, of course! Read it again, "For you have..." Already! But my friends we aren't yet (we will be one day!) completely free from this body of our flesh. Some do experience a miraculous delivery from addiction, health, or mental issues... sometimes this occurs at the time of salvation, acceptance of the Grace of Jesus, and sometimes afterward, and sometimes never!

God is not limited in the way He interacts with His children.

Remember that even Paul suffered some undefined affliction and prayed for release from it and heard God's wonderful and reassuring reply, *"My Grace is sufficient."* (2 Corinthians 12:9 ESV)

So, it seems that putting off the old self and putting on the new self... is an ongoing concept. When we find ourselves living in, "putting on," our old self, our sinful nature, we can, and must consciously, decide to turn from that nature, to "strip it off," and to instead "put on" the new nature, to clothe ourselves with Christ. This decision is ours. This choice is called repentance, turning away from (stripping off) our sinful nature, and turning to the grace of Christ! We put on and put off—what we choose.

We can do this! (All things! Philippians 4:13) We are well-advised to do this! The alternative is to remain in, to "leave on" the flesh... and that is death for us.

Father, help us to put on our new nature! To clothe ourselves with Christ! We pray this in Jesus' Name!

"Only Jesus"
Casting Crowns
https://youtu.be/TAtx1y58jS0

May 29

Today's Encouragement is Acts 26:29 NLT *Paul replied, "Whether quickly or not, I pray to God that both you and everyone here in this audience might become the same as I am, except for these chains."*

The same as I am –

Paul spoke this to King Agrippa, as he began to explain how Jesus was the Messiah. Paul said, I pray, I'm asking God, now, that everyone who hears me would become the same as I am... except for my chains.

He spoke of course about the faith that he had in Christ, the hope, the forgiveness, and the Love of God which belongs to us as believers. He wanted everyone, regardless of race, background, or status in this world, to become a true believer in Christ!

Can we say this? Is it your desire, your prayer, that everyone becomes, as you are, except for... the chains.

My friends, the freedom in Christ we enjoy is the greatest gift; it is the greatest blessing that we could ever pray for another to receive. It isn't really our gift to give. We can talk about it, testify to its effect on our lives, and explain how to accept the gift, but it is God's gift to give.

And yet, we are too often reluctant, timid, and tenuous in sharing the greatest blessing of our life! Me too.

Father God, please grant us bold hearts to share Your Love, the joy of our Salvation with everyone, always, without fear of their response. We ask in Jesus' Name.

"For the One"
Jenn Johnson
https://youtu.be/2Y1ROPUdUNU

May 30

Today's Encouragement is Habakkuk 3:17-18 NLT *Even though the fig trees have no blossoms, and there are no grapes on the vines; even though the olive crop fails, and the fields lie empty and barren; even though the flocks die in the fields, and the cattle barns are empty, yet I will rejoice in the Lord! I will be joyful in the God of my salvation!*

Yet I will rejoice –

Several wonderful passages encourage us to continue to rejoice and be joyful in our God, despite the difficult, even painful, sometimes hopeless, circumstances we are facing. Job said after losing everything he had...Job 1:21b NLT *"The Lord gave me what I had, and the Lord has taken it away. Praise the name of the Lord!"* And James 1:2 NLT *Dear brothers and sisters, when troubles of any kind come your way, consider it an opportunity for great joy."*

Great joy when we have troubles? "I've lost everything, and I'm supposed to praise God?" There's no hope, no way out of this terrible circumstance, and YET I'm supposed to be joyful and rejoicing in God?"

Yes! My friends this is exactly what the Bible repeats many times. Why?

Because our peace, our security, our provision, our contentment, and our JOY, are found only in Christ! His grace, mercy, and love... this is our joy... eternal hope of life with Him! We have every reason – in Him alone– to rejoice!

Father, we know we can do all things through Christ! Help us to rejoice always, even when we are in the midst of our troubles because You are still God! Jesus is still our Savior! We are still Loved by You!

"Shout for Joy"
Paul Baloche
https://youtu.be/zR2ukx6to7I

May 31

Today's Encouragement is Colossians 1:9-12 NLT *So we have not stopped praying for you since we first heard about you. We ask God to give you complete knowledge of his will and to give you spiritual wisdom and understanding. Then the way you live will always honor and please the Lord, and your lives will produce every kind of good fruit. All the while, you will grow as you learn to know God better and better. We also pray that you will be strengthened with all his glorious power so you will have all the endurance and patience you need. May you be filled with joy, always thanking the Father. He has enabled you to share in the inheritance that belongs to his people, who live in the light.*

Have not stopped praying –

- For complete knowledge, wisdom, and understanding... To live to honor and please God

- To produce good fruit

- To learn to know God better

- To be strengthened with His power To have endurance and patience To be filled with Joy!

- Always thanking Him!

Because (v12) He has enabled us... to do all these things and to share in the inheritance, and to live in the light!

My friends, this prayer is for you and me also. And we are invited to live in this way, honoring God, pleasing Him, producing every kind of good fruit... growing in our knowledge of God!... and more! This blessed life is available to us, it is not a fantasy, "Someday I wish that...", No! It is ours, now, today! Live in the light!

Lord God, open our hearts and lives to the blessed inheritance you have already provided us... to live in the Light!

"In the Light"
DC Talk
https://youtu.be/CUGD4gsQ3C0

June 1

Today's Encouragement is 1 Thessalonians 4:17 NLT *Then, together with them, we who are still alive and remain on the earth will be caught up in the clouds to meet the Lord in the air. Then we will be with the Lord forever.*

We will be with the Lord forever –

And the next verse (v18) *So encourage each other with these words.*

Are you encouraged? Does it strengthen your heart to consider ... that one day, much sooner than later, we will be with the Lord... forever!

Focus with me just for this moment on that phrase... "We will be with the Lord forever..." My friends, when this certain future awaits us, don't the cares, worries, and troubles of this life just quietly fade away? As in His brilliant light, the darkness of this life—ceases to exist, so also, in the truth of Eternity with Christ, all our current concerns simply dissolve.

What changed? Only our focus. He's always been there, always will be, forever. We've always belonged to Him, as His adopted children, chosen before our birth... His promises – eternal. But what we choose to focus upon has control over our entire lives.

So, what is it, that is our focus: the predominant thought that we each choose, or allow to occupy our minds, hearts, and spirits?

May I suggest this?... Lift your spiritual gaze to Him now, at this moment. And consider that He is your true home, now and forever!

Help us, Father God, to focus on You, and Your eternal Truths, that the cares of this life might fade away.

"We Shall Always Be with the Lord"
Ellie Holcomb
https://youtu.be/HEicxb7pTDc

June 2

Today's Encouragement is 1 Thessalonians 2:13 NLT *Therefore, we never stop thanking God that when you received his message from us, you didn't think of our words as mere human ideas. You accepted what we said as the very word of God-which, of course, it is. And this word continues to work in you who believe.*

The very word –

Paul expressed gratitude to God and to the church because they accepted the message as God's Word, His Truth, and not as "mere human ideas."

What do you think? Is this true for us? Do we accept this message, as it is recorded in the Bible, handed down through the centuries... as God's own Words? Or is this book filled with "mere human ideas"?

If it is "mere human ideas" then it's perfectly fine to ignore the parts we don't like, to pick and choose what we will believe and what we consider to be errors or outdated ideas...

But, my friends, that is a slippery slope... because once you remove one passage or one concept... the next removal comes easier, and then we begin to erode the virtual foundation of our faith. Where does such "human editing" cease? Sadly, it cannot end, except in humanizing the entire message.

Rather than sliding down this slippery slope into mediocrity and ultimately, disbelief... the alternative is the belief, the acceptance of this message as "The very Word of God"!

Father God, help your children to cling to Your Truth, as Your very Word! Help us choose to Believe YOU!

"The Word of God "
Vertical worship
https://youtu.be/waUt8KTk5no

June 3

Today's Encouragement is 2 Thessalonians 2:13 NLT *As for us, we can't help but thank God for you, dear brothers and sisters loved by the Lord. We are always thankful that God chose you to be among the first to experience salvation - a salvation that came through the Spirit who makes you holy and through your belief in the truth.*

Belief in the truth –

It's fascinating to consider who we are in Christ – and in this verse, we see another expression of our true identity.

Through our belief in the Truth, we are:

- Loved by the Lord Jesus!
- Chosen by God the Father to experience salvation!
- Brought to salvation by the Holy Spirit who makes us holy!

Each of these truths is incredibly rich in meaning and power and deserves to be studied and understood in depth... but here's just a moment's thought today...

We are Loved by Jesus... known by Him, watched over, and provided for, He loves us perfectly! Our own, our best concept of, Love for another comes close to– but still is far from – His perfect Love.

We are chosen by God—what an identity! We are His chosen adopted children! Individually selected, by His Grace, not by our merits – We are His selected ones!

The Spirit lives within us to bring us to holy living, by the Grace and forgiveness of our God, which we could never earn.

All this – through our belief in the truth –

This song beautifully describes our beliefs... sing with it and make this your prayer today... participate in this proclamation of faith... and so come to recognize more fully who you are in Christ!

Father God, we do believe, help us in our doubts and questions. Help us to firmly stand on the Truth in which we believe.

"We Believe"
Steve Green
https://youtu.be/6-U4z-_mxb8

June 4

Today's Encouragement is 1 Thessalonians 3:12 NLT *And may the Lord make your love for one another and for all people grow and overflow, just as our love for you overflows.*

May the Lord make –

Friends, it is God! He makes. He creates! He does a work in us! He transforms. He recreates. He brings rebirth, renewal, and regeneration to our hearts, minds, and spirits... to our entire lives.

Read the passage again... this is a prayer that God will make this happen! God alone can make our love grow for others! We cannot! He is the Source of Love.

But we are truthfully only selfish, weak, sin-filled people... and because we are this way, God made a New Way! Through faith in Jesus, we are reborn and now can live a life of Love – for God and for others, made possible only by His power living within us, His Love flowing through us. "May the Lord make your love...grow and overflow."

Father God, our desire is to be Yours, to live daily in Your ways, and You alone can enable us to live so. We ask Lord that Your Love, from, and through You, would grow in us, fill us, and overflow our lives, to You and to others. We ask in Jesus' Name.

"Your Love Is Life"

Eileen Walker

https://youtu.be/Fk7NbVqgyEc

June 5

Today's Encouragement is Galatians 3:3 NLT *How foolish can you be? After starting your new lives in the Spirit, why are you now trying to become perfect by your own human effort?*

Human effort –

The Galatians were trying to "become perfect" by their own human effort—specifically, by obeying the law of Moses. Living according to the historical Jewish laws and rules. This foolish thinking is refuted here with this clear question. He essentially asks them, "Where does your new life come from? From God's Spirit living within you or from your human efforts?"

Jesus gave us a new commandment, that we Love God and one another. His life, death, burial, and resurrection fulfilled the old requirement of the Law in every way... perfectly. We can add nothing, nor take away anything from His Perfect fulfillment of the law!

It's good for us, as believers in Christ, to try to live "a good life." We are examples to this world, Ambassadors of Christ, and we reflect God's nature to this world around us. Yet, we cannot rely on our human effort, or our good behavior (for we all fall short!) as our right-standing before God. We can ONLY RELY on the perfect completed work of Jesus, our Lord, in His death, burial, and resurrection so that we are forever made right with God.

Not by our human efforts! But by His Blood!

We recognize Lord that our own efforts to live right, even in the smallest details, fall miserably short of the perfection of Jesus. We need Him, His grace, and His blood to save us. Thank You for providing The Way for us to be saved, through faith in Christ.

"Only the Blood"

Del Way

https://youtu.be/lw6iVOPFnjY

June 6

Today's Encouragement is Ephesians 5:33 NLT *So again I say, each man must love his wife as he loves himself, and the wife must respect her husband.*

Love and Respect –

This isn't an original thought. I first heard it years ago from Dr. James Dobson on his radio program, "Focus on the Family." He said something to the effect of "A woman's greatest need is love from her husband, and a husband's greatest need is respect from his wife."

This rings true with most married folks! Because – it's ancient wisdom, not modern psychology or new revelation or something someone thinks might be true. The source is Biblical Truth.

Marriages fall apart when this Love and Respect are not offered. When a man doesn't demonstrate love to his wife, the marriage dies! When a wife doesn't demonstrate respect for her husband, the marriage dies! The two cannot become one without this essential truth. And notice: there is no provision for "deserving it."

Final thought, is it possible that – this brief description of marriage is a type, an example, of the nature of our relationship with God? He is the husband we are to respect, and we are the spouse who is showered with love. Is it possible? And then does this truth apply to both relationships equally? Who created the idea of marriage? The previous verse reads *This is a great mystery, but it is an illustration of the way that Christ and the church are one.* Ephesians 5:32 NLT

Father God, we thank You for the unlimited love which You have already poured out on us, help us, Lord, to properly respect You!

"You Have Been So Good to Me"

Paul Baloche

https://youtu.be/XTrgqImWxYU

June 7

Today's Encouragement is 1 Timothy 6:17 NLT *Teach those who are rich in this world not to be proud and not to trust in their money, which is so unreliable. Their trust should be in God, who richly gives us all we need for our enjoyment.*

So unreliable –

The wisdom of biblical truth is so often confirmed in experience!

We've all seen our comfortable and seemingly secure financial situations worsen in recent months at a frightening pace! Costs have soared, investments have drastically declined, shelves are empty, and we scream out, "What is going on!?"

We all go through seasons in this life, seasons of growth, and decline, health and illness, comfort, and struggles, hope, and despair... it is an essential element of maturity, to recognize that change is inevitable, and that seasons come and go. (Eccles. 3:1)

But as believers in Christ, we have the opportunity to see from the eternal perspective, by considering that "this world," "this life," is NOT all there is.

Our money, our comforts, our security, and our very lives are transitory, temporary, and all are "so unreliable" as today's verse clarifies. And we are blessed in the sense that this concept is so clear for us all today, much more so than just a few years ago! As we see our "security," our trusted financial stability, begin to fail us... we now have the opportunity, if we will... to consider the biblical truth, that everything in this life... will fail us!

Our health declines, our wealth comes and goes, our friends, even our families disappoint us... and YET!... God is where we place our Trust! He alone "richly gives us all we need for our enjoyment!"

Help us Lord to look only to You... You alone, can and do provide us with all we need! My worth is not in what I own.

"What I Own"

Fernando Ortega, Keith and Kristyn Getty

https://youtu.be/05jKxv8ApuI

June 8

Today's Encouragement is 2 Timothy 1:14 NLT *Through the power of the Holy Spirit who lives within us, carefully guard the precious truth that has been entrusted to you.*

Carefully guard –

Through the power of the Holy Spirit (we cannot do this on our own), we are advised to "carefully guard" this treasure, "the precious truth," which is the Good News of Jesus Christ, which was entrusted and given as a blessing for us to care for and use properly.

So, how do we guard this precious truth? We nurture it. We "feed" it "oxygen" so that it is alive and vibrant and flaming within our lives. We've all seen others, perhaps ourselves, "on fire for God" at times, and this is a life fanned into flames! (V6)

And we work carefully to guard this precious truth, to keep it untainted by the world, by the latest ideas, fads, trends, philosophies, and all untruths.

Today's culture is constantly screaming at us – "Change!" "Express yourself," "Don't tell me... anything!" "Listen to Me," "Be like Me," "You do You!" And a myriad of similar ideas

– all throwing off any restraint and any sound definition of Truth.

For us, the believers in Jesus, the remnant of His church, the salt and light of this world, we must carefully guard the Truth of Jesus Christ. We must not allow the Truth of His Good News, which is dwelling within each of us, to be perverted, infected, and distorted by the ranting of the masses.

God's Truth is eternal. The Bible describes Him. Jesus is The Truth.

Lord, help us carefully to guard this precious Truth, through the Power of Your Holy Spirit.

"The Voice of Truth"
Casting Crowns
https://youtu.be/D7JTx1ScD-w

June 9

Today's Encouragement is John 9:2-3 NLT *"Rabbi," his disciples asked him, "why was this man born blind? Was it because of his own sins or his parents' sins?" "It was not because of his sins or his parents' sins," Jesus answered. "This happened so the power of God could be seen in him.*

Who sinned --

We often think this way, both about others and about ourselves... "This or that bad thing happened because of their (my) sin."

Jesus forever set the record straight, though at times we still don't fully grasp the amazing truth He reveals here.

First, Jesus explained that the man was born blind, not because of his sin nor his parent's sin (of course, both had sinned because... we all sin! Romans 3:23) but so that God's power could be seen in him! Jesus stated clearly: "It was not because of sin!"

Consider for a moment... If the man's blindness was caused by sin, his or his parents, wouldn't we all then be blind, because all have sinned? Wouldn't all afflictions, birth defects, diseases, tragedies, all suffering... be handed out by God as punishments? Is this idea—in any way—consistent with the God who offered Jesus Christ to save us, free us, and make us sons and daughters of the Living God? NO! This is not how God treats His beloved children!

Instead, God can and will USE our disability, our weakness, our troubles, and our tragedies for demonstration of His power. None of us is perfect, we all have weaknesses, whether it is physical, emotional, or mental, each person has weaknesses... some weaknesses are more visible than others, and some easier to hide.

But... Is it possible that – Our weaknesses are God's opportunity to show His Power, to compensate, to heal, to complete, to overcome. 2 Corinthians 12:10 NLT) *That's why I take pleasure in my weaknesses, and in the insults, hardships, persecutions, and troubles that I suffer for Christ. For when I am weak, then I am strong.*

Father God, help us to recognize our need for You, in every weakness, every hardship, and every trouble... so that Your strength can work in and through us to make us strong!

"Your Grace Is Enough"

Matt Maher

https://youtu.be/LISbMRp0Y64 '

June 10

Today's Encouragement is Psalm 103:10-12 NLT *He does not punish us for all our sins; he does not deal harshly with us, as we deserve. For his unfailing love toward those who fear him is as great as the height of the heavens above the earth. He has removed our sins as far from us as the East is from the West.*

He does not punish –

Facing a terrible tragedy, the loss of his son, a new believer in Christ cried out, "Why did God do this to me?" He might also have asked, "Why did God let this happen?" Or "Couldn't God have stopped this?"

We can't address the huge challenge of "why do bad things happen to good people?" in a few sentences... yet this passage makes it clear...

God Does NOT punish us for all our sins!

God does NOT deal harshly with us (as we deserve).

NO! We falsely accuse God! He, the Almighty One who provided Jesus as the perfect eternal cleansing of all our sins past, present, and future! Would this God of Grace, now set about to now punish us for our sins, no matter how great or small? He would Himself be ignoring, erasing the once-for-all-time, perfect atonement of Jesus!

We live in a fallen world my friends, and death, destruction, decay is evident everywhere. This world is, and our lives within this world are, passing away; tragedy will come!

But no tragedy, no suffering, no punishment comes into the life of a believer by the hand of God!

In Jesus' own words...John 16:33 NLT *"I have told you all this so that you may have peace in me. Here on earth you will have many trials and sorrows. But take heart, because I have overcome the world."*

Father God, forgive us when we have falsely accused You of punishing us for our sin. Help us to clearly focus on Your unfailing Love, and to recognize that all our sins are perfectly erased by the perfect work of Jesus! Thank You, our Loving Father!

"How Great Is the Love"

Elevation Worship

https://youtu.be/sXNdeVxEsic

June 11

Today's Encouragement is 2 Timothy 3:1-2 NLT *You should know this, Timothy, that in the last days there will be very difficult times. For people will love only themselves and their money. They will be boastful and proud, scoffing at God, disobedient to their parents, and ungrateful. They will consider nothing sacred.*

Love only themselves –

Friends, we see this everywhere, don't we, every day. In the last days... I don't know where we are in this timeline but consider for a moment the predominant view of "Self" in today's world.

Here are just a few examples, familiar phrases in today's world:

"Be true to yourself," "Decide for yourself what is true," "My truth," "My body, my choice," "I decide what's right for me," "I have to do this for me."

We even take "selfies"! And we spend inordinate amounts of money on clothing, makeup, plastic surgery, etc. to make our "Self" look better, younger, healthier!

"Self" has become "god" in our culture.

Now, it is important to take care of yourself, respect yourself, and have a proper attitude toward your — Self. But we too often go far beyond healthy self-respect into self-worship, self-adoration, and constantly seeking affirmation from others of our worth!

Jesus clarified the proper perspective of Self in these instructions, (my paraphrase) ... First, Love God with all you are, with all of your Self; Secondly love others just as much as you love your-Self.

The Self is equal to others, but all is secondary to God, Himself! He is to be our focus, the one we adore, the one we draw the attention of others to! We are but grass, all our beauty, our accomplishments, and our lives fade quickly — and the Self we protected, promoted, and pampered becomes dust again!

"People will love only themselves..."

Father God, help us to care for ourselves with love and respect as we recognize You as our God first, and also to genuinely love, honor, and respect our neighbors equally with ourselves.

"Nothing Without You"
Bebo Norman
https://youtu.be/W4wxxG_GRB0

June 12

Today's Encouragement is 2 Timothy 3:16 NLT *All Scripture is inspired by God and is useful to teach us what is true and to make us realize what is wrong in our lives. It corrects us when we are wrong and teaches us to do what is right.*

All scripture –

Paul wrote this letter to his student and friend Timothy to encourage and strengthen him in his growing faith. Timothy was a man of God (see 1 Tim. 6:11) already well acquainted with scripture, which at the time Paul wrote this... was only what we call the Old Testament books... and which some consider outdated, unimportant, or just historical information, even today.

Yet Paul said it is– inspired by God, other translations read "is God-breathed." All of it! It is useful! It is necessary for wisdom! It is what guides us to God, what tells us about God, and what describes God's interaction with His own children throughout many ages of history–and it is God-breathed, inspired–all of it!

And all scripture, which God has breathed out for us, is revealing Him to us, who He is, His nature, His wisdom, His justice, His power, and His mercy! And finally, to conclude the matter, to finish the God-breathed teaching we now call the Bible, God breathed the message of His Son Jesus, the Final Word!

Thank You, Father, for breathing out all scripture for us and for Jesus who completes scripture; Your Final Word to us.

"The Final Word"
Michael Card
https://youtu.be/7MH1OEToxp0

June 13

Today's Encouragement is 2 Timothy 4:11 NLT *Only Luke is with me. Bring Mark with you when you come, for he will be helpful to me in my ministry.*

Helpful in ministry –

Paul ends this letter to his friend Timothy with a listing of several of the people he has worked with, some friends, co-workers, supporters, and some of the opposition.

Only Luke remained with him at this time, a faithful friend and servant of Christ. Friends come and go, don't they? And here Paul asks Timothy to bring Mark with him because Mark is helpful in ministry.

So, reflecting on this thought... who is your Mark? Who is helpful to you in ministry? Who is alongside you, supporting, praying, and assisting you in your service to God? Do they know how grateful you are for them? Might it be a good idea to tell them?

And who is your "Paul," the one that you are helpful to in ministry? This helpfulness in ministry could be in any number of ways, financial support, prayer support, and/or physical support... the question is—Are we helpful, in ministry, to God?

Being available to be – ambassadors of Christ, prayer warriors, servants of the Church, teachers of the Word, even a doorkeeper in His house (Psalm 84:10), there are numerous ways to serve, my friend, ways to be helpful in ministry.

Don't feel qualified? Just ask God to make you qualified, to equip you to serve Him in some way. He will!

Father, help us to serve You, to be helpful first to You and also to those who serve You in ministry.

"Serve the Lord"

Carmen

https://youtu.be/xPGcEAIPYxQ

June 14

Today's Encouragement is Psalm 107:43 NLT *Those who are wise will take all this to heart; they will see in our history the faithful love of the Lord.*

See in our history –

We all generally acknowledge that perspective is a good thing. The younger folks get pretty upset by minor setbacks which don't affect the older folks nearly as much... the difference is not age as much as it is...perspective.

The older folks have the benefit of more years and more experiences of both the seemingly good and the seemingly bad types. They have come to realize that often the difference becomes less distinct with time.

Is it possible that... just as the seniors among us have a greater perspective of this life than the young... those who consider history, beyond just personal experience, also gain an even broader, and clearer perspective as well?

This seems to be the thought behind today's scripture. Those who are wise... will consider these truths and will see—in our history—the Faithful Love of God.

Psalm 107 describes God's interaction with and merciful Love for His people in various glimpses of their history. And we can clearly see how God has been Faithful... throughout time... to His people.

And He never changes!

Father, we offer our sincere thanks for Your Faithfulness and Love for Your own, throughout all time. Thank You for choosing us, adopting us, cleansing us by the blood of Jesus, and bringing us to You!

"You Have Been Good"

Twila Paris

https://youtu.be/hRsHehoRA7o

June 15

Today's Encouragement is Isaiah 55:8-9 NLT *"My thoughts are nothing like your thoughts," says the Lord. "And my ways are far beyond anything you could imagine. For just as the heavens are higher than the earth, so my ways are higher than your ways and my thoughts higher than your thoughts.*

Far beyond –

My father reminded me the other day, just before his 103rd birthday, of a theology professor who told him, about 65 years ago (Yes, he is still that sharp!), "Stop thinking that you can understand God, stop trying to understand and just believe. You can't even understand yourself-much less God!"

Through believing, through our faith in Jesus, we can "know God" and become His own, even when we do not fully understand Him – because we just aren't capable of fully understanding God. See today's passage – His "ways are Far Beyond anything YOU COULD IMAGINE!"

Jesus clearly revealed God's nature to us, John 10:30 NLT *"The Father and I are one."* And from John 14:9 NLT *"...Anyone who has seen me has seen the Father!"* So, we can know ABOUT God through Jesus, we can learn ABOUT God from studying the Bible, we can know enough about God to "accept Christ Jesus as our Lord," But God's thoughts, His ways, His reasoning, His mind... these are beyond us... far beyond anything we could even imagine!

And this is why we are called to BELIEVE... to live by Faith, to place our FAITH in Jesus... Because we are not intended, not created to, and not capable of – understanding God.

Father God, help us to trust You in Faith, for our understanding is far too inadequate to fathom all of who You are.

"The Greatness of Our God"

Hillsong

https://youtu.be/5BSAayiCKO8

June 16

Today's Encouragement is Mark 12:30-31 NLT *"And you must love the Lord your God with all your heart, all your soul, all your mind, and all your strength. The second is equally important: 'Love your neighbor as yourself.' No other commandment is greater than these."*

And you must –

So how do we do what Jesus commanded? Remember God can – but I cannot! – Without Him, we can do nothing (John 15:5); but we can do all things through Christ who gives us Strength (Philippians. 4:13).

Love comes from God, and fills us, and overflows to others. 1 Thessalonians 3:12 *NLT And may the Lord make your love for one another and for all people grow and overflow, just as our love for you overflows.*

It starts with the Source of Love, our Father God, and flows from Him, through us, and then—back to Him and then—flows to others who also love Him and then flows—to others. This is what Jesus said we Must do; there is no greater commandment! Love!

So, what is it that you are now striving to do, to overcome, or to remove from your life, to stop doing? Is it possible that to Love (as Jesus commanded us to do) is far more important?

Father God, help us, selfish creatures that we are, to look to You alone for the Love we need. To seek You so sincerely that Your Love fills us, and overflows back to You and then to this lost world around us.

"Living in the Overflow"
Charity Gayle
https://youtu.be/4UsY4tSDRiE

June 17

Today's Encouragement is 2 Timothy 1:6-7 NLT *This is why I remind you to fan into flames the spiritual gift God gave you when I laid my hands on you. For God has not given us a spirit of fear and timidity, but of power, love, and self-discipline.*

Fan into flames –

The clear message is that 1) God has given each of us the Gift of His Holy Spirit, which we are to 2) fan into flames – that is, to allow, even help, to grow in His power within our lives.

This Spirit which God has given us as a gift (it cannot be earned!) is His Holy Spirit of power, love, and self-discipline!

Most of us don't question God's Power – but we question His power, through the Holy Spirit – living within me

Most of us don't question God's Love – but we question His Love, through the Holy Spirit – living within me

Most of us don't question God's Self Discipline – but we question His self-discipline, through the Holy Spirit – living within me

We are told to fan this gift, God's Holy Spirit, into flames. Is it still only a smoldering ember within you? Is it being fed fuel and oxygen... the breath of God? Or is this gift lying dormant, unfed, covered with the ashes of spiritual neglect....

Wherever you are spiritually, this Gift, this ember, whether you realize it or not... still glows within you... all we must do is to fan it into flames! We do so by opening our hearts to the oxygen of God's love, grace, and mercy, by renewing our minds with the fresh wind of His Word, and by choosing daily, – perhaps several times each day, – to Trust Him with every need, every issue, every concern, so that we remain free of fear and worry.

Lord, help us to fan into flames the priceless spiritual Gift You have given to each of us so that we might live lives of spiritual power, love, and self-discipline rather than fear and timidity.

"Light the Fire Again"
Brian Doerksen
https://youtu.be/1pD2O3FarRM

June 18

Today's Encouragement is Hebrews 7:25 AMPC *Therefore He is able also to save to the uttermost (completely, perfectly, finally, and for all time and eternity) those who come to God through Him, since He is always living to make petition to God and intercede with Him and intervene for them.*

Intercede –

Listen to the finality, the absoluteness, completeness, the permanence in this verse. Jesus is able to save... *To The Uttermost—further described so beautifully as (completely, perfectly, finally, and for all time and eternity)*!

Do you hear it? Once and For All—in Jesus' own words, "It IS Finished!"

And He is Always Living in order to petition, intercede, and intervene... for you and me! More permanence, more eternal... always! Jesus lives and speaks for us, stands between, and He even takes our place! In the Presence of God!

Is it possible, my friends, that Jesus is speaking for us, in God's Presence, for our sin, saying-"Father, this one is Mine, this one believes in Me, this one is covered by my blood." God doesn't need reminding of this, my friends, but we certainly do.

Jesus always lives to intercede for you and me.

Lord, how can we thank You enough, that You would live to intercede for us, we are unworthy, but oh, so grateful Lord Jesus. Thank You, Lord!

"Born in Zion"

Wayne Watson

https://youtu.be/T3pOTzGOlqQ

June 19

Today's Encouragement is Hebrews 10:25 NLT *And let us not neglect our meeting together, as some people do, but encourage one another, especially now that the day of his return is drawing near.*

Meeting together –

We often think we meet together, go to church, to hear from God, to hear His Truth, to worship Him, and of course all these are true. And then we quickly say, "Yeah, but I can do all of that at home, or on the lake, or on the golf course, or walking in the woods, or..." And of course, all of those situations are true.

But there is one thing we do by gathering that, only "meeting together" can do.... Encouraging each other. We cannot encourage each other, and we cannot love each other... alone.

John 13:34 NLT *So now I am giving you a new commandment: Love each other. Just as I have loved you, you should love each other.*

Is it possible that - We love others best when we worship with them?

Being together, meeting with each other and with God, singing, praying, studying God's word... together. We are not alone, not isolated units, we are a family, the body of Christ (1 Corinthians 12:27), and only together, do we experience what God has created us to be...One! *"That they may be one as You and I are one."* (John 17:21).

We are encouraged not to neglect this... it is easy to neglect meeting together, church is often "messy," people aren't all sweet and loving and kind, the church is far from perfect... and yet, it is still the Body of Christ! And you and I are parts of that Body!

Father God, help us to gather, messy and challenging as it may be, and extend Your Love to each other.

"By Our Love"
For King and Country
https://youtu.be/d9zoq3k-3K0

June 20

Today's Encouragement is Hebrews 10:21-22 NLT *And since we have a great High Priest who rules over God's house, let us go right into the presence of God with sincere hearts fully trusting him. For our guilty consciences have been sprinkled with Christ's blood to make us clean, and our bodies have been washed with pure water.*

Fully trusting Him –

Can you envision this? Going "right into the Presence of God"? Without fear? Without shame? Without any consciousness of our sinful lives? Just with sincere hearts totally filled with Trust, Faith, and Confidence in Jesus!

Only Jesus can make the way, give us the strength to enter the very presence of our Father God, Creator, Almighty, The Most Holy God of all!

Only because we belong to Christ because He has done the perfect cleansing of our lives – which we could never do. Jesus prepares us for this moment, this experience, this life-transforming privilege: entering the Presence of Almighty God... without fear, shame, or remorse... but as dearly loved children coming to our Father. We are perfectly clean by the blood of Christ, so clean that we are welcomed in the presence of God Himself.

And this is

- not someday,
- not when we pass from this life,
- not a nice thought that 'one day maybe if I'm good enough...'

This is our opportunity Now!

We can enter the Presence of Our Father at any time! Because we are perfectly cleansed already, now, completely, and eternally! We cannot add to the work, the sacrifice of Christ, nor can we detract from it! It is Finished already, by Jesus... not by us!

Thank You, Father, for the privilege of coming into Your presence, fully clean and loved. Help us to come often, and just spend time in Your presence.

"Throne Room"
Kim Walker-Smith
https://youtu.be/A1Ljl32SqRc

June 21

Today's Encouragement is Hebrews 12:1-2a NLT *Therefore, since we are surrounded by such a huge crowd of witnesses to the life of faith, let us strip off every weight that slows us down, especially the sin that so easily trips us up. And let us run with endurance the race God has set before us. We do this by keeping our eyes on Jesus, the champion who initiates and perfects our faith.*

Strip off every weight –

We all want to run with endurance the race God has set before us! It is the sincere desire of every believer as we recognize that God's way, His plan, and His race, is where we need to be, to focus our lives, time, and attention.

So, we prepare for His "race," the challenge that God places before each of His beloved children. Interesting that we each are challenged by the "race God has set before us." Each of us has our own "race" to run!

Let's focus on stripping off every weight. This doesn't refer to sin because that is separately addressed, so what else could hinder us in the race we are given?

Is it possible that this "weight"' includes all the "good" things we get involved with, which have the result of slowing us down in the Race which God has set before us? Some possibilities include work, exercise, watching TV, social media, sports, – and even church busyness... there's no limit to places we can spend time.... which "slows us down" in the race God has set before us.

Recognize a few key points: we all have a race, and running this race is not an option. Sin trips us, "weight" slows us down, and we can only run God's race with endurance when we throw off the weight and the sin that works against us.

Father, open our eyes to the weight, as well as the sin, which keeps us from running well the race You have set before us. We need Your help, always, as we keep our eyes on Jesus, the champion.

"Runner"

Twila Paris

https://youtu.be/YSPORhV2eZY

June 22

Today's Encouragement is Hebrews 12:2a NLT *We do this by keeping our eyes on Jesus, the champion who initiates and perfects our faith.*

Eyes on Jesus –

Continuing the thought of running the race that "God has set before us" (v1), let's look a bit further at how we are to run this race.

"Eyes on me!" The leader reminds his followers to keep looking to, at, for Him—for the right thing to do, for the courage, strength, and direction needed for the task at hand. Whether fighting a battle, or running a race, or caring for a neighbor in need, our answer... as followers of Christ... is to keep our eyes on Jesus.

Notice the brief description of Jesus which follows: He is the champion, and He began our faith, and He perfects our faith. He does the initiating and completing, the perfecting of our faith!

Our task is just this, to run the race that God placed before us (v1) and keep our eyes focused on Jesus, our Champion, our Leader, Guide, Enabler, and our Perfector!

Father, help us continue to keep our focus clearly and firmly fixed on Jesus, and Him alone, as we continue to run the race You have set before us. We trust that He will strengthen, complete, and perfect us in true Faith!

"Fix My Eyes"
For King and Country
https://youtu.be/iXGuWHb5INk

June 23

Today's Encouragement is Colossians 3:15 NLT *And let the peace that comes from Christ rule in your hearts. For as members of one body, you are called to live in peace. And always be thankful.*

Rule in your hearts –

Do you notice the sentence style here? It isn't a prayer, not a hope, nor a question, but an imperative, an instruction, a command... Let the Peace that comes from Christ—rule in your hearts!

We choose, my friends, as so often God allows us to do so, what it is that "rules" —all the authority, all the control,—in our hearts, minds, and emotions.

Is it fear and anxiety that rules our hearts? The worries and cares of this life, or gossip, rumors, despair, depression, doubts, hopelessness... the list of options (all destructive!) is endless... But only one choice, one "ruler" for our hearts is the wise choice... and that is God's Peace, the Peace that comes from Christ. He is the Prince of Peace!

And we are counseled to "Let" His peace have all control! We allow – or we disallow this!

Do you notice how throughout the New Testament, with only a few rare exceptions, Jesus was always at peace? When the crowds wanted to throw Him off a cliff, called Him names, and mocked His teachings... whatever His circumstances, Jesus was at Peace.

Is it possible that Jesus' mind was fixed upon His Father rather than the threatening circumstances? Isaiah 26:3 NLT

You will keep in perfect peace
all who trust in you,
all whose thoughts are fixed on you!

Help us, Lord, to Let, to allow Your Peace to rule our hearts and minds, by fixing our thoughts on You.

"I Fix My Eyes on You"
Tommy Walker
https://youtu.be/K_b6UnKvEF8

June 24

Today's Encouragement is Psalm 119:18 NLT *Open my eyes to see the wonderful truths in your instructions.*

Wonderful truths –

We are free of course... by God's immeasurable Grace... to choose what we listen to, what we believe and decide about every concept, idea, suggestion, and instruction of God. Yet, my friend, consider this...

Is it possible that God's truth, His Word, His wisdom, His desire for us (His Will) is always, always, always... in our best interest!?!? Is it possible?

Since we believe that, He is Love, and He is our Loving, Perfect, all Wise, Heavenly Father... would He not want to give all the wisdom, instruction, and guidance that He can... to His dearly loved children?

Wouldn't you do this, imperfect, fallible being that you are... for your own children? Teach them the best way to live?

God's Word is chock-full of His instruction: His wisdom, guidance, and advice for us on how to live this life, how to survive, how to worship Him, how to live joyfully, even how to be victorious over life and death! The handbook for life, some have called it. Our obedience to His instruction is our choice, we can't do this perfectly, and it is not a requirement to be saved... only faith in Christ can save us.... Yet we are wise to consider His wisdom in how we live!

Since God took so many years– centuries– and hundreds of authors, carefully guided by His hand, to compose this book of Life, might it not be kinda smart to choose to believe it?! To read it, study it, and learn the many wonderful truths within our Bible?

Father, we can do nothing without You, we even need You to "Open our eyes to the wonderful truths in Your instructions!"

"The Truth"
The Belonging Company
https://youtu.be/QmHwFURtQx0

June 25

Today's Encouragement is Colossians 1:22 NLT *Yet now he has reconciled you to himself through the death of Christ in his physical body. As a result, he has brought you into his own presence, and you are holy and blameless as you stand before him without a single fault.*

Without a single fault –

Did you hear that? Do you believe that?

It is one thing to recognize that we are saved, brought to a right relationship with God because of Christ's suffering and death for us. This is one thing. And we believe it, though at times it's still hard to conceive of this incredible, unimaginable gift of forgiveness. Yet, we know it is true, and this is exactly, precisely what – we believe!

Yet, Paul doesn't stop there in his teaching to the believers who make up the church... he goes on to teach us... God has brought you into His OWN PRESENCE! This isn't "one day," "in the great beyond," or "someday, maybe, I hope," No! This is present, NOW! God has NOW brought you into HIS PRESENCE!

AND my friends – as if being saved, reconciled, and brought into God's Presence isn't enough! Read it again carefully and slowly...

YOU are Holy and Blameless as you stand before the CREATOR, ALMIGHTY GOD... Without – a – single – fault.

Really? Is this true? Do You believe?

Father God, such kindness, and such power, to cleanse us completely, perfectly, forever... so that we are just like Jesus—holy, blameless and without a single fault as we stand in Your Presence... Help us to grasp the amazing Truth of the Cleansing Power of the blood of Jesus!

"Clean"

Natalie Grant

https://youtu.be/2BfZ3KKKg9c

June 26

Today's Encouragement is James 1:5-6 NLT *If you need wisdom, ask our generous God, and he will give it to you. He will not rebuke you for asking. But when you ask him, be sure that your faith is in God alone. Do not waver, for a person with divided loyalty is as unsettled as a wave of the sea that is blown and tossed by the wind.*

If you need –

Wavering, doubting, questioning...

Doubting is clearly described as a sign of divided loyalty, an unsettled mind.

The alternative is a settled mind, a mind that has decided, is fixed in determination, not tossed around from here to there like the waves, or blown this way and that, by the wind.

Friends, a believer is one who has decided, chosen, and continues to choose to believe!

"Believe what?" You may ask...

- The Truth of Jesus Christ, that He is the Truth, the Life, and the Way!
- That God has plans for you that are for your good, to bless you, to give you hope and a future.
- That God has not, and never will abandon you.
- That these trials and troubles will someday pass away.
- That Jesus died for you, to give you eternal life, beginning now.

Don't have this faith, this confidence? Just "ask our generous God." Jesus is waiting. Patiently. Lovingly.

Father God, strengthen our faith, so that we do not waver, blow around by the craziness of life and our unsettled minds. Help us to decide, now, for all time, to place our faith in God alone. You are our Hope!

"The Master Is Waiting"

Marty Stuart

https://youtu.be/ryoQktrAgVo

June 27

Today's Encouragement is Hebrews 13:5 NLT *Don't love money; be satisfied with what you have. For God has said, "I will never fail you. I will never abandon you."*

Be satisfied –

In other versions, this satisfaction is called contentment. Here it is used in reference to money, but in context, it applies to all situations, including relationships, as the writer begins this passage with, Hebrews 13:1 NLT "Keep on loving each other as brothers and sisters." Then, he mentions also, loving strangers, those in prison, and our spouses.

Be satisfied with what you have—What does this have to do with loving others? Is it possible that... we are to be satisfied, and content, with the people in our lives whom God has allowed there? Of course, those who are destructive, abusive, full of anger and resentment, these we are to flee from, because they are not honoring God with their lives... but our brothers, sisters, spouses in Faith... these are the people whom God has placed, or allowed, next to us... Be content with them, live with them in satisfaction, because you and I are just as flawed as they. Our satisfaction comes from God, not from money, or relationships, or prestige... He is the source of all we need!

Father God, help us to practice satisfaction, and sincere contentment in all areas of our lives, including relationships, as we consider that we are as imperfect as they are.

"Hallelujah (Satisfied)"
Gaither Vocal Band
https://youtu.be/W8Z8NTsHDu

June 28

Today's Encouragement is Psalm 121:1-2 NLT *I look up to the mountains- does my help come from there? My help comes from the Lord, who made heaven and earth!*

I look –

The idea is frequently repeated in the Bible. Fix your eyes on Jesus, I look to You for help, and numerous other times this concept is used to help us to understand, to "see," that what we choose to focus on, look to, and for, is essential to our direction!

Years ago, I heard my driver's education teacher say, "If you focus on the lines in the highway you will start to drift over to them, because you move toward what you are focused on." Additionally, we've all heard that we need to "set our sights" on a goal.

The world recognizes this truth. We are drawn to what we focus on.

So, what is our focus? What are we looking at, looking for? May I suggest that the only focus with any positive, lasting value is Our God! Not career, health, wealth, power, prestige, or even family, nor friendship, nor any other pursuit, any other focus... all these will disappoint, fail, fade like the grass.

Father God, help us to turn our eyes, our focus, our pursuit to You alone! May we choose to make You the focal point of our lives... lift our eyes, our gaze, our focus to You, Your Grace, Love, Perfection, and Your ways, Your Truth, Your Hope. We ask in Jesus' Name.

"Psalm 121"

Kristyn Getty

https://youtu.be/RxtMjBsN2FE

June 29

Today's Encouragement is Psalm 123:1-2 NLT *I lift my eyes to you, O God, enthroned in heaven. We keep looking to the Lord our God for his mercy, just as servants keep their eyes on their master, as a slave girl watches her mistress for the slightest signal.*

Keep looking –

Eyes on the master, watching, waiting, keep looking... patience is implied, calmly but actively waiting for God to act, to speak, to direct us. He is our Master, Lord, and King and we are privileged to serve Him.

So, we watch Him, with spiritual eyes, we see Him through eyes of faith, and we respond to Him as He directs us. He directs us in unlimited ways, remember He is The Creator, but His direction is always consistent with His Word, our guide and measuring stick for all truth.

So, we keep looking to You, Lord! For Your Mercy, for Your direction, "this is the way you should go" Isaiah. 30:21, for our every need, every day, every breath. You alone are Life. Help us keep looking to You alone Lord.

"God, I Look to You"

Francesca Battistelli

https://youtu.be/KP1QKueGK-o

June 30

Today's Encouragement is James 4:1 NLT *What is causing the quarrels and fights among you? Don't they come from the evil desires at war within you?*

Causing the quarrels –

What is it? What causes us to be in turmoil, in a fight with this or that person, in the ceaseless drama of rocky relationships? Why are we like this? Here we have the answer.

Friends, it has absolutely nothing to do with what they said or did or thought! We have fights with others because we have-evil-desires-at war within ourselves!

It is then, our own selfishness, greed, jealousy, and covetousness which causes us to be caught up in fights, and arguments. Even bullying, excluding, and generally doing all we can to hurt others... all own evil, selfish desires cause us to get caught up in quarreling and arguing.

Ouch! Ok, what's the answer? Read on! James 4:7-8a NLT *So humble yourselves before God. Resist the devil, and he will flee from you. Come close to God, and God will come close to you.*

The enemy of our souls, the devil, loves to see us fighting and quarreling! It's his turf! We can resist him by turning away from our selfish desires and instead drawing closer to God. And as we do come close to God, like the returning prodigal son, God will run to meet us!

Lord God, please give us strength to resist the evil one, and the sinful desires of our own hearts, which cause us to fight with others. Help us to live in Peace with others, and with You, as we draw close to You through prayer and worship.

"Jesus Draw Me Close"
Lenny LeBlanc
https://youtu.be/kvKQZBH5rZU

July 1

Today's Encouragement is Psalm 113:5-9 NLT *Who can be compared with the Lord our God, who is enthroned on high? He stoops to look down on heaven and on earth. He lifts the poor from the dust and the needy from the garbage dump. He sets them among princes, even the princes of his own people! He gives the childless woman a family, making her a happy mother. Praise the Lord!*

Who can be compared –

Who or what compares to God? The almighty Creator of Life, who cares for His own creation so deeply that He gave Jesus, His Son, to restore us to a right relationship with Himself?

Compare Him to the other things which some consider to be "gods": Mother Nature, a self-achieved higher state of consciousness, a "prophet" or "'enlightened one" who wrote a book about what he thinks is the way we should live, ancestor worship, bowing before idols, kissing icons, and a myriad of other ways people try to connect with their concepts of god...

Yet, we are privileged to know Him! THE Truth, THE God who IS Love, Creator, Almighty, Omnipotent, and much, much more.... He has too many other amazing, unlimited attributes to list here!

As you worship Him with this song, consider His power, His greatness, His mercy, kindness, and His love... just a few of the unlimited aspects of the Wonder of Our God!

There truly is no one like You, Father! We will choose to worship You and You alone!

"Who Is Like Our God"

Vineyard Worship

https://youtu.be/xu0QLD1MtdE

July 2

Today's Encouragement is James 1:12 NLT *God blesses those who patiently endure testing and temptation. Afterward they will receive the crown of life that God has promised to those who love him.*

Patiently endure –

We all know some folks, perhaps they are ourselves, who complain loudly and freely, to anyone and everyone, when they are hurting, experiencing difficulties, or discomfort. They're not happy and they want to make sure everyone is well aware of their undeserved suffering!

This response to difficulty is natural. It's a very human but also a very self-centered response: "I want my way... and this is not it!"

God's wisdom for us describes what He desires from His children, "Patiently endure [both] testing and temptation." And notice that He blesses those who endure... with the "crown of life"!

Now it is only possible to "endure with patience" the many, varied, and sometimes unimaginable, difficulties and temptations of this life... when we focus our hearts and minds beyond this day, this moment, this painful experience that we are presently confronting face to face.

(This may seem contrary to the idea of being grateful for, and living just today, allowing God to hold tomorrow and not worry about the future... but it isn't the same.)

The endurance of pain – must focus on – the hope for tomorrow. This pain shall pass, this will ultimately end, I must endure this for this day... yet I am trusting God and hoping for a better tomorrow. This is patient endurance.

Father God, we need Your help, Your strength, to be able to endure with patience. We cannot do this in our own strength. Help us to honor You by trusting that You will bring us through the many trials of this life, with patient endurance.

"While I Wait"

Lincoln Brewster

https://youtu.be/NswPPVgMaPE

July 3

Today's Encouragement is 1 Peter 1:7 NLT *These trials will show that your faith is genuine. It is being tested as fire tests and purifies gold-though your faith is far more precious than mere gold. So, when your faith remains strong through many trials, it will bring you much praise and glory and honor on the day when Jesus Christ is revealed to the whole world.*

Far more precious –

This is our Faith, tiny or mountain-moving, —just as it is at this moment... Our Faith is far more precious... than gold!

We too often begin to discount, minimize, and devalue the power of scriptural truth by adding our own "buts" to it. As if we could change God's Truth.... We read the words, "Your faith is far more precious than mere gold." And add, "But... my faith isn't very strong" or "my faith is so weak, inconsistent, wavering...." Friends, we can take God's Words, His Truth, as it is—without our adding doubts and fears to it! What if we instead responded to Him with, "Yes, Lord, thank You!" rather than our critical doubts?

This passage is about both trials and faith, how trials influence our faith, and how our faith can remain strong through the many trials of this life. We don't know what trials lay ahead, but if the past is any indication... we have some still in store! So just as fire purifies gold, trials purify our faith. And this is a far more critical process than refining gold because our Faith is far more precious than gold or anything else that we can imagine.

Father God, strengthen us as we go through the trials of this life so that our Faith becomes purer and stronger and brings us ever closer to You.

"More Precious than Silver"
Lynn DeShazo
https://youtu.be/DKmlrlzTHXY

July 4

Today's Encouragement is 1 Kings 8:27 NLT *"But will God really live on earth? Why, even the highest heavens cannot contain you. How much less this Temple I have built!"*

Heaven cannot contain –

King Solomon built the first and greatest temple for God in Jerusalem around 3000 years ago. It was magnificent! Everything was covered in gold. And here Solomon prays, dedicating it to God, and the glory of the Lord filled the Temple (v 10-11).

Yet this wisest man, King Solomon, recognized that, as beautiful, as magnificent, as well-intentioned as this Temple was... nothing on earth, nor even the heavens above, can contain our God. He is far beyond our ability to understand Him... He is so much greater, my friends, than we give Him credit for!

And here is a mystery. God is too great for us to understand Him, Isaiah 55:8 NLT *"My thoughts are nothing like your thoughts," says the Lord. "And my ways are far beyond anything you could imagine."* And yet... He gave us Jesus, to show us, to reveal to us—Himself! Jesus said, *"The Father and I are one."* (John 10:30 NLT)

Jesus introduced us to the heart of God, to the Love of God for us (John 3:16). So, while we cannot understand God, whom all the heavens cannot contain, nor can we know His ways and thoughts, yet we Can know Him—by knowing Jesus! Jesus is God with us, Immanuel, so that can know Him... even though "the highest heavens cannot contain" Him!

Thank You, Father, for allowing us to see You, to know You, through Jesus. Help us to grasp the mystery: how vast is Your Greatness, and yet how genuine Your Love for, and Your knowledge of, each of us—Your adopted children, sinners saved only by the Grace of Jesus.

"The Greatness of Our God"
Hillsong Worship
https://youtu.be/5BSAayiCKO8

July 5

Today's Encouragement is 1 Peter 3:21 NLT *And that water is a picture of baptism, which now saves you, not by removing dirt from your body, but as a response to God from a clean conscience. It is effective because of the resurrection of Jesus Christ.*

A clean conscience –

There seems to be much confusion, or at least disagreement, about baptism. Does it save us? Does it cleanse us from sin? Is it required for salvation? This brief devotional thought isn't intended to answer all our questions, even about only one verse of Scripture. [The Word of God is far too vast, too powerful- it is living and alive! (Heb. 4:12), to be adequately explained in just a few paragraphs!]

This verse introduces the idea that baptism is "a response to God from a clear conscience." And this baptism is effective because Jesus was resurrected.

So, we choose baptism – as a response to God, a recognition of all He has done for us through Christ... that He has given us the gift of ... a clean conscience!

Are we living in this gift, my friends, a clean conscience before God? Are we recognizing that Jesus has paid the unimaginable price to cleanse us, (including our conscience!) from all the sin we have done and ever will do?

Tragically, some of us continue to hold on to, and feel guilt and shame for, the terrible things we have done when Jesus' death and resurrection has already provided for us ... a clean conscience! Freedom from all guilt and shame!

Is it possible, my friends, that when we pray, "Father, please forgive me for my sins." that He would respond to us, "What sin are you talking about? I only see Jesus when I look at you, my child!"

A clean conscience... this is for you and me!

Thank You, Lord, for a clean conscience! Only You can do that! Help us believe it, Lord!

"Clean"
Natalie Grant
https://youtu.be/2BfZ3KKKg9c

July 6

Today's Encouragement is Luke 10:41-42 NLT *But the Lord said to her, "My dear Martha, you are worried and upset over all these details! There is only one thing worth being concerned about. Mary has discovered it, and it will not be taken away from her."*

Only one thing –

Jesus visited the home of Mary, Martha, and Lazarus. While Martha is busily preparing the meal, Mary sits at Jesus' feet, intently listening to His every word. Martha naturally becomes upset because she was doing all the work! Concerned about the many details of serving Jesus, she asks Jesus to tell Mary to help her.

Jesus' response is today's passage.

We too often become very busy with the many details of this life; we can even become consumed by busyness! Even serving the Lord, as Martha did, can leave us frustrated, upset, and eventually burned out. There is a place and time for serving of course...

Hear Jesus speak this directly to us, today — "My friend, there's only one thing that matters, only one thing that is so important that you need to be concerned about. It is above and beyond and far exceeds the busy details of this life. It is listening to and being with Me."

In John 6:68 NLT Simon Peter replied, *"Lord, to whom would we go? You have the words that give eternal life."*

Mary discovered that Jesus' words, the words of Eternal Life, were (and are still now, and ever will be!) The—Only—Thing—That—Matters!

Friends, will we set aside our busyness, the many details of this life, in order to choose, as Mary did, the One Thing—listening to Jesus, sitting at His feet, hearing His words of Eternal life? Nothing Else Matters!

Lord, help us understand that resting in Your presence is far superior to any work that we or any other person can do.

"Find Me at The Feet of Jesus"
Christy Nockels
https://youtu.be/GThyC6ZFUgI

July 7

Today's Encouragement is 2 Peter 1:1 NLT *This letter is from Simon Peter, a slave and apostle of Jesus Christ. I am writing to you who share the same precious faith we have. This faith was given to you because of the justice and fairness of Jesus Christ, our God and Savior.*

The same precious faith –

Did you get that? Peter, the disciple who was one of Jesus' closest friends, wrote this letter to us, his fellow believers, "who share the same precious faith...."

How can this be? Surely his faith is far greater than others of his day, and greater than ours today, right? Surely his experiences with Christ, the time Peter spent in close contact with Him, the struggles and suffering that he endured... surely, we presume, Peter had great faith, he even walked on water with Jesus!

Yet his words, not mine, speak to believers of his day and forever, that we all "share this same precious faith"!

He goes on to explain... this precious faith was given... a gift not earned by us in any way... because it is a perfect gift of the just and fair Lord Jesus.

Every good gift comes from God and His gifts are perfect! (James 1:17) And we cannot add to these perfect gifts... we can use them, exercise them, practice them, and thus grow in our faith, but the precious gift of faith is graciously and fairly given to us undeserving humans.

Is it possible my friends, that Jesus has, already, in His justice and fairness, given us "this same precious faith"... and everything else will ever need (see v3)?!?! Already Given!?!?

Thank you, Jesus, for Your perfect mercy and love.

"Already All I Need"

Christy Nockels

https://youtu.be/zByzjJ4nvH8

July 8

Today's Encouragement is 2 Peter 1:4 NLT *And because of his glory and excellence, he has given us great and precious promises. These are the promises that enable you to share his divine nature and escape the world's corruption caused by human desires.*

Great and precious promises –

He has (already) given us His great and precious promises! The Word of God is full of wonderful promises, which we can choose to believe, to trust, to rely on. Some promises we recognize are fulfilled, and some we understand are not yet, but they are still the great, and precious, promises of our God to us!

These wonderful truths of what is, and what will be,– are given to us because God is Good! In His Glory and His Excellence... He gives us wonderful gifts... these great and precious promises.

And notice carefully, my friends, the effect of God's great and precious promises in our lives... they enable us to "share his divine nature and escape the world's corruption caused by human desires." God's promises do this!

His great and precious promises are what bring us to Him, to share His divine nature (become like Christ!) and to escape from sin... because we choose, to believe, His great and precious promises to us!

And His greatest promise? Everlasting life! Because of His Love and our belief! John 3:16 NLT *For this is how God loved the world: He gave his one and only Son, so that everyone who believes in him will not perish but have eternal life.*

Thank You, Father, for your promises; help us continue in faith, to trust You, to believe You, and to be transformed by Your promises!

"God So Loved"
We the Kingdom
https://youtu.be/jasoo3UDSwY

July 9

Today's Encouragement is Psalm 139:6 NLT *Such knowledge is too wonderful for me, too great for me to understand!*

Too wonderful –

In this Psalm, David writes about God's perfect and complete knowledge of... everything! He knows everything about us, when we sit, when we stand, and when we lie down... He even knows the words we will say before we speak....

And this same God, (v5) "He goes before me and follows me. He places His hand of blessing on my head."

As David writes these words, he is overcome, overwhelmed, and overshadowed by the wonder of our God... and in this state, he recognizes how truly vast, and yet amazingly intimate, our God really is.... David can only say, "Father God, You are too wonderful, too magnificent. This knowledge of You is too much for me, I am overwhelmed by You!"

Lord, when we see, through eyes of faith, how immeasurably magnificent You are, and then how tenderly You care for us... truly such knowledge is too wonderful for us, mere humans, to understand.

Father, all we can say is Thank You; we Praise You! You are so wonderful! You truly are magnificent! Our words fail to express Your glory!!

"Wonderful"
Christy Nockels
https://youtu.be/vlTHjBjq2t4

July 10

Today's Encouragement is Psalm 130:3-4 NLT *Lord, if you kept a record of our sins, who, O Lord, could ever survive? But you offer forgiveness, that we might learn to fear you.*

If You kept –

Recently we were talking to a friend who shared several grievances they had towards us. It was very uncomfortable and rather sad in hindsight. We recognized that while these issues were certainly the result of our shortcomings, mistakes, and our generally human behavior... this person was essentially—"keeping a record of our sins." These are things we cannot undo, we cannot erase, and the harm done to our relationship is already final. Additionally, and very importantly, this record of our sins continues to hurt this friend... each time they remember the harm done to them, they are harmed again!

Yet our God, our Perfect Loving Father, has not only erased any past record of our sins, even mistakes, even our minor insults ... He has provided complete erasure of our future sins! We cannot undo our past; we cannot restore our damaged relationship with our friend... only their forgiveness will heal our friendship! And this is exactly what God has done for us, granted us complete forgiveness; He has forgotten our sin! (Heb 8:12)

And we now have a restored, proper, and grace-filled relationship with Him because of His forgiveness... bought by Jesus, so that we can be close to, in relationship with, our loving Father God!

Thank You, Jesus, for purchasing our forgiveness with your life; Thank You, Father, that you do not keep any record of our sins!

"Cleansed"

Charity Gayle

https://youtu.be/vQSber6psjg

July 11

Today's Encouragement is John 20:29 NLT *Then Jesus told him* [Thomas], *"You believe because you have seen me. Blessed are those who believe without seeing me."*

Believe without seeing –

In the preceding verses, Jesus is resurrected, has appeared to the disciples, and Thomas, now that he has seen Jesus, believes. As always, Jesus' words have profound and eternal depth... and He speaks here, 2000 years ago, of you and me!

I admit it... I want to see! Don't you? To see Jesus, to see His miraculous power at work, to see people healed, prisoners (of all types of bondage) set free! We have friends who are serving overseas who report that they are experiencing a great harvest of people coming to faith in Jesus! I want to see that! We all want to, we long for our faith to become sight! We think, "That would be such a great blessing!"

And yet, Jesus says it is those (including you and me!) who do not see Him face to face, nor His miracle-working power... who are "blessed"!

This word "blessed" is also translated in the Amplified as "happy" and "to be envied," and this is you and me!

Because we walk by, live by, Faith and not by sight... we are blessed, happy and to be envied!

Friends, anyone can believe what they can see... no faith is required. We, however, believe in what our physical eyes cannot see. The redeeming Love of our God through Jesus Christ!

And so, we are blessed!

Thank You, Father, for Your truth and wisdom, designing us that we may please You by our faith in what we cannot see. You are so wise and so good to us!

"Blessed"

Hillsong

https://youtu.be/hI-02ly6-0Q

July 12

Today's Encouragement is 1 John 1:5 NLT *This is the message we heard from Jesus and now declare to you: God is light, and there is no darkness in him at all.*

God is Light –

What happens when we are in the darkness? We stumble, bump into things, each other, we fall down, and generally get lost.... When were you last in deep physical darkness? We grope for something to anchor us, to obtain our bearings, to orient us to the world around us... and any tiny glimmer of light, no matter how far away from us... brings hope, it draws us to it, we naturally seek it... just a tiny light and we have direction, a purpose, a renewed strength. If it were extinguished, we'd be lost again, in the darkness.

John describes God here as "Light," and in 4:16 as "Love." He personifies God as Light and Love. God is the source of both, and indeed, all of Life! And as the Source, He provides to us what we need, and we need the Light He provides.

As we walk in His Light... we see clearly, we do not stumble, we do not have to grope for an anchor, we are aware of our circumstances and situation, our eyes are open and functioning.

Father God, thank You for being our Light, allowing us to see, to learn, and to move toward You!

"In the Light"
DC Talk
https://youtu.be/e2qzxY5a37o

July 13

Today's Encouragement is 2 Peter 1:3 NLT *By his divine power, God has given us everything we need for living a godly life. We have received all of this by coming to know him, the one who called us to himself by means of his marvelous glory and excellence.*

Everything we need –

We pray for strength, courage, faith, patience, wisdom, hope, success, and so many things. We are constantly asking for something from Our Father. Now, it is good to ask Him for our needs, it is good to recognize He is the source of every good and perfect gift (James 1:17) and that we desperately need Him!

Yet, my friends, before we ask Him, wouldn't it be wise to look into what He has already given to us? "God has given us everything we need for living a godly life." God has ALREADY given us... Everything we need... for living a godly life! Sorta shocking, isn't it? we can come up with a long list of things, attributes, gifts, and skills which we think that need for living a godly life. Yet God's word says... we ALREADY have... EVERTHING... And we have (ALREADY) received all this by coming to know Jesus!

Father God, please reveal to us how you have already equipped us, with everything that we need to live a godly life, a life pleasing to you. You are so good to us, Lord. Open our eyes to this truth!

"Already All I Need"
Christy Nockels
https://youtu.be/zByzjJ4nvH8

July 14

Today's Encouragement is Isaiah 40:7-8 NLT *The grass withers and the flowers fade beneath the breath of the Lord. And so it is with people. The grass withers and the flowers fade, but the word of our God stands forever.*

Stands forever –

You don't need to live too very long on this earth to understand the brevity of this life. Just like the grass, which withers away in a drought, or flowers which bloom for only a few days... so it is with people.

Sometimes people die young; sometimes they live to old age. When you attend the funeral of the young... the brevity of life can become a very sharp and painful reality.

My friends, the words, ideas, theories and popular movements of people, are human, fallible, faltering, and often false... just like the grass. Quickly appearing and quickly fading away.

While there truly is nothing new under the sun (Eccles. 1:9) things can seem new to a new generation... because sin repackages itself to make fools of the unsuspecting in its never ceasing effort to deceive humanity.

The antidote to such deception? "The word of our God stands forever!"

John 1:1 NLT *In the beginning the Word already existed. The Word was with God, and the Word was God.*

Jesus is the Eternal Word of God.

Father God, help us as Your children, to look only to the truth of Your Word for guidance. "You [Jesus] have the words of eternal life, where else would we go?" (John 6:68)

"All Flesh Is Like the Grass"

Fernando Ortega

https://youtu.be/cb4xp9XkKsk

July 15

Today's Encouragement is Isaiah 40:29 NLT *He gives power to the weak and strength to the powerless.*

Strength to the powerless –

Our God often mystifies. He turns things around or upside-down or throws them into reverse. He is not limited. Especially not by our human logic or expectations.

A few examples-

- He calls things that are not - into existence
- The first shall be last
- When I am weak, then I am strong
- The meek shall inherit the earth

In each reference above God reveals how wrong our human expectations, our logical inferences, our limited understanding can be, when operating in the realm of His Truth, His Power, His Reality.

This life, this earth, our physical bodies, our human minds, are like the grass... withering away, it is "but a mist."

God's truths, His Wisdom, His Word, is the True Reality... and very different from our earthly perspective of what is real. This is why we have His Word to teach us His Truth, this is why Jesus came to reveal to us the Truth, about this life and plan out eternity.

Is it possible my friends that this life is merely like boot camp? A relatively short time (compared to eternity) when we are tested, strengthened, trained, and developed for what lies ahead? In this training camp we learn the basic principles of the reality which we are approaching.

Wouldn't it be a good idea to pay close attention to the training, so that we are well prepared for the reality of our eternal future?

We begin our training as powerless, weak, ignorant, and fearful; but by God's Grace, His Strength, His Plans..., we emerge from this life into Eternity with Him... as Powerful and Strong sons and daughters of the Most High God!

Thank You Lord that you choose the weak, and You strengthen us for this life and for Life Eternal with You!

"His Strength Is Perfect"

Shanna Thompson

https://youtu.be/gGqzaakuRLE

July 16

Today's Encouragement is Psalm 139:23-24 NLT *Search me, O God, and know my heart; test me and know my anxious thoughts. Point out anything in me that offends you, and lead me along the path of everlasting life.*

Search me –

David asks God– invites Him– to search, to know his heart and mind, to examine, and purify him and to lead him.

Now, David didn't know of Jesus' perfect cleansing from every offensive thing for the children of God, but today we know that there is nothing offensive within us, for we are (already, now) washed clean by the blood of Jesus!

So, because we are cleansed by Jesus, we too can invite God to know our hearts, to search us, and to know our thoughts.

While God already knows everything, He still responds to our invitation.... He even gives us the gift of a desire for Him... no one can come to me unless the Father draws him (John 6:44) so Lord, we now invite You to search us, and know us, and to lead us along the path of Your Everlasting Life!

Thank You, Jesus, for Your cleansing blood, the perfect undeserved gift of righteousness, right standing, before God Himself! We truly are nothing without You, Lord!

"Change My Heart O God"

Maranatha Music

https://youtu.be/IlSmG-_eJTU

July 17

Today's Encouragement is 1 John 4:12 NLT *No one has ever seen God. But if we love each other, God lives in us, and his love is brought to full expression in us.*

Brought to full expression –

Seems curious, doesn't it? God's love is brought to full expression... IF we love each other! Later John said, (v19) We love each other because he loved us first.

Seems there is an important message here: God loved us first—and gave Jesus' life to demonstrate the depth of His perfect love for us. And now, if and when, we love each other, God's love is brought to full expression, or as other translations read, His Love is perfected or made complete!

So, is it possible that... as amazing, even incomprehensible as God's immeasurable Love is for us... that this Love of God, which far exceeds all we can understand... is somehow incomplete, lacking just a bit, and needing...our response? ... In loving each other!?!? Is it possible?

In human terms it becomes a bit clearer. As we greatly love our own children and grandchildren, we experience even more love for them and also a taste of this completeness, this perfection... when we see these people that we love... also loving others.

So, in a similar way, Love comes from God to us, and then through us, to each other (and of course is reflected back to God). Then others also love God, and love others as well... This "circle of Love" becomes complete, perfected, and brought to full expression.

Remember God IS Love. This is His plan! His idea! His creation!

Father, we stand in amazement and awe as we gain only just a glimpse of Your wonderful Love for us, Your plan for Love to be the rule and measure of our lives. May we be so filled by Your Love that we overflow with Your Love for each other, so that we are fulfilling our role in bringing Your Love to full expression!

"The Love of God"
The Isaacs
https://youtu.be/6UTV6vmDx-s

July 18

Today's Encouragement is John 14:1 NLT *"Don't let your hearts be troubled. Trust in God, and trust also in me."*

Don't let –

God has provided so much for us! ... complete forgiveness through faith in Jesus... cleansing of our lives from all sin... eternal life with Him... everlasting hope... joy even in times of sorrow... confidence to enter God's very presence without shame... complete rebirth... access to God through prayer... the Holy Spirit to guide and comfort us. He has declared us more than conquerors, called us His children and named us as His friends..., and there are countless other gifts and blessings through "His very great and precious promises"!

God has, already, done more for us than we can recount, or even remember!

And we are in a relationship with Him. Each of us individually in relationship with God the Father, Jesus the Son, and the Holy Spirit. A relationship that is (all up to us!) either growing or dormant. Like a friendship or even marriage, this relationship needs time, attention, thought, and intentional purpose. Unlike our human relationships, it is rather one-sided, but not as that term usually implies. It is one-sided in that God is completely ready, willing, and available to grow in relationship with you and me—the depth of this relationship depends on us alone. He cannot be more ready, willing nor more available than He already is.

The springboard for this thought is the phrase "don't let." We have the power to "Let" our hearts be troubled... or to "Don't Let" our hearts be troubled. By choosing to Trust! And in this same vein, we have the power to grow in deeper relationship with God, or to remain dormant and unengaged in relationship with Him... by choosing not to Trust.

Thank You, Lord, for granting us the privilege of determining to Trust you or not, to grow in relationship with You, or not... to allow our hearts to be troubled... or not! You are so very wise.

"Same Power"
Jeremy Camp
https://youtu.be/InsifiZxVXU

July 19

Today's Encouragement is 1 John 4:18-19 NLT *Such love has no fear, because perfect love expels all fear. If we are afraid, it is for fear of punishment, and this shows that we have not fully experienced his perfect love. We love each other because he loved us first.*

Such love has no fear –

My friends, as the adopted children of God, chosen, cleansed, blessed, reborn, redeemed, and deeply loved by our Creator... How could we—Why would we—What could we possibly... Fear?

Reread with me this key thought.... "If we are afraid, it is for fear of punishment, and this shows... that we have not fully experienced His perfect Love!" This explains WHY we are sometimes, too often, or always afraid! We haven't fully experienced His Perfect Love!

We say it all the time, casually, or with a note of concern, or with genuine terror... "I'm afraid that it may be cancer;" "I don't believe this is going to turn out well;" "I fear you're making a grave mistake;" "I'm afraid to fully surrender myself to God because then He might send me to Africa!" And a million other uses (and misuses) of the concept of fear! Fear leads to doubt, depression, panic attacks, isolation, and a host of other social, emotional, medical, and mental ills! Our Enemy loves it when we Fear!

Yet, my friends, there is NO FEAR in the life of God's Love – into which we are reborn! None! Remember it is First – God – who loved us (v 19), then we love others because of His Love dwelling in and flowing through us. This cleansing Love removes, and "expels all fear" ... Do you see that? Do we believe it? NO FEAR IN LOVE!

Max Lucado wrote a beautiful, powerful, short book which I highly recommend titled *Fearless: Imagine Your Life without Fear.*

Thank You ,Father, for Your Perfect Love, which expels All Fear!

"Stand in Your Love"

Josh Baldwin

https://youtu.be/1T2tMt0Ky6g

July 20

Today's Encouragement is 1 John 4:16a ESV *So we have come to know and to believe the love that God has for us.*

We have come to know –

This phrase implies a development, the creation of an idea, a concept, and finally a belief, a confident assurance... of the Love which God has for us.

For some, this confident recognition is immediate and for others it is a gradual process... but however we may come to this understanding, the truth is astounding.

God loves you!

Can you pause for a divine moment at that statement?

God... our Creator, the Almighty, and Father of all... Loves ... with perfect Love...

You... just as you (and I) are, sinful, yet washed to purity by the sacrifice of Jesus. God Loves You!

Have you confidently come to know this truth yet? Is it still developing? Are you certain of this truth? Is it possible that we never fully comprehend the depth of God's Love for us? That in the growing love relationship which we have with Him, we might be able to continually see new evidence of His Love? Like a romantic spouse who leaves love notes throughout the house, doing kind things, preparing a favorite meal, cleaning up a mess they didn't make... numerous other expressions of Love... ongoing, never ceasing, ever growing, ever giving, ever Loving... there is evidence all around us of His unending love.

We grow in our understanding of His Perfect Love for us, as we ...come to know... how great is His love, active and alive today!

Loving Father, open our eyes to see; help us continue, every day, to come to know and believe that You truly do continuously Love us! You are Unending Love; You are Perfect Love. Thank You for the way that You Love us!

"How Great Is the Love"

Vertical Church Band

https://youtu.be/sXNdeVxEsic

July 21

Today's Encouragement is 1 John 5:11-12a NLT *And this is what God has testified: He has given us eternal life, and this life is in his Son. Whoever has the Son has life.*

Whoever has the Son –

Remember that word in John 3:16, "Gave"? God Gave us Jesus! We Have the Son because God already Gave Him to us, for us.

We have (because God Gave) Life Eternal, now... already! Not one day, by and by... Now!

We Already, Now, have this treasure (the Son, Eternal Life, the Love of God, complete Grace, and forgiveness...and so much more!) in these clay jars, our frail human bodies (2 Cor. 4:7)

You Have the Son of God! God already gave Him to us! And Eternal Life is in Him, and so in us! Assuredly, my friends, we can be confident that we now, already, have Eternal Life!

Often, we wrongly think when our bodies die on this earth, that only then will we begin the Eternal Life. But this isn't what scripture portrays. Read the passage again.

Eternal Life is in the Son, and we have the Son... now... already... Our Eternal Life has already begun!

Father, help us to recognize the immensity of Your Gift and the transformation we have now, already undergone through faith in Jesus! That we now, already, have Eternal Life through Jesus! We pray in His Name.

"Christ Our Hope in Life and Death"

Keith and Kristyn Getty

https://youtu.be/OibIi1rz7mw

July 22

Today's Encouragement is Isaiah 46:4 NLT *I will be your God throughout your lifetime-until your hair is white with age. I made you, and I will care for you. I will carry you along and save you.*

I will carry –

In the preceding verses, Isaiah compares how man's idols are carried as burdens by livestock, and how God Himself carries His own. Friends, our idols weigh us down... *Both the idols and their owners are bowed down. The gods cannot protect the people, and the people cannot protect the gods. They go off into captivity together.* Isaiah 46:2 NLT

In contrast to the idols which we create (wealth, popularity, beauty, freedom, intellect, independence, power...) and which only burden us... God says, "I made you! And I care for you, and I do the carrying in this relationship!"

He is our strength and provider! He is Father, Shepherd, Savior! And so much more!

Father God, You are the only Omnipotent, All-Powerful God of all!!! Thank You for Your immeasurable Love and Grace and Mercy for us. Thank You that You carry us... throughout our entire lifetime, short or long, in joy and pain, in Your Perfect Faithfulness to us! How can we say thanks enough? Open our eyes, Lord, to see and understand and know... that always, yesterday, today, and forever... You. Carry. Us!

"I Will Carry You"
Ellie Holcomb
https://youtu.be/IziBz0d5yOk

July 23

Today's Encouragement is Matthew 1:21 NLT *"And she will have a son, and you are to name him Jesus, for he will save his people from their sins."*

Name him Jesus –

What do you call Him?

An arms-length term -

The man upstairs, The Good Lord, The Big man, or The Big Guy?

Or a term of Affection -

Abba, Our Father, Dear Lord, Dear God, Father God, Dear Master, Lord Jesus, or Dear Jesus?

Perhaps something recognizing His Power—

Almighty God, Creator Lord, King of Kings?

Is it possible that the way we address Him has an effect on our relationship with Him? Or at least is an indication of the type of relationship we have with Him?

This verse connects the Name of Jesus, the Name that is above every other name (Phil. 2:9) with Salvation! His name means "God saves."

My friends, we are wise to respect, revere, and honor His Name. The only name by which—we are saved! (Acts 4:12)

Lord, help us be unashamed of the Name above all Names, Jesus!

"Your Great Name"

Natalie Grant

https://youtu.be/PasbQx0VilQ

July 24

Today's Encouragement is 1 Peter 1:3 ESV *Blessed be the God and Father of our Lord Jesus Christ! According to his great mercy, he has caused us to be born again to a living hope through the resurrection of Jesus Christ from the dead,*

Living Hope –

We are – already, now – born again, according to God's mercy, not according to our worthiness or unworthiness. We are born again to something... to a Living Hope... a Hope in Jesus, His Salvation, His Redemption, His Love and Mercy for us... and all this comes through Him, through Jesus' resurrection from the dead.

When Jesus was resurrected, everything changed! Death was defeated, Sin was banished, our enemy was put in his place... and a way was made for us to be born again to a Living Hope! Jesus IS Alive... He is our Living Hope!

If you have ever lost Hope, for whatever reason, or even considered giving up Hope, you have a clearer idea of how critical Hope is to life. It is said that people who "give up Hope" don't live very long. It seems Hope is essential to life.

People place their Hope in many different things, but all those will fail! Only Jesus never fails!
Jesus Christ is
Savior, Friend, Brother,
Prince of peace, Lord of all lords, King of all kings,
Eternal, Returning
And
He is our Living Hope!
And we, who are born again, are born into Jesus, into this Living Hope.

Lord, You know how much we desperately need to have Hope. Help us cling to Christ in hope.

"Living Hope"
By Phil Wickham
https://youtu.be/9f2FXxDVO6w

July 25

Today's Encouragement is Hebrews 13:16 NLT *And don't forget to do good and to share with those in need. These are the sacrifices that please God.*

Share with those in need –

We immediately think of people on the street corners with "Need Help" signs, but is it possible that this applies to more than giving a few dollars to the obviously needy ones? Could it also apply to honoring God and to blessing those around you with All that He has given you?

Musical talent, teaching ability, cooking skills, mechanic skills, biblical wisdom—what do you have that can be shared with others? Does God give us skills and abilities to please only ourselves?

If we are to Love God and to love others—His greatest commandment— would this not include sharing the gifts He has given us with Him first, then with others?

He has made each of us as seasoning salt and as lights to the darkness around us (Matthew 5:13-14). Will we withhold this salt and light from others? Whether we know or understand exactly how, or what, or when, to share with people who are in need... God knows, and what we are sharing is ultimately His, because my friends, we belong to Him, everything we have—comes from, and belongs to, God alone!

Father, open our hearts to share with those in need, the obvious and not so obvious. More than just our money, but also our time, skills, our Hope and Faith in You... and most of all Father, help us to share Your Love!

"What Can I Do"
Paul Baloche
https://youtu.be/_NqtgE22w58

July 26

Today's Encouragement is 1 Peter 3:15a NLT *Instead, you must worship Christ as Lord of your life.*

Lord of your life –

We all have accepted Christ as our Savior, but Is He the Lord of our life? What does that mean?

The New Testament was written in the Greek language, and the Greek word translated here as "Lord" is *kurios*, which is defined as "Lord, master, sir, and owner." (Recognize that there is no one English word that matches perfectly and exclusively with Greek. Just as "Senor" in Spanish can mean "sir, Lord, mister, or master.")

So, let's briefly explore "Lord" and a few of its synonyms.

Master – one who is in charge, an overseer, one with absolute control. **Owner** – the one with all the rights, power, and authority to direct, manage, control, and use something (someone).

Remember, in various places, we are called His servants, His sheep, His followers, His friends, His brothers and sisters... There's no getting around it my friends. Jesus is Lord! Whether people accept it or not.

And because He is Lord... and because we acknowledge it, accept it, and believe it... we need to live it... Live today, in the Truth that Jesus is Lord of your Life. He's got you and me... He is our Owner. He is going to take care of us today and always!

*Lord Jesus, help us to submit our entire lives to You as our Lord, our **Master**, our **Owner**, and our **Shepherd**. That we may go where You lead us, say what You want us to say, and do what You want us to do. We fail at times; thank You for Your Grace and Forgiveness for those failures. We choose now and always, to worship You, Jesus, as Lord of our lives! We surrender our lives to You as Lord.*

"I Surrender"
Hillsong
https://youtu.be/kJTKU5oX_XE

July 27

Today's Encouragement is 1 Peter 3:15 NLT *Instead, you must worship Christ as Lord of your life. And if someone asks about your hope as a believer, always be ready to explain it.*

Always be ready –

Many may say to us:

- "The Bible is just a really old book of stories."

- "You know there are many religions and some people who practice them are very good people." "It's ridiculous to claim to have the only way, everyone knows that there are many roads that lead to God."

- "There are lots of contradictions in the Bible, everyone knows that!"

- "It's impossible to live the "Christian life," no one can really do that! Didn't Jesus say we should be perfect? How crazy is that?"

These questions, claims, arguments, and accusations go on and on.... And always have my friends, and always will. Some of these are from non-believers, who just "can't accept" the Bible and the Truth of Jesus. Yet at times, we believers have questions also; we are tempted to listen to the questions, to consider the arguments of the world against our beliefs. For this likelihood, we are wise to follow Peter's counsel... "Worship Christ as Lord and be ready to explain your hope as a believer."

We all have accepted Christ as Lord, He is our Savior, Redeemer, and Friend! Yet are we ready to explain our hope?

Father God, help us to learn, to study, and to be ready, always, to explain our Hope in Jesus.

"All My Hope"
Crowder
https://youtu.be/94KbIGWdKa4

July 28

Today's Encouragement is John 16:7 NLT *"But in fact, it is best for you that I go away, because if I don't, the Advocate won't come. If I do go away, then I will send him to you."*

It is best for you –

This amazing statement of Jesus has always challenged my thinking. It's as if He is telling his disciples… 'Look guys, it's best for you! Best that I go away! Best for you that I leave you! Because when I go, I will send the Holy Spirit!'

And this is even better than having Jesus physically present with us!?! Still shakes the ground around me! How can anything be better than being in the presence of Jesus Himself?! Yet, He said this, my friends!

So, there must be a much deeper truth here than mere words can describe… something deeper than we may have seen before.

This Holy Spirit, God's presence, is dwelling, living within every believer, and He is eternal, all-wise, and all-powerful! *For God has not given us a spirit of fear and timidity, but of power, love, and self-discipline.* (2 Timothy 1:7 NLT)

It truly is The Best for you and me—that God's Presence is living within, dwelling inside, abiding with us… even better than being with, walking beside, or talking face-to-face with Jesus!

Father God, please open our hearts to the truth of Your Holy Spirit dwelling in, living in, and guiding us! We long to be close to You!

"He Lives!"

Alan Jackson

https://youtu.be/pv-ibJHsgy8

July 29

Today's Encouragement is John 16:8 NLT *And when he [Holy Spirit] comes, he will convict the world of its sin, and of God's righteousness, and of the coming judgment.*

When he comes –

Jesus is speaking to his disciples about his leaving them, but He will send (has already sent) the Holy Spirit in His place, and says, The Spirit will convict the world: of its sin, of the righteousness of God, and of the coming judgment.

In my life, the Spirit has led me to this "conviction of sin" in several ways, first was the recognition that I was full of sin, there was nothing good, really, about me and I needed a Savior!

Then, later as a believer in Christ, I began to choose a bit more wisely, to grow, and to strive to obey Him. Then the Holy Spirit gently began to reveal some of my hidden, deeper sins. And as I became able to deal with it, He then worked within me to overcome. It is a process directed by the Spirit, as He sees fit for me.

I don't believe that this process will ever be completed in this life (Philippians 3:12), but I wouldn't trade for the victory that He has achieved in my life! All the while remembering "His Grace is all I need" for all my sin (2 Corinthians 12:9).

I believe the same is true for each individual believer. The Holy Spirit individually guides each of us, corrects, molds, fills, and strengthens us to live as Christ! He is not finished with any of us.

Thank You, Lord, that you are the source of everything we need! We rely on You and the Son and the Holy Spirit... You are truly all that we need!

"Spirit of the Living God"

Rosemary Siemens

https://youtu.be/eyZsVxUz7aA

July 30

Today's Encouragement is James 4:8a NLT *Come close to God, and God will come close to you.*

Come close –

There are so many wonderful promises in the Bible! Here is another... as we come close to God, He comes close to us.

Like the prodigal son returning to his father in desperation, in the hope of safety... and finding his father running toward him! When we turn toward God, from whatever situation, or position we may be in... we find God watching and waiting for us.

Returning from our selfish sinful ways, or just beginning our day with a few moments in His presence... He is Always... Always... ready to meet us, to be with us, to lovingly embrace us, to come close to us... to draw us close.

Because He is Love, and God [Love] never fails, never gets tired of waiting, never says "You did it again!?!"

Love never brings up our sin or failures... God [Love] never turns away from us even when we have turned away from Him.

How do we come close to God? How can we draw near? Only in our hearts and minds... a spiritual encounter. A few suggestions might help, but aren't required... A quiet room, alone, on your knees or lying prone, worship music like this song, and sincere prayer... talking to Him, not asking for all your needs, He knows them already...but, rather asking Him to come close to you. He is Creator God. He is Creative... He will come as He sees fit, as you need Him, but possibly not as you may expect. Just wait, my friend... as you wait for him, as you do what you can to come close... the promise is... God will come close to you!

Lord, we long to be close to You. Draw us close to You, we ask in Jesus' Name.
"Draw Me Close"
Michael W Smith
https://youtu.be/7d_oYr-P16M

July 31

Today's Encouragement is 2 Corinthians 1:11 NLT *And you are helping us by praying for us. Then many people will give thanks because God has graciously answered so many prayers for our safety.*

So many prayers –

We can only do so much, my friends. Our own time, skills, and resources are limited. We have friends in another country which is war-torn, they are in danger of being killed and live under the constant threat of death. —All we can do is pray.

Another friend has terminal cancer, he's on hospice care and awaiting his death, there is nothing anyone can do for him.—All we can do is pray.

Whatever the need, the situation, or the circumstances... we often don't have a single option of something physical that we can do to help others in need. It's so frustrating we feel, to see the need, to want to "do something" to help, and yet... we can't! —All we can do is pray.

May I suggest a change in language and attitude? For us as believers, our greatest gift, blessing, assistance, our greatest demonstration of Love... is Prayer!

Friends, it isn't "All I can do is pray," or "The least that I can do is pray"'... No! it is the Greatest, the Best, the most Loving, the Wisest thing we can do!

When we pray for the needs of others... we're asking God in His Wisdom and Omnipotence (unlimited power) to do for others what He knows is the absolute best! What better gift could we give?

Father, thank You for the gift of prayer! ...That we can come at any time and ask You about anything. ...that we can rest in complete assurance that You hear, You love, You choose, that You will graciously answer "so many prayers."

"All I Can Do Is Pray"

Lisa Bevill

https://youtu.be/sleH3UsCqQg?t=16

August 1

Today's Encouragement is Mark 6:31 NLT *Then Jesus said, "Let's go off by ourselves to a quiet place and rest awhile." He said this because there were so many people coming and going that Jesus and his apostles didn't even have time to eat.*

Rest awhile–

Jesus was busy. He was often surrounded by people with needs, asking Him for healing. They had questions about faith, who He was, and some even tried to trap Him in one way or another. He was busy!

His disciples were also busy; and today, we are busy too!

Jesus and His disciples were busy doing God's will, carrying out the Mission of preaching and teaching the Gospel of God's Love and Grace, Hope and Forgiveness, His Strength, and His Power! What are you and I busy doing?

Regardless of the type of busyness we may be occupied with, at times, we too need to "go off by ourselves to a quiet place and rest awhile" with Jesus.

Thoughts for the busy believer:

What are we busy doing? Remember Mary and Martha. Martha was busy preparing her home and a meal for Jesus; while Mary "was busy" sitting at His feet, absorbing His every word.

And, My friends, even Jesus and His disciples, needed a break, a time to get away and rest.

Father, help us to rest in You, to rest with You. And then to return to what You've called us to... refreshed, renewed to serve You.

"You Speak"
Audry Assad
https://youtu.be/L22Q3_McBOI

August 2

Today's Encouragement is Deuteronomy 17:19-20 NLT *He must always keep that copy with him and read it daily as long as he lives. That way he will learn to fear the Lord his God by obeying all the terms of these instructions and decrees. This regular reading will prevent him from becoming proud and acting as if he is above his fellow citizens. It will also prevent him from turning away from these commands in the smallest way. And it will ensure that he and his descendants will reign for many generations in Israel.*

Regular reading –

These instructions were directed to the future kings which God knew the people of Israel would want to have, just like all the other nations.

The regular reading of God's Word, which at that time only consisted of the first few books of the law of Moses, would provide the king with wisdom and keep him from becoming proud and turning away from God, in even the smallest way, and ensure his descendants would also follow God's ways. He would learn to fear and respect God,

That sounds like a pretty good result from spending some time... regularly, daily, reading His Word!

God Himself, through the Holy Spirit who lives inside us, works a transformation in the lives of His chosen children, in any way He pleases... but here, explicitly, He explains that the regular reading of His Word will bring about these direct benefits in the life and character of His children.

Father, help us to read Your Word regularly, to believe It and to put into practice what You say; to eat and drink from the riches of Your Truth, daily. So that we can live as Your beloved children!

"Word of God Speak"
MercyMe
https://youtu.be/4JK_6osCH74

August 3

Today's Encouragement is 1 Corinthians 3:16 ESV *Do you not know that you are God's temple and that God's Spirit dwells in you?*

You are God's temple –

Pretty clear, huh? There is now no external, physical Temple of God which we are to "go to" in order to meet God or to hear His voice... because He lives within us! The church you attend (hopefully) is not God's temple. No, You are that Temple!

Sadly, many deny this truth, minimizing the significance of His Spirit dwelling in our lives... and within those lives His Spirit certainly lies dormant, awaiting a day of surrender, an opportunity of clarity, for this person to "come to himself" as the prodigal did (Luke 15:17), and to realize:

"God is WITH me (Immanuel), He is FOR me! He will never leave me nor forsake me! He is my Strength, my Protector, my Ever-present help! He is all I ever need, and He lives within me!"

God's Spirit dwells, lives, remains, works, acts, and speaks... within you!

We can ignore Him and die... or we can listen, sense, follow, and obey Him! The choice is always ours. The results of the choice... is life or death!

Father, we confess that we don't fully understand this, but we do know that You will live within us, and by faith we accept it... help us to believe it and to experience Your spirit living within us.

"Where Could I Go from Your Spirit"
Kelly Willard
https://youtu.be/6llPUeJLVkQ

August 4

Today's Encouragement is Romans 1:5 NLT *Through Christ, God has given us the privilege and authority as apostles to tell Gentiles everywhere what God has done for them, so that they will believe and obey him, bringing glory to his name.*

Believe and obey –

Two components to Faith are Belief and Obedience. **Belief** is first, and it is by this Faith that we are saved (Eph. 2:8). Yet, we are not to stop there. Faith and belief are the essential steps into His Salvation, and this salvation is assured! Now the next focus is **Obedience**. We recoil at the word, "No one is gonna tell me what to do!" And certainly, we are not to obey, to follow devotedly, nor stand in reverent awe, any human being... but only Jesus.

Yet that word—"Obey"—is clearly prevalent throughout the Word! James 1:22 NLT *But don't just listen to God's word. You must do what it says. Otherwise, you are only fooling yourselves.*

We often make the excuse, "We can't really obey because, well, nobody's perfect!" Certainly, we aren't! But does this mean we don't need to try, to strive, to work to obey? Ok then, how do we obey? What do we obey? It's much clearer and simpler than many think. We are not bound to Obey 10, or 100, or 1000 commands. But only 2!

1 John 5:3 NLT *Loving God means keeping his commandments, and his commandments are not burdensome.* Mark 12:30-31 NLT [Jesus said the greatest commandment is] *"And you must love the Lord your God with all your heart, all your soul, all your mind, and all your strength. The second is equally important: 'Love your neighbor as yourself.' No other commandment is greater than these."*

Father, please help us to Obey, to support and verify our Faith in You by obeying You, by loving You and those around us. And so—to bring Glory to Your Name.

"Trust and Obey"

Chelsea Moon and the Franz Brothers

https://youtu.be/Lwi0VSrwbGI

August 5

Today's Encouragement is Romans 1:12 NLT *When we get together, I want to encourage you in your faith, but I also want to be encouraged by yours.*

To encourage you –

He writes to his brothers and sisters, of how he longs to see them, so that they can be encouraged by each other – in their faith. The ESV translates this as that we may be mutually encouraged."

Friends this is why "we get together," this is the fellowship of the gospel, gathering to worship Him, hear the Word preached, and to encourage each other in the faith!

We all need encouragement from time to time, and we can seek it directly from the Lord, through the Word, and also through other believers, — and we are wise to utilize all three sources.

Beware of those in the fellowship who do not reciprocate the encouragement in faith which you offer. There are a few who will try to turn every word of encouragement into doubt; questioning and refusing to trust the Lord's mercy and grace. They seem bent on discouraging others, as they themselves are discouraged. Offer them His Love and prayer, but do not try to change them, that is God's work.

Seek instead, the friends who are full of faith, those who will encourage you and be encouraged by you, this is your brother and sister in Christ! From time to time, we all need some encouragement, we have setbacks, losses, sorrows, and trials. So, we turn to Him, His Word, and His people for the courage to continue this journey of faith.

And this mutual encouragement is God's plan for His children. We are being built together into the dwelling place of God (Ephesians 2:22). We need each other.

Father, please help us to find encouraging and faithful friends. Open our eyes to see them, not that we will place our faith in them, but that we may mutually encourage each other in our Faith in You!

"Faithful Friend"

Twila Paris & Steven Curtis Chapman

https://youtu.be/HiDas6erOGo

August 6

Today's Encouragement is Romans 1:16a NLT *For I am not ashamed of this Good News about Christ.*

Not ashamed –

It's a curious choice of words, don't you think? He says, "I'm not ashamed of this Good News"! When he could have said something like, "I'm so very grateful for this Good News!" or, "I'm so happy to share the Gospel!" Or anything a bit more on the positive side. Yet there is no twisting of the Word that ends in Truth. So, accepting it as written... he chose to focus a bit on the word "ashamed."

Perhaps it is because we all struggle (so odd, isn't it?), from time to time, with being "ashamed of the gospel"!

We're in a situation with unbelievers, and we "hide" our faith, when Jesus' Name is used as trash, when ungodly talk is in charge. This is one of the moments when we are tempted to be ashamed of Christ... embarrassing to admit, but true for most all of us.

Is it possible that this, or a similar moment in time, is a great spiritual battle? One where we are facing a powerful, evil force with only our faith and maybe a slingshot and five stones?

First, remember God's Grace is sufficient, all our sin is cleansed!

Second, man cannot harm us, we belong to God.

Third, being tempted isn't sin, but yielding to the temptation becomes sin.

Fourth, it is Fear that tells us to be silent, "they might get mean or may not like you anymore..." and fear of man is surrender to our enemy.

Fifth, God is our strength, He doesn't Need us to defend His Name, but when we do speak up for Him, when we Stand up for Jesus, He is our strength!

My friends, we wouldn't let others mock our mothers, would we? Why then would we tolerate the mockery of Our Savior?

Father God, in all situations, may we recognize that being unashamed of You is our best choice. While You need no one to defend You... We have the need to be Unashamed of Your Love and Mercy and Strength and Holiness! Please give us the strength to be unashamed!

"Stand Up, Stand Up for Jesus"
Stuart Townend
https://youtu.be/xUII9PabHPE

August 7

Today's Encouragement is Romans 4:23-24 NLT *And when God counted him as righteous, it wasn't just for Abraham's benefit. It was recorded for our benefit, too, assuring us that God will also count us as righteous if we believe in him, the one who raised Jesus our Lord from the dead.*

Will also count us –

Like Abraham, you, and I – all who believe in Him, are counted, considered, deemed to be... righteous... like Abraham!

Now, Abraham was the model of Faith, the man whom God first called out, set apart, to become the Father of the Lord's chosen nation, His very own people, Israel.

Far from perfect, as we all are, Abraham often fell short, yet he continued to trust God, to believe God over what his eyes and thoughts and the world around might say... And as the result of that faith... (v22*) And because of Abraham's faith, God counted him as righteous.*

"If we believe in Him, the One who raised the Lord Jesus from the dead", my friends, God "will also count us" as righteous... just like Abraham! No other person in biblical history was a model of faith like Abraham... and, my friend, that right standing with God... also belongs to you and me and all who believe! Only because of God's Amazing Grace!

And if that wasn't enough, my friends,... *For our sake he made him to be sin who knew no sin, so that in him we might become the righteousness of God.* 2 Corinthians 5:21 ESV

Father God, help us to believe, though we may never be able to fully understand... that we are counted as righteous; and even more amazingly, that we are, in Christ, The Righteousness of God! You are so good to us Father!

"Jesus Messiah"

Chris Tomlin

https://youtu.be/IL7BlrwZHf8

August 8

Today's Encouragement is Isaiah 40:31 ESV *But they who wait for the Lord shall renew their strength; they shall mount up with wings like eagles; they shall run and not be weary; they shall walk and not faint.*

They who wait –

We just don't like to wait! On anything! We want food fast, we want convenience stores, we want instant response to our texts... we are obsessed with NOW!

God's ways are not our ways (Isaiah 55:8) and His timeframe is not ours. He deals in all aspects of time, in moments, in years and in millennia... He is unlimited by time, He created it, and He is above all aspects of time. Yet we are too often obsessed by time! We consider our days, planning our accomplishments, deciding if it is a "good day" or a "bad day"... we are obsessed with time, and so we don't want to, we fight hard against... the wisdom of God as He says... "Wait."

We wait for the Lord by praying for our needs and desires and yielding to "not my will but Yours be done Lord." We wait by reading His Word and resting in His Truth and His Promises, even when we don't understand or see any evidence of His response or His action. We wait for our hopes, our dreams, His promises, His Power to be displayed... for so much my friends... We Wait!

And what is His promise to those who wait for Him?—By waiting, our strength is renewed, like an eagle, we will rise; we will run and walk and not get tired.

Now, we can get discouraged by waiting, can't we? "When Lord will You do something! When will You answer my prayer?" And He replies... "Wait."

Lord, Help us to wait on You, to trust Your timing, and Your wisdom. As we pray in Jesus' Name.

"While I Wait"
Lincoln Brewster
https://youtu.be/NswPPVgMaPE

August 9

Today's Encouragement is Revelation 15:2b-3a ESV ... *standing beside the sea of glass with harps of God in their hands. And they sing ...*

Harps of God –

My friends, we all, too often, become overburdened by the reality of this life, our problems, needs, illnesses, – the suffering of those we love... it is easy to become discouraged at times. May I suggest a refreshing break for your soul... a short visit to the Throne of God —

The harps of God! As a music lover, (a passion I recognize is not shared by everyone) I am continuously amazed by the truth that God's Presence is continually surrounded, engulfed, and permeated by worship music. "Holy, Holy, Holy!" sing all the angels, and even other creatures we can't conceive of. It is never-ceasing, glorious praise from countless voices, from every nation, tribe, and tongue. These unlimited voices are accompanied by every known and yet to be known musical instrument, like the harps of God—in unlimited scales, octaves, and registers. This sound is the most beautiful music, far beyond what we have ever heard! And our minds cannot even imagine it!

Consider the greatness of Handel's *Messiah*, Beethoven's "Ode to Joy," and similar masterpieces created by man... and yet, all these fall woefully short when compared to the ceaseless, eternal worship of Heaven.

From today's song, "Hear heavens voices sing, their thunderous anthem rings, Through emerald courts and sapphire skies... their praises rise!"

As you listen, and worship along with this anthem of Praise to the One who sits on the Throne and reigns forevermore... imagine yourself there now, one voice of millions... in perfect song... before His throne!

What Glory!

Lord, grant us a glimpse, just a taste of what it is like before Your throne. Help us to worship you now, as we will then.

"There Is a Higher Throne"
Keith and Kristyn Getty
https://youtu.be/BAGX9iWQ8kI

August 10

Today's Encouragement is Romans 5:21 NLT *So just as sin ruled over all people and brought them to death, now God's wonderful grace rules instead, giving us right standing with God and resulting in eternal life through Jesus Christ our Lord.*

Grace rules –

In the time before Christ, everyone who wanted to please God was burdened by guilt and shame for their sin and was allowed to make sacrificial offerings of various types to relieve themselves of this guilt, by doing as the law required. This was the time referred to here as "sin ruled over all people and brought them to death"... this was before Christ.

But—now that "eternal life through Jesus has come"'; He has brought the pathway to Peace between God and Man, created a righteousness for mankind, and provided the restoration of a genuine, close, personal, forgiving, accepting Father-to-child relationship for all who will believe in Him.

And for all believers, it is God's wonderful Grace that now rules! His Grace is now in control of our life and our relationship with Him is under the rule of Grace, and not of sin! Now, Shame, Guilt, Fear, Doubt, and any sin which separates us from God, is no longer in control! We are not "subject to the rule" of Sin, in any form! Instead, Now, because of Christ...

Grace rules!

Friends, this means for you and me today:

- Shame is a lie – because Grace rules.
- Guilt is erased – because Grace rules.
- Sin is powerless – because Grace rules.
- Death is defeated – because Grace rules.
- Fear is impotent – because Grace rules.

We are free to rest in God's abundant Love—because—Grace rules.

Whatever you may struggle with today... Grace rules over it... God's wonderful Grace!

Thank You, Lord, that Your Grace is greater than everything, including our sin!

"Grace that is Greater"

Bart Millard

https://youtu.be/WT0z0tIasEg

August 11

Today's Encouragement is Romans 5:20 NLT *God's law was given so that all people could see how sinful they were. But as people sinned more and more, God's wonderful grace became more abundant.*

Grace became more abundant –

Read it again with me, "But as people sinned more and more, God's wonderful grace became more abundant."

God's Grace is unlimited! Of course, everything about Him is unlimited!

Yet with our human (limited) perspective we often think-God is eventually going to… "run out of patience" with us. Similar thoughts we may have are, "God is disappointed with me," or "He is tired of hearing my prayers." Or similar thoughts… which all share the same error—that error is… we think that God is like us… human and limited in His patience and compassion and His grace.

Friends, we are limited in so many ways; He is not! He isn't limited in Time, in Power, in Wisdom, in Patience, nor in Grace.

Because of His Love – which is far beyond our understanding—He extends Grace, Mercy, and Forgiveness in abundance!

Remember Jesus said in His last words before death… "It is Finished!"? The purchase of our forgiveness, the Grace of God forever for all who believe, that price was fully paid! The finished work of Jesus, perfectly and forever, is the Grace of God for His children!

Thank You, Lord, that Your Grace is Abundant! Help us to rest in Your Grace and be at peace.

"This Is Amazing Grace"
Phil Wickham
https://youtu.be/cgsbaBIaoVc

August 12

Today's Encouragement is 1 Chronicles 9:33 ESV *Now these, the singers, the heads of fathers' houses of the Levites, were in the chambers of the temple free from other service, for they were on duty day and night.*

Day and night –

Around the clock, day and night, singing praises and worshipping the Lord in His holy temple! Imagine!

This occurred in the Temple centuries before Christ, and we know this is still happening now in heaven, in God's Presence! Revelation 4:8 NLT *Each of these living beings had six wings, and their wings were covered all over with eyes, inside and out. Day after day and night after night they keep on saying, "Holy, holy, holy is the Lord God, the Almighty- the one who always was, who is, and who is still to come."*

We have friends living in Jerusalem, who are part of a group, I suppose it truly is a church, where they praise and worship the Lord 24/7/365 in their worship center in Jerusalem. The north wall of this worship center faces the Temple Mount and the Mount of Olives next to it, a solid glass wall, and all the chairs face this sight... we visited there once. And the supporters, the church, the worshippers, sign up for a one- or two-hour shift at all hours of the day and night... and the praise and the worship of God never stops! In this one tiny spot on earth, just as in the Temple thousands of years ago, and just as happens at all times in God's Presence... there is continuous Praise and Worship!

Father, help us to worship You now, at all times, 24/7/365 singing praises and worshiping You in our hearts and our souls. You are what matters... nothing else in this life does...

"Throne Room Song"
May Angeles & Ryan Kennedy
https://youtu.be/n80qmc3BDAM

August 13

Today's Encouragement is Luke 7:47 *NLT* [Jesus said] *"I tell you, her sins-and they are many-have been forgiven, so she has shown me much love. But a person who is forgiven little shows only little love."*

Shown me much love –

It's clear, from all biblical perspectives, where there is great sin, there is great forgiveness and grace, and then there is the result—great Godly Love.

Grace is unlimited for those who believe in Jesus... and that Grace is greater than all our sin! And it doesn't stop at Forgiveness... the process continues, into Godly Love.

Matthew 18:21-35 tells of a man who was forgiven a huge debt, but soon after, failed to forgive his neighbor a very small debt. He quickly forgot how great his own sin was, how great a debt that he had been forgiven. So, he had little (no) love nor grace to share with the man who owed him just a little.

Is it possible that the more we recognize the "depths of our depravity," our desperate need for God's Grace and Forgiveness, then the greater our gratitude, appreciation, and Love for God?

His Grace is always abundantly available. Those who realize how badly they need His Grace, and then ask for and accept His Grace... are then filled with His Grace (to overflowing) and are also filled (to overflowing) with Love... both for God and for others.

Father, help us to see how deeply we need Your Grace, to deal with, to cleanse us from, to erase forever... all our sin. The sins of yesterday, today, and forever.... And rather than guilt, shame, and remorse, we believe that You will replace these with grateful hearts and Your perfect Love — Because of Jesus.

"Grace"

Kenny Rogers

https://youtu.be/2r7W8eCkS0A

August 14

Today's Encouragement is Romans 6:4 NLT *For we died and were buried with Christ by baptism. And just as Christ was raised from the dead by the glorious power of the Father, now we also may live new lives.*

Live new lives –

Now, we also – may live – new lives! We are reborn to a new life when we accept Jesus as our savior. And—his mercies are new every morning (Lamentations 3:23) Is it possible that we are reborn each day—to a new life?

We often hear the expression, "Today is the first day of the rest of my life", and this is true! How will our life today be different, better than yesterday? A new life today?

Unencumbered by yesterday sins....

Sadly, many of us seem intently determined to "live OLD lives." Remembering our past, wallowing like pigs in slop, in our guilt, shame, and regret for old sins. By doing this, my friends, we choose to refuse, reject, and erase the immeasurable Grace of our God. He gives us a new life, a new start, a clean slate, and erased, forgotten sins, for not only yesterday but today and tomorrow also!

New Life now! Now!

Now we may also live... new... lives...

Lord, we admit we don't understand it, but we do long to live new lives! Help us to embrace this truth and begin to live a new life today!

"All Things New
Hillsong
https://youtu.be/JAM5biaV3Xs

August 15

Today's Encouragement is Romans 5:17b NLT *...But even greater is God's wonderful grace and his gift of righteousness, for all who receive it will live in triumph over sin and death through this one man, Jesus Christ.*

Live in triumph –

All who receive God's wonderful grace... and gift of His righteousness... All – anyone, even you, and me!

Who receive—accept, embrace, believe –

God's wonderful Grace – His favor and blessing which we have not, and never can earn...

And gift of righteousness – friends, we are made holy, perfect, and pure... just as Jesus is pure... by God's astounding gift of righteousness. In fact, we ourselves are His righteousness! (2 Corinthians 5:21)

All these people, (this is us!) will live in triumph! And our Triumph is over both sin and death!

Triumph is also translated as "Victory" in other versions. We are victorious and triumphant over both sin and death, when we have accepted the amazing gift of God's Grace.

Now, we all still sin, and we will all still die, so we may reasonably ask, "How exactly is there triumph, victory over sin and death?" The distinction is outcome, and the perspective of God. In God's sight, in His perspective (which of course, is the one which really counts!)... we are made perfectly righteous, clean, forgiven,— as if we had never sinned. And again, in His perspective, our death, as His children, is merely stepping out of this life, this world, and into His World... eternity, Heaven, paradise.—where Jesus has gone ahead of us... to prepare a place for us!

So, it's true, we see it and know it only by faith, by choosing God's perspective, and accepting His Gift of Living, now, in this life, in complete Triumph over sin and death!

Thank You, Lord, for the amazing gifts You have already provided for us, if we will only believe! Help us to live in Victory this day and always, because of Jesus' triumph!

"Overcome"

Jeremy Camp

https://youtu.be/L0csB3us2gA

August 16

Today's Encouragement is Luke 23:43 NLT *And Jesus replied, "I assure you, today you will be with me in paradise."*

You will be with me –

As these two men were dying an excruciating death, this amazing conversation was heard. One, wrongly accused and innocent; one clearly deserving his execution. One lived a life of blessing, caring for others, healing, teaching God's Love and wisdom, loving and performing miracles; the other a relentless thief living a life of crime and selfishness. Both dying... in the final moments of life....

This thief teaches us humility, repentance, surrender, and utter dependence on the Grace of God. In just these few words, we see Redemption described. Luke 23:40-42 NLT *But the other criminal protested, "Don't you fear God even when you have been sentenced to die? We deserve to die for our crimes, but this man hasn't done anything wrong." Then he said, "Jesus, remember me when you come into your Kingdom."*

This man recognized his guilt (we deserve to die), he recognized Jesus' innocence (this man hasn't done anything wrong) and finally he recognized Jesus as Lord (remember me when you come into Your Kingdom)! This is faith, my friends! They were both clearly and rapidly dying... and yet the thief believed! He believed that Jesus was going to come into His Kingdom! This is truly remarkable faith!

And Jesus responded with Assurance...Salvation... Hope...! "Today you will be with me in paradise!"

No good deeds done, no water baptism, no other acts of repentance nor other words... just a desperate plea!

"Jesus! Remember me!"

Father, Your Grace for us sinners, undeserved, unearned, is truly wonderful, amazing, and even... irrational. It just doesn't make sense to our minds... Yet Father, like this dying thief... we believe in You!

"How Love Wins" (Thief)
Steven Curtis Chapman
https://youtu.be/5JIWgMQBlhE

August 17

Today's Encouragement is Isaiah 64:4 NLT *For since the world began, no ear has heard and no eye has seen a God like you, who works for those who wait for him!*

Who Wait for Him –

But we, too often, get tired of waiting, we get impatient, decide we need to "do something even if it's wrong"... and, my friends, this is disastrous. Our impatience with God is really our distrust of Him, we start to question Him, "When will You do something about this Lord? I've been praying about it for (days, months, years)."

So, in our frustration, in our impatience, we take some action. This is the strength of man, we want to prove (to whom?) that we are strong, "take-charge" people. And spiritually what has happened? We have stopped waiting on the Lord, stopped patiently trusting and relying on Him, and substituted our own strength for His.

When seen from this perspective it seems obvious that our own efforts will fail. His ways are higher than our ways (Isaiah 55:9).

There's a reason that we are so often compared to sheep in the Bible. Sheep follow their Shepherd "blindly," They have no idea what is good for them, where there is good grass and water, where they are safe or in danger... they are NOT Independent self-willed, take-charge creatures. They surrender to the Shepherd. They wait for Him. And the Shepherd provides for them, every need, guiding them in safe paths....

Lord, teach us to wait, to trust, to depend on You. To follow You, as Your sheep, Your children. And to trust that You will work for us!

"Teach Me Lord, to Wait"

Gaithers

https://youtu.be/aCNoFkzhT9o

August 18

Today's Encouragement is Colossians 3:2 NLT *Think about the things of heaven, not the things of earth.*

Things of heaven –

Perhaps you've known them,– people who say things like, "He's so heavenly-minded that he's no earthly good!" Seems a wise and logical saying. How can we be thinking about Things of Heaven? We've never been there! Don't know anyone who's ever been there. Can't buy a travel guidebook on great places to stay and eat and sights to see while we're there" Or... can we? Maybe we do know someone who has been there, and maybe there is something written about it...

Friends, this world is not our home, it is a fallen place, and it is passing away. But Heaven is our eternal home, the residence of God Himself and our Savior Jesus. It is our true Home, Perfect, and Eternal.

"But," you may ask, "how do we live this life, go to work, pay our bills, raise the kids, and life live in this world while we're thinking about Heaven? Seems rather impractical!" Friends, we do this all the time... we live in this world, our current reality, taking care of the necessities of this life... while thinking about something else! The something else we often think about is, "Someday, I won't have to do this mundane stuff any longer. someday I'll have a better car, house, income. Someday, the kids will be gone, and I'll be free! Someday, my adult kids will come visit me!" We are always, in our thoughts, thinking about how things might be, could be, should be... someday!

That Someday, my friends, can be One Day in Heaven. The Bible contains several descriptions of Heaven, Jesus came from there and has returned there and he has told us what the Kingdom of Heaven is like! We will be blessed to spend some time understanding what the Bible really says, (not our conception from TV and cartoons!) and then we are well-advised to—Think about the things of heaven!

Father God, help us to think about heaven, to think about You and being in Your presence as we worship and praise You.

"Hymn of Heaven"
Phil Wickham
https://youtu.be/VbqSm-_pDxA

August 19

Today's Encouragement is Hebrews 6:18b-19 NLT *Therefore, we who have fled to him for refuge can have great confidence as we hold to the hope that lies before us. This hope is a strong and trustworthy anchor for our souls. It leads us through the curtain into God's inner sanctuary.*

Anchor for our souls –

We who have fled to Him for refuge. Friends, we are clearly identified as people in need of a great savior; we are sinful, foolish, willful, rebellious, stubborn, complaining... the list goes on.... We are not as we would like to see ourselves: Noble, Powerful, Strong, Honest, Capable, Stalwart. We may be tempted to falsely see ourselves, or others in this way... but we all have "feet of clay." Even great people falter and stumble, disappointing others, and themselves. This is why we NEED a Savior! Romans 3:23 NLT *For everyone has sinned; we all fall short of God's glorious standard.*

So, God, in His glorious mercy and love for us provided Salvation for us in Jesus, and my friends, His provision is not limited to cleansing us. Jesus is an Anchor for our souls, a strong and trustworthy anchor, granting us Hope and Confidence throughout the terrible storms, even the mighty hurricanes of this life — Jesus is our Hope, our Anchor, our strong and trustworthy Anchor!

Our Kind and Omnipotent Father, we thank You for Your kindness to us, your foolish and weak children... that You have provided Salvation for us through Christ and a Strong and Trustworthy anchor for our souls. Help us to anchor our souls in Christ, now and always!

" My Anchor"
Christy Nockels
https://youtu.be/fCymt6cZY5w

August 20

Today's Encouragement is Jeremiah 9:24 NLT *But those who wish to boast should boast in this alone: that they truly know me and understand that I am the Lord who demonstrates unfailing love and who brings justice and righteousness to the earth, and that I delight in these things. I, the Lord, have spoken!*

Truly know Me –

In our relationship with Our Father God and our Brother Jesus, we are the adopted members of His family. We have the privilege of being one of this family, not second-rate in any fashion, but chosen, selected, adopted, and deeply loved members of His family with full rights, privileges, blessings, and honors as the sons and daughters of the Most High God! Almost unimaginable! Yet still, His Truth, from His Word!

This verse is not about boasting, but about what we should aspire to be proud of, not the pride of our accomplishments, but pride in our relationship with God our Father. Pride implies our own worth, value, status... and as God's children, He is our source of Pride, we can be proud to be His, that He is our Father, that we are saved and set free. All our worth, value, and our status... comes from Him alone!

And notice friends, we can Know Him... and understand that He is the Lord. As we study Jesus in the New Testament, we are studying the Father (John 14:9). We can be proud of being His children, that we Know Him and understand that He is Lord!

Father God, help us to yearn to know You more, to eagerly desire a growing personal relationship with You as your deeply loved, chosen children. That we may know You and understand how magnificent You truly are!

"I Will Boast"
Paul Baloche
https://youtu.be/pBfOcJGEKUU

August 21

Today's Encouragement is Psalm 127:1-2 NLT *Unless the Lord builds a house, the work of the builders is wasted. Unless the Lord protects a city, guarding it with sentries will do no good. It is useless for you to work so hard from early morning until late at night, anxiously working for food to eat; for God gives rest to his loved ones.*

Unless the Lord –

Many a young person, full of strength, sets to work building a home for their family. They are diligent, dedicated, and determined; working tirelessly to build a home, a business, wealth, reputation, and success. And ultimately, they may achieve all these goals.

Yet they also will achieve a few other things which they don't anticipate. The ten- and twelve-hour workdays, seven days a week may well yield their desires: home built, business built, wealth built, reputation built. Yet, the cost may be a spouse who was second place to the work and often a cold faith,— some things occasionally considered, when they could find the time. They may even claim to believe in God, to trust in Jesus, but other than a quick prayer before meals, there is no evidence of a real relationship with Him.

They have built their home, a "house on sand." When troubles come, just as tough times come to us all, this world will begin to crumble, and they may soon be in danger of losing this family – the very reason they had built the home and built the business and worked so diligently.

Friends, when we place God first, honoring Him above everything... our marriage, family, work, reputation, wealth, and health.... He guides, helps, and strengthens. Friends... he even "gives rest to His loved ones."

Father, we need Your help to focus first on You, we need Your strength to do what You lead us to do, and we also need Your rest. You truly are our Home, Father.

"I Will Bring You Home"
Michael Card
https://youtu.be/6O5Es0etqTM

August 22

Today's Encouragement is Matthew 6:20 NLT *"Store your treasures in heaven, where moths and rust cannot destroy, and thieves do not break in and steal."*

Store your treasures –

In Heaven? How do we do that, Lord?

I have a few things that I would consider to be my "treasures." Recently we were briefly threatened by a brush fire nearby, and it caused me to give a few moments thought to my "treasures"! First, I thought of my precious wife, then a few "things" that are important to me... these seem to be my earthly treasures.

Yet, Jesus clearly is not speaking of storing up our earthly things in heaven... so, it must be "things" which are not of this world, not anything physical. So, what are these treasures, and how do we store them up in heaven, and then—Why? What use will we have in heaven for these "treasures"?

Is it possible my friends, that the only treasures we could possibly store in heaven... are what Jesus was speaking about in this "sermon on the mount"? He has just taught about giving to the needy, praying, forgiving, fasting, and about not doing any of these things to be seen by others, but to do these things in secret so that God alone knows the good we have done. Love God and love others... this alone stores up treasure for us in heaven!

And so, in this manner my friends, we store treasures in heaven.

And why? It only seems reasonable that these treasures will have value to us... eternally... in heaven these are our true and lasting treasures.

Help us recognize, Lord, that You... doing Your will, loving You and loving others... are our true and eternal Treasures!

"My Worth Is Not in What I Own"

Fernando Ortega & Gettys

https://youtu.be/Ls_Fjep1j98

August 23

Today's Encouragement is 2 Corinthians 5:20 NLT *So we are Christ's ambassadors; God is making his appeal through us. We speak for Christ when we plead, "Come back to God!"*

We are ambassadors –

We each have our own sphere of influence. Most of us aren't called to change the world, BUT there still is a group of people over which we each have some measure of influence... one person or many, we are Christ's ambassador to them.

Now friends, we can be either a good, effective, and honorable ambassador, by sharing God's love with them, (if necessary, use words...) Or we can be poor ambassadors, either by being ashamed of the gospel, or worse..., by our sin, bringing shame to His Name. We get to choose.

Recognize that we are, already, His ambassadors, and whether we do that job well or poorly, we cannot escape that we still represent Him to this world! And we represent Him well when we simply Love others as He loves us!

Lord God, help us to be good ambassadors, representing You and Your love to the world around us, to the people You've placed in our sphere of influence. Equip us, and speak Your Love through us, we ask in Jesus' Name.

"Oh, How He Loves You and Me"
Unknown
https://youtu.be/LmtFxnQsl6Q

August 24

Today's Encouragement is Matthew 6:31 NLT *"So don't worry about these things, saying, 'What will we eat? What will we drink? What will we wear?'"*

So don't worry –

In this passage, (vs25-34) Jesus speaks repeatedly and clearly about how useless it is to worry or be anxious. He essentially tells us, "Just Stop It!"

Also, He then clarifies what we do need to choose to focus on, instead of our own needs... Matthew 6:33 NLT *"Seek the Kingdom of God above all else, and live righteously, and he will give you everything you need."*

Friends, our worry and anxiety only result in crippling fear... no good comes from it, only a mental and emotional prison. Panic attacks, health problems, and many other mental, emotional, and physical problems find their root in a decision, a choice to worry, to fear.

Repeatedly, throughout the New Testament, He said "Don't Fear!" (Just Stop it!) And all our Worry... is based on Fear.

Jesus prescribed the way out, freedom from the prison of our tormented minds... In essence, He said, "Don't worry about these earthly things... instead, focus your thinking on God's kingdom and living right, and He will take care of everything that worries you!"

Father God, help us to choose to trust You and just stop the worrying! It does no good for anyone. But, trusting in You, seeking You instead, blesses us and those around us. Thank You for helping us to choose to seek You, Trust You, and Rest in You.

"Seek Ye First"

Maranatha Music

https://youtu.be/EsBpM9IcBts

August 25

Today's Encouragement is Mark 4:40 NLT *Then he asked them, "Why are you afraid? Do you still have no faith?"*

Why are you afraid –

Jesus was speaking to his disciples just after He has calmed the terrible storm which had so badly frightened them. Jesus was with them on the boat, but he was asleep. The storm was terrible! Even the experienced fishermen were frightened by its power and violence.

But after Jesus simply spoke to the storm, "Peace, be still" ... all was calm and quiet.

Then He made this remarkable revelation, in the form of a question... "Why are you afraid? Do you still have no faith?"

My friends, Fear cannot exist in the presence of Faith. If we are living in Faith, practicing our Faith, Trusting God in Faith, relying on Him for our every need including physical safety...

we will not fear! Fear happens when we don't have Faith. And the seeds of fears grow into worry, anxiety, and sometimes panic.

Faith is God's good alternative to the fear, anxiety, worry and panic which torment many of us today. We feed our fears, in all these forms, when we look at life from this earthly perspective. We feed our faith, which grows into strength, courage, and hope, when we look at this life from the perspective of Jesus. That is, Jesus is in the boat with us, and the terrible storm around us—is subject to the Master who is with us!

We either choose Faith in Him, and are at peace within the storm, or we choose to focus on the storm and worry and panic instead. Faith or Fear. Trust or Worry. Hope or Despair. We either choose Jesus or the world.

Father God, we choose Jesus—Faith, Trust, and Hope in You. Strengthen us so that when the storms of life come, our Faith in You will rule our hearts and minds, and fear, worry, and anxiety will be washed away.

"Give Me Faith"
Elevation Worship
https://youtu.be/bBfhfV9WcNI

August 26

Today's Encouragement is Mark 4:37-38 NLT *But soon a fierce storm came up. High waves were breaking into the boat, and it began to fill with water. Jesus was sleeping at the back of the boat with his head on a cushion. The disciples woke him up, shouting, "Teacher, don't you care that we're going to drown?"*

Jesus was sleeping –

As the storm blew in, and the waves tossed, water began to fill the boat, the men shouted at each other to bail water or tie down the cargo, and the wind blew fiercely, and the noise level had to be deafening... yet Jesus was asleep!

Why didn't He wake up earlier? Why didn't He rebuke the storm before it even started? How could anyone sleep in such conditions?

Of course, Jesus knew beforehand the storm was coming, yet He didn't prevent it, or even warn His disciples, he just went to sleep.

Is it possible my friends that Jesus was waiting for the right time to wake and calm the storm? His time, His conditions, His decision. We want to avoid the storm completely, clear skies and smooth sailing always... but God has other plans.

We are designed to Need Him! Not manipulated but all are created, as one philosopher said, "with a God-shaped hole that nothing else can fill."

My friends, we are often in the midst of the storm. Somewhere between the calm beginning and the miraculous restoration of peace. This is the place of Faith, a school where we learn to Trust Him, to pray for our needs and rely on Him to deliver us... in His Time, as when He woke up in midst of the storm and said, "Be Still!"

Father God, as we endure, by Faith, the storms of this life, the trials, and even the suffering, help us be confident that, You are with us, and that You will act when You know the time is right! Strengthen our Faith Father, we pray in Jesus' Name.

"Peace in the Storm"

Sinach

https://youtu.be/EaxlVfPx7TY

August 27

Today's Encouragement is Romans 8:28 NIV *And we know that in all things God works for the good of those who love him, who have been called according to his purpose.*

In all things –

This is a great verse to memorize. It is a constant source of encouragement to me. When bad things happen, I remember this. When good things come out of bad circumstances, I remember this. When I don't understand how anything good could possibly come out of this situation, I remember this.

God sees, thinks, acts differently than you and I do, He knows the beginning and ending and how things will happen. He's in charge; He is Sovereign.

For you and me, my friends,— His dearly loved children, we who love Him, and are called by Him to be His own — He moves all things; He causes all things, He arranges for all things to work for our good! He is That Good... and His Love for us is That Deep, that True!

Help us, Lord, to hide Your word in our hearts! To strengthen our faith by memorizing Your Truths! To remember that You are in absolute control, and You love us. To trust in Your plans, Your purposes, and Your timing. "When I cannot see it, God, I still believe it... You are working all things for our good!" (from this song)

"All Things"

Covenant Worship

https://youtu.be/dR-WF7J6Sf8

August 28

Today's Encouragement is Romans 6:22a NLT *But now you are free from the power of sin and have become slaves of God.*

Now you are free –

Let that thought sink in, allow it to take root in your heart. Now, my friend, You Are Free! Free from Sin's power over your life, free from condemnation, guilt, and shame!

We're all too quick to add the word "But" onto the truth of the gospel. Avoid that for another moment or two. Absorb the Word of God, as Jesus speaks these words to you ... You are Free!

Can you accept it? The freedom we have in Christ! The freedom from our past and future sin, freedom to become new creations, freedom to start each day with a new overflowing measure of God's mercy and love, can you, have you accepted this?

And just as we are freed from these destructive things, we are freed to be fully His...Slaves of God! People who live to serve Him, to do as He instructs!

We are Free!—to be the strong, confident, peaceful, and loving person God designed us to be. Independent of Sin; Free to Depend on God!

Thank You, Jesus, for purchasing our freedom from the past, from all guilt, shame, and addictions, for paving the way for us to live as Your Free Servants!

"I'm Free"
Lynda Randle
https://youtu.be/coR_MANuXKQ

August 29

Today's Encouragement is Philippians 4:6 NLT *Don't worry about anything; instead, pray about everything. Tell God what you need and thank him for all he has done.*

Instead, Pray –

The Bible is God's Wisdom for how to live wisely, the way He intends for us.

Here, God's Word speaks to us about worry, and how to choose a better way. This is God's wisdom for us my friends, it's not some man's teaching, but the Wisdom of God.

Just don't worry... Stop it! Refuse worry and anxiety and fretting! Choose as a matter of your own will to turn away from worry.... And instead of worry...

Pray!

This is choosing to turn from focusing on what we humans can do, wish we could do, think we ought to do, wish someone else would do... from the world of man. This is choosing to turn to the world of God... recognizing we are so often powerless to "fix" the broken things of this life. God is fully able, fully powerful, to address these things... and to do so in the wisest, most beneficial manner possible... in God's wisdom, timing and power.

Worry, fretting and anxiety all focus on ME... Prayer is focused on God, what He can and will and might do... in His best for His beloved children!

Father God, please help us to choose prayer, trusting You, over worry and trusting ourselves or others. You are in control.

"Do Not Worry"

Ellie Holcomb

https://youtu.be/QhbK2GpbKTY

August 30

Today's Encouragement is Philippians 4:7 NLT *Then you will experience God's peace, which exceeds anything we can understand. His peace will guard your hearts and minds as you live in Christ Jesus.*

God's peace –

Then you will experience God's peace... when is that? After you choose not to worry but to pray (v 6—see yesterday's devotional).

My friends, when we choose to say "Yes" to God's ways, His plans, His best... we must say "No" to our own ways, our will, our self-determination... this is Surrendering to Him. As Jesus did always, but most clearly, He prayed the night he was arrested... Luke 22:42 (NLT) *"Father, if you are willing, please take this cup of suffering away from me. Yet I want your will to be done, not mine."* Your Will be done, not mine! But don't stop there my friends... read on! (v43) *"Then an angel from heaven appeared and strengthened him."*

God's perfect peace and strength came to Jesus as He surrendered to God's will, turning away from worry, fear, and anxiety (and Jesus was very anxious at this time!), and by Praying, turning TO God, asking Him for help, and —Trusting Him, His ways, His plans— then peace comes. And not "just any peace," but God's Peace.

"Then you WILL experience God's Peace".... This is Assurance. Not maybe, not occasionally.... YOU WILL! And God's Peace exceeds anything we can understand. It guards our hearts and minds... when we choose to live in Jesus. surrendering to and trusting in God's will and plan.

Help us, Father, to turn from worry to prayer, to choose You over our own ways and thoughts, to Trust You. We long to experience Your Peace which exceeds anything we can understand!

"Peace"
We The Kingdom
https://youtu.be/_UREG0ZRhlY

August 31

Today's Encouragement is Romans 5:11 NLT *So now we can rejoice in our wonderful new relationship with God because our Lord Jesus Christ has made us friends of God.*

New relationship –

It's a good practice sometimes to read scripture very slowly, savoring each word, phrase and thought. His Word is living and alive (Hebrews 4:12) and is our food (Matthew 4:4).

- So now - (at this time, as the saved children of God...)
- We can rejoice - (celebrate, relax, be at peace and content...)
- In our wonderful new relationship with God – (it is Wonderful to belong to Him, to be In Him, to be a part of Him, to have Him living within us! ... No other relationship can even come close!)
- Because our Lord Jesus Christ - (when Jesus became our Lord... everything changed... we became new creations, we were cleansed forever of every flaw, every sin, every wound we've ever received or inflicted on others... completely clean... without fault or even a blemish)
- has made us friends with God - (How amazing is this? ...we are God's Friends!? We realize we are His children, His sheep, His followers, His people... these are a little easier to accept... but seriously – His Friends? Friends of God?

My friends, approach God as your friend... recognizing who He is, as Almighty Creator, Eternal Father... and also—Our Friend! This is our Wonderful New Relationship! Rejoice in Him!

Thank You, Father God, for creating for us a wonderful new relationship with You... that we are now, already, your friends and You are now, already, our Friend. Help us to rejoice in our friendship with you! To spend time with You, to talk frequently with You, and to listen carefully as You speak to us! We thank You and we pray in Jesus' Name.

"Friend of God"
Phillips, Craig, and Dean
https://youtu.be/YthdqrT-D3o

September 1

Today's Encouragement is 1 Chronicles 22:14a NLT *I have worked hard to provide materials for building the Temple of the Lord—nearly 4,000 tons of gold, 40,000 tons of silver, and so much iron and bronze that it cannot be weighed.*

Worked hard –

King David, in his final years, spoke this to his young son Solomon. David really wanted to build a Temple for the Lord! A permanent home for the Ark of the Covenant, representing God's presence on this earth. But God made it clear that it was not David, but his son, who would be allowed to build this magnificent Temple.

So, King David did what he could do... he worked hard (the original Greek translates, "in my affliction and troubles") to provide richly for the building materials of the temple! His hard work was this—he sacrificed his own wealth, it cost him dearly, he took great pains, made great sacrifices and he 'worked hard' at it!

How does this encourage us today?

David recognized what he could NOT do, yet he "worked hard" to do the things that he COULD do! There may be major obstacles between you and what you want to do for the Lord—But are we doing what we CAN do? I have a friend who is severely limited in physical ability and mobility, but she can talk and use a phone, so she regularly calls people to encourage them, maybe just a few words of blessing, love, and hope... from one who is extremely limited. Though severely constrained by physical limitations, her spirit is still free to honor God and share His Love.

Father, help us to see what we can do to bring You honor and glory, and then to "work hard" at it. Because only what is done for You will last or have any real value.

"Only One Life"

unknown

https://youtu.be/56PMgMG3G8c

September 2

Today's Encouragement is Proverbs 19:11 NLT *Sensible people control their temper; they earn respect by overlooking wrongs.*

Overlooking wrongs –

There seems to be a great shortage of sensible people these days.

Sensible... Wouldn't we all want to be considered as sensible people? It makes you think of someone cool, calm, and collected, not easily rattled or angry!

Yet today's culture seems to honor, in a way, the hurt feelings, anger, sulking, and the "poor pitiful me" behavior of spoiled children... and adults! How many times a day do you hear someone say, "I am offended by... (you name it!)"? We are all so easily offended by each other... our words, our pronouns, our looks, our thoughts! It's getting, no, it has already become, ridiculous! It seems there are very few "Sensible people" these days.

God's Wisdom, from the Book He provided for us, says... Sensible people control their anger (and all emotions) and they become respected when they overlook wrongs...

The Wrong is done... and some harm has come. It may be physical, financial, emotional, mental, work-related, or personal. The wrong is real! –and yet, sensible people ...wise, calm, thinking, people... overlook the wrong! Most of us want to fight! "I'll show YOU!" We seethe with anger desiring revenge!... but wait... *Human anger does not produce the righteousness God desires.* (James 1:20 NLT)

Instead... Overlook it! Choose God's way over your human emotional response... this will allow you to be free from all Offenses!

Father God, help us, for we always need Your help in everything, to overlook wrongs. It seems these wrongs are everywhere, and we long to be Your people, free from the control of our emotions, free to choose to honor You with all our lives.

"Forgiveness"

Matthew West

https://youtu.be/h1Lu5udXEZI

September 3

Today's Encouragement is Mark 6:5-6a NLT *And because of their unbelief, he couldn't do any miracles among them except to place his hands on a few sick people and heal them. And he was amazed at their unbelief.*

Their Unbelief –

Matthew 8:26 NLT *Jesus responded, "Why are you afraid? You have so little faith!" Then he got up and rebuked the wind and waves, and suddenly there was a great calm.*

Matthew 15:28 NLT *"Dear woman," Jesus said to her, "your faith is great. Your request is granted." And her daughter was instantly healed.*

Notice the difference in Faith in these three? Unbelief, little faith, and great faith.

Unbelief is no faith, refusing to believe... a choice. And in this absence of faith, Jesus will do little. A hard teaching... but, because He is unlimited in power it must be His choice, to limit His miraculous power to a few healings. (which is actually—extremely miraculous!) Note also, this was among His own friends and neighbors.

Little faith, describing His own disciples, might be termed an immature faith. Even among the disciples there was a variance of faith, Judas clearly had none, and Peter professed, "You are the Messiah!"

Great faith, oh to be granted such a gift!! This faith resulted in "instantly healed." And this great faith was from a Gentile woman!

Is it possible, my friends, that once we choose to believe in Jesus, we've moved from unbelief to "little faith?" And then, by prayer, choosing to trust, and a conscious growing acceptance of God's will... we too, can move from "little faith" to "great faith." Is it possible?

Thank You, Father God, that You are patient with us, knowing that we are all beginning with only a little faith. Grow us Father into people of Great Faith, we ask in Jesus Name.

"Oh Me, of Little Faith"
Ashton/Becker/Dente
https://youtu.be/mkyK3-Z0M3o

September 4

Today's Encouragement is Matthew 13:23 NLT *"The seed that fell on good soil represents those who truly hear and understand God's word and produce a harvest of thirty, sixty, or even a hundred times as much as had been planted!"*

Good soil –

My friends, this wonderful parable of the Sower describes the widespread scattering of the seed of the word of God, the Good News of Jesus Christ to the world. And we, those who believe, who truly hear and understand... are the "good soil" of this parable! And we, who "hear and understand"... we shall inevitably, produce a harvest! Not just any harvest... (the ESV study Bible footnote says a 5-15x harvest is normal!) but an abnormally large harvest!

What is the harvest? It must be souls... only the soul of man has eternal value. No riches, honor, nor fame has lasting value in the kingdom of heaven (v11).

This is not saying that we must produce such a harvest to be worthy of the kingdom, nor by our own efforts and striving will we produce a large harvest... Jesus simply says... good soil will produce... a bountiful harvest. It is the "natural" result of God's supernatural work! Good seed (the word of God) planted in good soil (believers who hear and understand) results in a good harvest.

Is it possible, my brothers and sisters, that God is using your life to produce a bountiful harvest of 30, 60, or 100 times...?

Examine the parable again. Of the four types of soil, only the good soil "hears and understands" the Good News... the salvation by faith in Jesus... and that is you and me!

God, we thank You for the wonderful promises of Your Word. Though we may not see it, help us to know that You are working within us to grow Your Kingdom... that we each have value and usefulness to You! And you are working through us, in all things for Good!

"All Things"
Covenant Worship
https://youtu.be/dR-WF7J6Sf8

September 5

Today's Encouragement is Matthew 5:20 NLT *"But I warn you—unless your righteousness is better than the righteousness of the teachers of religious law and the Pharisees, you will never enter the Kingdom of Heaven!"*

Your righteousness –

The righteousness of the teachers of the law and the Pharisees was their own works. These men were, as He reveals in several places in the gospels, literally "self-righteous" and it was a false righteousness, full of pride at their own accomplishments. The people to whom He preached really considered these religious leaders to be truly righteous.

But here, Jesus condemned their self-righteousness saying that we must be truly, perfectly righteous. Friends, we can only be truly righteous, truly in a right relationship with God (this is what righteousness is) when we are IN Christ! When we are IN Him, it is not our righteousness that is considered but His! We are clothed with Christ! (Galatians 3:27) We are one with Him (John 17:22-23). His grace is sufficient for us (2 Corinthians 12:9).

So, for everyone who believes in Jesus as Lord and Savior... our "righteous is far better that of the scribes and Pharisees"" better than anyone's good deeds or self-made righteousness! No matter how "religious" they may seem to be!

Much of the sermon on the mount was aimed at revealing to ordinary people the vast and impossible chasm between man and God. No sacrifice, no man's righteousness, is adequate to truly free man from sin... only Jesus can do that... and He did!

Father, we are grateful for Your amazing gift of Grace, that we can be clothed, covered with Christ and His righteousness, and that He is In us today!

"Clothed With Christ"

Genevieve Falleur

https://youtu.be/bDViFl57IKQ

September 6

Today's Encouragement is Matthew 15:32 NLT *Then Jesus called his disciples and told them, "I feel sorry for these people. They have been here with me for three days, and they have nothing left to eat. I don't want to send them away hungry, or they will faint along the way."*

Here with me –

For three days these people followed Jesus, hanging on His every word, amazed by dozens of miracles (v30), and praising God (v31).

Can you imagine such an experience? Spending 3 days with Jesus? All the food they'd brought was gone, they had to see that it was running out... and what about their work, their homes... all the responsibilities of this life?

All things had been set aside for worship! Everything set aside in order to just –

Be. With. Jesus.

Selah- pause and consider that...

Notice Jesus' response to this great crowd of people... the ESV reads, *"I have compassion for them...."* What kindness and Love from our Lord!

So, ...He feeds them, meets their need, kindly, graciously, freely, He fed thousands... who had spent three days following, watching, listening to Him... and worshipping God. (v31b) "And they praised the God of Israel."

Thank You, Father, for the Love and compassion You have for Your children. Help us to be so amazed in Your Presence that we, too, forget to eat, forget about all the cares of this life, and are simply amazed by Who You are!

"I Stand Amazed"

Chris Tomlin

https://youtu.be/ue8ZCAc9xQ8

September 7

Today's Encouragement is 1 John 3:1a NLT *See how very much our Father loves us, for he calls us his children, and that is what we are!*

How very much –

My friends, brothers and sisters in Christ, we are deeply, even immeasurably, loved by our Father!

Just consider this sampling of blessings He has (Already!) granted us...

We are His sons and daughters

We are made Righteous by the Blood of Jesus Filled with the Holy Spirit

We are Clothed with Christ

We are protected–No weapon formed against us will prevail More than Conquerors

We have a spirit of power, love, and self-control Have the Mind of Christ

We are the righteousness of God.

We can do all things through Christ who gives us Strength... And there is even more!

Friends don't fall prey to the idea that, "There is some truth in the Bible, but you can't believe everything in it." Instead, take God at His Word! Choose to accept, to believe all of it, all of what God says, and set aside your opinions, what your think, and what others say is true. Jesus is the Truth! And God's word contains all of the Truth about you and me as His children.

Whether we Feel it or not, whether we Understand it or not, whether the great academic minds, philosophers, and theologians of this fallen world Believe it or not... we Accept His Word as The Truth!

Just consider... how immeasurable is the Love the Father has for you... and in addition to all this... He gave His Son to bring us into His Family.

Father God, such Great, Wonderful, and Amazing Love is just too much for our human minds to conceive. Please help us to accept Your amazing Love even though we understand it so little.

"How Great Is the Love"

Paul Baloche

https://youtu.be/huGSh3sUyBE

September 8

Today's Encouragement is Romans 12:2 NLT *Don't copy the behavior and customs of this world, but let God transform you into a new person by changing the way you think. Then you will learn to know God's will for you, which is good and pleasing and perfect.*

Let God transform you –

Don't we all want to know God's will? His will for us is "good, pleasing and perfect!" Friends, this comes about as a process, which God Himself manages... as He transforms us into new people! It's His work to transform us. Our own efforts at transformation are usually short-lived, half-hearted attempts to "do better," "get my life right," "clean up my act," etc. a good try maybe ,but unless God is doing the transformation, you and I will make a mess of it! (John 15:5b " *For apart from Me you can do nothing.*")

Friends, our part is, "Don't copy the behavior and customs of this world." This "world" with its behavior and customs, is corrupt and dying. We can live as ambassadors of Christ, freed from the behavior and customs of this decaying world culture... as we allow God to transform us!

As we turn away from this world, in faith toward Our God, then we allow Him to transform us... by changing the way we think! And friend, this transformation is the same word used in Matthew 17:2 NLT "*...Jesus' appearance was transformed so that his face shone like the sun, and his clothes became as white as light.*"

This is the transformation God is doing with us! And then we will know His good and perfect will for us! What a wonderful, merciful God we serve!

Father God, we need You to transform us, we cannot do this ourselves. We choose to "Let You" transform us!

"Thank You, Jesus, for the Blood"

Charity Gayle

https://youtu.be/2ms-IasUFBs

September 9

Today's Encouragement is Matthew 11:6 *ESV* *"And blessed is the one who is not offended by me."*

Offended –

Many were in His day—offended by Him. Because He flaunted their petty religious traditions. He did things like healing on the sabbath day... highly offensive to their religion. And most offensive of all, he claimed to be equal to God! (v27)

All the religious leaders were highly offended! Incensed! Enraged! So much that they chose to kill Him.

We too, can be offended! Even by the teachings of Jesus. We don't call it that... we say, "Well, nobody's perfect, no one can live up to His teachings!" And we use this as an excuse to continue living as we choose.

Friends, His teaching, the Sermon on the Mount for example, is intended to "set the bar" at the highest level possible, so high that no one could attain it; so high that, without Jesus, without the Perfect, Amazing Grace of God... no salvation is possible!

Offended by Jesus? May we rather be enthralled by Him! And overwhelmingly grateful!

For not only has He told us the Truth (He IS the Truth)—He also has provided the (only) Way for us to be saved! *Jesus said to him, "I am the way, and the truth, and the life. No one comes to the Father except through me."* (John 14:6 ESV)

Thank You, Lord, that Jesus wasn't concerned at all about how people perceived Him, He was true to You and to Himself, and He spoke Truth, whether the people believed Him or not.

"The Outlaw"
Larry Norman
https://youtu.be/9cq6SFHlkHc

September 10

Today's Encouragement is Hebrews 13:8 NLT *Jesus Christ is the same yesterday and today and forever.*

Jesus Christ is the same –

Many of us would like to have a closer relationship with God. We know we would be better off. We know that prayer can and would help us be better people and be better Christians.

But we just get busy, too busy for our own good. Or... we get discouraged, we've waited so long, prayed so many times, for years even.

Reread the verse... and try to imagine that. Jesus is the SAME! He isn't frustrated by what we did or didn't do yesterday. Not disappointed in our current performance or failures... He just IS. Remember in Exodus 3:14, God said, 'I AM'? There's no need to say more!

"I Am" what?" We might ask ... Well, ...

"I Am" – "The same yesterday today and forever,"

"I Am the Lord who heals you!"

"I Am the beginning and the end."

"I Am the way, the truth, and the life."

So, no matter how long it's been, in our perspective, since you spoke with God through prayer... Jesus is the same... He is unperturbed, patient, kind, loving, all-knowing, all- gracious, all-forgiving. And no matter how long you have asked Him for your heart's desire, your prayer request of so very many years... He's not holding out on you! He's not waiting for you to "get right" so He can bless you... He knows what we need before we ask Him... He is the "I Am," the same yesterday, today and forever. And He wants a real, personal, and growing relationship with you.

Thank You, Lord, that Jesus is the same, always. Help us to know that we and rely on and trust You both because You never change.

"Jesus the Same"
Hillsong
https://youtu.be/hre2GJUUnaA

September 11

Today's Encouragement is Philippians 4:6-7 NLT *Don't worry about anything; instead, pray about everything. Tell God what you need, and thank him for all he has done. Then you will experience God's peace, which exceeds anything we can understand. His peace will guard your hearts and minds as you live in Christ Jesus.*

God's Peace –

God's Peace is beyond our comprehension, it's supernatural (beyond the natural world) and it is not rational nor logical to our human minds. As when we say, "How can you be calm at a moment like this?" This Peace is only possible when it is beyond our own abilities, and only God's Peace has the power to guard in our hearts and minds while the world around us is in chaos.

Jesus is the Prince of Peace. He said in John 14:27 NLT *"I am leaving you with a gift—peace of mind and heart. And the peace I give is a gift the world cannot give. So don't be troubled or afraid."*

Take a moment, right now, and "don't be troubled or afraid," let go of fear, instead, embrace, accept the Peace of Christ... Peace beyond human understanding...

Silence the noise around you. Close your eyes and consider this: He has saved you; He has prepared an eternal home for you; He knows your name, every aspect of your life; He loves you and will provide for you always. Be at Peace; experience His Peace for this one moment. Still your soul, regardless of the circumstances surrounding you. Recognize that because of the finished work of Jesus Christ, It is Well with Your Soul.

Father God, Help us to rest in Your Perfect, Divine Peace—this moment, this day. Regardless of the chaos, confusion, or clamoring around us... we look to You for Your Peace!

"It Is Well"
Bethel Music
https://youtu.be/8Wb_WD1emFQ

September 12

Today's Encouragement is Colossians 2:6-7 NLT *And now, just as you accepted Christ Jesus as your Lord, you must continue to follow him. Let your roots grow down into him, and let your lives be built on him. Then your faith will grow strong in the truth you were taught, and you will overflow with thankfulness.*

Continue to follow –

Do you see the process in this passage?

- Accept Jesus As Lord
- Continue to Follow
- Let roots grow deep
- Build life upon Him - and then –
- Our faith is strong in truth - and
- Thankfulness Overflows!

This is the Christian life... a growing life ("roots" and "grow strong") till the overflowing of thankfulness occurs.

It begins with "Accepted." God invites us, welcomes us, beckons us, calls us. And our role is to Accept Jesus. We Accept Him, as our Lord – our Master, Guide, Shepherd, as our God. And we then Continue to Follow Him. We persevere, we remain, we dwell with Him... as part of His Church. We Continue.... Next, we Let (allow) our roots grow deep—We build our lives upon Him... He guides us in this, but WE DO this... we Allow our roots to grow, and we Allow our lives to be built upon Him— a Choice we make, a Decision...

Then – my friends, and THEN! Our faith becomes Strong in Truth, because—we Accept Jesus as Lord, we continue to follow, we let our roots grow deep, and we build our life upon Him! And then, we Overflow with grateful Thanks!

Father, Help us to choose to Continue to Follow... that You may become Strong in us... that our lives may overflow with Thankfulness for Who you are, for What You have done, and for What you are going to Do!

"For Your Splendor"
Christy Nockels
https://youtu.be/DC_QCKCuAM8

September 13

Today's Encouragement is Psalm 51:1 NLT *Have mercy on me, O God, because of your unfailing love. Because of your great compassion, blot out the stain of my sins.*

Blot out –

Think of the pen and ink used to write in ancient times. Erasing wasn't possible. The only way to remove a mistake, or to change a written word? Blot it out! Cover it completely with more ink.

My friends, our sins are covered with something which makes them unrecognizable, something infinitely greater than the "ink" with which we "wrote" them. The blood of Jesus covers all our sin. His blood 'blots out' our sin, it's no longer recognizable, and cannot be held against us!

All our sin was future sin when Christ died for us on the cross. Our future sins as well as our past, are blotted out, covered completely by the priceless blood of Christ.

Father God, may we then live as Your freed, forgiven, and beloved children—Granted complete pardon, unshackled from our past pain, our future fears, and our daily doubts. Help us to realize that we are no longer slaves to our sins, our pasts, or our fears. Father, please blot out all our sin from our memories as well, Lord. We ask in Jesus' Name.

"No Longer Slaves"
Zack Williams
https://youtu.be/xJ4XR2iuOIk

September 14

Today's Encouragement is 2 Chronicles 6:18 NLT *"But will God really live on earth among people? Why, even the highest heavens cannot contain you. How much less this Temple I have built!"*

Really live on earth –

As Solomon dedicated the Temple to God centuries ago, he recognized that God is too great to be limited to one location, even the beautiful Temple. And he asks this question: "will You really live on earth among people?"

Jesus certainly did just that—many centuries later! And just in case you feel like you missed out, missed those three years in ancient Israel, only a moment in time—which transformed eternity... when God really did "live on earth among people," consider Jesus' words in His final talk with His disciples... John 16:7 NLT *"But in fact, it is best for you that I go away, because if I don't, the Advocate [Holy Spirit] won't come. If I do go away, then I will send him to you."*

"It is best for you"!? *"That I* [Jesus] *go away"*!? What??? How can that be good?

Friends, is it possible that... WE are MORE blessed now, (Jesus said, "It is BEST"!) to have the Holy Spirit within us, than the disciples who walked and talked with Jesus!? Is it possible? Read John 16:7 one more time... It seems clear that this is exactly what Jesus said!

Father, help us to recognize that: just as Your Glory filled the temple of Solomon, just as Jesus lived on Earth, now, in this day, Your Holy Spirit lives within each believer. Thank You, Father, that You have given us Your Best, and that You really do, still today, "live on earth among people"!

"Spirit of the Living God"
Vertical Worship
https://youtu.be/ZPZrxZgQjrg

September 15

Today's Encouragement is 2 Peter 1:3 NLT *By his divine power, God has given us everything we need for living a godly life. We have received all of this by coming to know him, the one who called us to himself by means of his marvelous glory and excellence.*

Everything we need –

Imagine having everything you need. Not only our physical needs, but also our emotional and spiritual needs, all completely satisfied.

It's rather surprising to learn... we already do! We have "everything we need for living a godly life!" Now, so, please explain to me... What. Else. Really. Matters...?

Admittedly, we may not "feel" like we have everything, at least not Yet! But our Feelings are not our true reality. Just because we are unaware of our blessings does not mean that we are impoverished; it is only rejection of the blessings God has provided us that makes us destitute.

Lord God, open our eyes and hearts to the amazing blessings You have given to us, Your deeply loved children. By Your divine power... You have given us everything we need!

"Already All I Need"

Christy Nockels

https://youtu.be/zByzjJ4nvH8

September 16

Today's Encouragement is 1 John 4:16 NLT *We know how much God loves us, and we have put our trust in his love. God is love, and all who live in love live in God, and God lives in them.*

God is Love –

This verse doesn't say, God loves only us. John 3:16 tells us He loves the whole world ... but this verse goes beyond describing what He does...to tell us Who He is—He IS love! It's His character, His Nature, the essence of His being!

It is possible that we cannot really love – any other person—without first experiencing God in some way. (Perhaps this is why Love is our greatest need?). Of course, as we humans always do, we contaminate love, bring it down to our basest level...But God isn't brought down, His Perfect Love remains as the truest example of Love to us all.

So, consider asking, allowing Him to refill you with His Love. And then His love will... through you... love others.

Because only when we experience Him, experience His Love, then we will have His love to share with others.

Without His love, there's nothing worthwhile for us to share with anyone else.

Lord God, refill us with You, with Your Love, so that we can love others.

"The Love of God"

The Isaacs

https://youtu.be/mbCqclLfWZo

September 17

Today's Encouragement is John 15:5 NKJV [Jesus said] *"I am the vine, you are the branches; he who abides in Me and I in him, he bears much fruit, for apart from Me you can do nothing."*

You can do nothing –

"I think I'm offended! Jesus is saying that, without Him, I can't do anything! But I can tie my shoes! I can eat lunch... so, what is He saying?"

Jesus explains that He is the vine, and that we are branches – attached to His

vine. Only by our remaining in His vine, in contact, abiding, with Him, through a life-giving connection with Him, by our relationship with Him, can we ever "bear fruit," or have any real success—have any lasting value.

The analogy goes on to be even more serious, because, without Jesus, the Vine, and our life-giving connection to Him, we can do Nothing. Because we are dead without Him...

Nothing.

But by remaining IN Him, attached to His Vine, we will bear much fruit. *For I can do everything through Christ, who gives me strength.* (Philippians 4:13) Through Christ... attached to Him, dwelling, abiding in Him.

Lord, Draw us nearer, make us more aware of the life-giving and life-sustaining relationship we can have with You. So that we have life, and we can "bear much fruit," the fruit of Your amazing love for this lost and dying world.

"Without You"
Paul Baloche
https://youtu.be/eBsE8VGW4C8

September 18

Today's Encouragement is John 15:15 NLT *I no longer call you slaves, because a master doesn't confide in his slaves. Now you are my friends, since I have told you everything the Father told me.*

You are my Friends –

Imagine... we are FRIENDS of Jesus Christ!... Wow!... Consider that for just a

moment. Think of the best friend you've ever had...multiply that love, affection, warmth, comfort, peace, happiness... by a hundred times, ...no, make that a million times... (still not enough). And that is only getting a little closer to describing the incredibly rich, immeasurable relationship and bond between... you and Jesus. You are His Friend.

Remember, His Love is a gift... we can never earn it... we are not worthy to be His friends... but—He Chose You and me to be His friends!

It's not about how you feel—"But I just don't feel close to Jesus!" No, it is a fact–a truth that Jesus has revealed to us. So, with this truth in your heart, turn your mind and spirit toward Him, and let Him be a real friend to you, and let Him be your very best and closest friend! He is always waiting patiently for you and me to come to Him.

Thank You, Lord Jesus, for choosing us as Your friends. Help me, to allow You, to draw me, ever closer to You.

"I am a Friend of God"
Phillips Craig and Dean
https://youtu.be/lcxKRsn-hGc

September 19

Today's Encouragement is Job 7:7 NLT *O God, remember that my life is but a breath, and I will never again feel happiness.*

Never again –

Job is a difficult book. We focus on only a short period of his lifetime, a tragic, horrifying time when he loses everything, his health, great possessions, respect, even his sons and daughters! His wife even advised him to "Curse God and die." (What a blessing she was!)

But this lengthy description of his suffering was not the entirety of his long lifetime! We don't know how long his suffering was, but we do know he was old enough that he had adult children when this greatest trial came upon him, and we know that, after his recovery... he lived another 140 years, and God blessed him with twice the wealth he had before, and 10 more children! (Job 42:12-16)

In this verse, Job admits his complete despair, essentially saying "My life is over, I'll never feel happy again!" Later he even wishes he had never even been born! That's deep despair!

Friends, we also, like Job in his great misery, see only a glimpse of life. Our current circumstances seem to overwhelm everything, but they are not forever, whether they are very pleasant or very, very difficult... this is not the end. This moment, this trial, this tragedy, is only a season, and it will pass.

Father, help us to trust in You. We do not know what tomorrow holds. We will choose to continue to hope in You regardless of how difficult life may be at this one moment.

"I Know Who Holds Tomorrow"

The Isaacs

https://youtu.be/9K9LPY9A1uI

September 20

Today's Encouragement is John 21:3 NLT *Simon Peter said, "I'm going fishing."*

"We'll come, too," they all said. So, they went out in the boat, but they caught nothing all night.

I'm going fishing –

Jesus had been killed a few days before. He later appeared to his disciples behind locked doors and ate with them and showed them the scars. And sometime shortly after these amazing days, Peter says, "Think I'll just go fishing."

It kinda sounds like Peter was saying, "Well, this has been fun, fellas, but it's over, Jesus is gone, we're all just sitting around here looking at each other, asking ourselves 'what's next?' So, I'm going back to what I know, where I can make a living again, and that's fishing!" Was he giving up?

Peter's plan didn't go too well. Notice that they caught nothing all night; nothing at all… until someone (Jesus) shouted from the shore, "Try the other side of the boat!" and then—there was a net-busting catch!

After three years with Jesus, Peter was quitting, or maybe he was just discouraged, or didn't know what to do. But remember Jesus talked with him after breakfast, and asked him, "Peter do you love me?"

Peter said, 'You know I do Lord," and Jesus replied… "Feed my sheep."

Sounds like Jesus was saying, "Peter, you're not to go back to fishing, you are going to feed my sheep." No scolding, no punishment, just loving correction.

Father, although we are tempted at times to give up on serving You, to give up on following Your way, and just go our own way… Yet You never give up on us… and for Your steadfastness, we are grateful. Thank you for gently correcting us, and for patiently loving us. You are a loving Father to us.

"You Never Give Up on Me"

Josh Bates

https://youtu.be/k45iSliZN-E

September 21

Today's Encouragement is 2 Chronicles 20:12 *NLT "O our God, won't you stop them? We are powerless against this mighty army that is about to attack us. We do not know what to do, but we are looking to you for help."*

We do not know what to do –

Jehoshaphat was a good king of Judah, and the Lord was with him. When they were attacked by a huge army of Moab and Ammon. They recognized the disaster facing them, so all of Judah gathered, fasted, and prayed. King Jehoshaphat led the nation in praying and closed his prayer with these words: "We do not know what to do, but we are looking to you for help."

And the rest of the story - 2 Chronicles 20:21-22 NLT *After consulting the people, the king appointed singers to walk ahead of the army, singing to the Lord and praising him for his holy splendor. This is what they sang: "Give thanks to the Lord; his faithful love endures forever!" At the very moment they began to sing and give praise, the Lord caused the armies of Ammon, Moab, and Mount Seir to start fighting among themselves.*

As Judah began to praise God, after praying and seeking His help... the mighty enemy force was completely destroyed from within! God had told His people, Judah, in verse 17, *"But you will not even need to fight. Take your positions; then stand still and watch the Lord's victory. He is with you, O people of Judah and Jerusalem. Do not be afraid or discouraged. Go out against them tomorrow, for the Lord is with you!"*

My friends, whatever we are facing, whatever enemy—physical, emotional, or spiritual—nothing is greater than our God! When you don't know what to do...Pray, fast, seek Him and then Praise Him...Thank Him for all His Love and Care... and you will see His Powerful Hand come to deliver you!

Father God, we look to You. We often don't know what to do... but still, we look to You!
"Pray Every Day"
Buck Owens
https://youtu.be/7A2SIu_wALw

September 22

Today's Encouragement is Romans 8:14-15 NLT *For all who are led by the Spirit of God are children of God. So you have not received a spirit that makes you fearful slaves. Instead, you received God's Spirit when he adopted you as his own children. Now we call him, "Abba, Father."*

His own children –

We often think to ourselves, yeah, God loves me, but He loves everybody... so, it's no big deal. Our minds are tricky things (deceitful) and the lies we believe will keep us broken, weak, and alone. How often we say "Yes, But..." when we read of God's promises and His love. "Yes, but that's for good people, who really love God, who live good lives, who don't have the past or problems that I have."

My friends, God's love is specific... He chose you to adopt as His beloved child. He makes no mistakes; he chooses His children carefully. We are among those who are privileged to call him Daddy (Abba is like Daddy in English). This is not adoption into an institution filled with lost and lonely children... this is the embrace of a Loving, Personal, Close, and Perfect Father. And You are chosen (by the One who knows everything about you, past and future) to be HIS!

This is the Good News... we just believe, and He does this (and even much more) for us... What loving father doesn't want to bless his kids with everything? And our God is so much greater than any loving father we can imagine.

Lord, open our hearts to accept Your Love and embrace the truth that we are your very – deeply– loved sons and daughters. Because of Jesus!

"Who You Say I Am"
Hillsong Worship
https://youtu.be/IcC1Bp13n_4

September 23

Today's Encouragement is John 1:5 ESV *The light shines in the darkness, and the darkness has not overcome it.*

The light shines –

Read these amazing words again with me in John 1:1-5 ESV *In the beginning was the Word, and the Word was with God, and the Word was God. He was in the beginning with God. All things were made through him, and without him was not anything made that was made. In him was life, and the life was the light of men. The light shines in the darkness, and the darkness has not overcome it.*

In just these few verses, we are introduced to Jesus, who is described here as The Word. And also, to His relationship to God. We're told that all of creation came about through Him, and that He is the Light and the Life of men.

And in this last sentence...

Can't you just hear this as a victory shout? THE DARKNESS HAS NOT OVERCOME IT!!! Amen! Thank God!

Friends, when we aren't certain which way to go, when our pathway, our future, all our options... are dark, Jesus is the Light. And no darkness, no evil, no sorrow, no depression, no despair... nothing of the darkness can – ever– overcome His Light.

We can turn away from the Light, and walk toward the Darkness if we choose, we always have the choice... But the Light Still Shines! And we can return to the Light, anytime we choose as well.

God's Light, the Hope and Salvation, Miracle Working Power, the Love, The Forgiveness of Jesus Christ... Still Shines—Eternally. Victoriously.

Father, help us to choose to walk in Your Light, and to return when we falter, doubt, or fear... because - Jesus Shines, even in the darkness.

"Shine Jesus Shine"

Graham Kendrick

https://youtu.be/AvMeTWAiUz8

September 24

Today's Encouragement is Matthew 7:8 NLT *"For everyone who asks, receives. Everyone who seeks, finds. And to everyone who knocks, the door will be opened."*

Everyone who seeks, finds –

We find what we're looking for—Jesus said seek and you will find! Of course, He was speaking of spiritual matters, but this is true in all cases!

One person believes that everyone is against her, everyone is abusive, and that her life is hopeless. And that's exactly what she finds. She finds exactly what she expects to find.

Years ago, I went to lunch several times with a very negative co-worker, he was especially negative towards our boss. I soon began to be very negative toward the boss also. Soon, I began to realize that my co-worker was negatively influencing me, and I stopped having lunch with him... and my boss somehow "became much smarter"! (This coworker was later fired!)

So, my friends, look for, seek, the blessings in this life and choose to pray about...and then to leave in God's hands... all the worries, anxiety, and problems of this life.

Philippians 4:6-7 NLT *Don't worry about anything; instead, pray about everything. Tell God what you need and thank him for all he has done. Then you will experience God's peace, which exceeds anything we can understand. His peace will guard your hearts and minds as you live in Christ Jesus.*

A friend told me about Ann Voskamp's book, *One Thousand Gifts.* In this book the author tells how she began looking for, seeking, any blessing, gift, or positive thing, no matter how small, that she could find in her daily life, and making a list of them... it transformed her life! And this practice also transformed the life of my friend. Why? Because they found what they sought: God's blessings!

What are you looking for? You can decide today to look for all the blessings of God around you. God is present and He will guide you... if you Ask and Seek.

Father, help us to seek You, and to recognize that You are already everywhere... already here with us.

"Counting Every Blessing"
Rend Collective
https://youtu.be/7X9d4ubvWH4

September 25

Today's Encouragement is John 16:33 NLT *"I have told you all this so that you may have peace in me. Here on earth you will have many trials and sorrows. But take heart, because I have overcome the world."*

Take heart –

It just happens. Setbacks, disappointments, sorrows, tragedy. We all suffer some of these in this life. These troubles, whether of our own making or by the hand of others... Will Come! Jesus didn't say, some of you might have little annoyances in your lifetime! He said, "You Will! Have many!" All of us—and—definitely.

What if this is within the church? It is not immune, my friends. Our family, workplace, friendships, and even our church family are all part of this world... in which we will... have trouble.

So, His counsel for us is this simple phrase. "Take Heart. Have peace in me."

The Amplified Bible translates this as "be courageous, be confident, be undaunted, be filled with joy"!

Why? How can we? We are facing a deeply painful situation, a tragic loss of someone or something vitally important to us! We can..."Because I have overcome the world. "

This world is full of trouble. It's inevitable. But God! But Jesus! He is over and above and beyond and transcends everything, including this world!

Our faith, our hope, our confidence—is not in a job, a spouse, a family, a friend, a pastor, an institution, a church, a routine, a government, or anything of this world. Our Faith is in Jesus! He is the One who has overcome everything, including this world! He is victorious over everything we face. And we are His!

Father God, please help us remember Your Truths. You have overcome this broken world. Our time here, our troubles here, are not for long. You hold us in Your Hands. Help us, Lord, to "Take Heart"!

"Broken World"
The Talleys
https://youtu.be/Y4vSjTcpdkQ

September 26

Today's Encouragement is Matthew 19:25-26 ESV *When the disciples heard this, they were greatly astonished, saying, "Who then can be saved?" But Jesus looked at them and said, "With man this is impossible, but with God all things are possible."*

Who then can be saved? –

Much of Jesus' teaching describes the Perfect, Ideal life. He set the highest possible standards of devotion to God, such as Love for God and for others, including our enemies, forgive endlessly, turn the other cheek, and lay down your life for others.

These are standards which no person can ever achieve! We are all imperfect, fallen, sinful human beings. (This is one of the many arguments which atheists use to declare the Christian life hopelessly impossible to "achieve.")

As if being a Christian was "achieved" by our own behaviors... it is Not!

We are Christians (which means "Christ-like") because we Believe and live out our faith and hope in Jesus as our Savior. *For God made Christ, who never sinned, to be the offering for our sin, so that we could be made right with God through Christ.* (2 Corinthians 5:21 NLT) It is not by our behavior, abiding by rules, living according to any definition of "right living." Our salvation is impossible "with man"; it is only possible "Through Christ"!

Only through Jesus, by our accepting the grace and mercy of God, being reborn (John 3:3), and becoming transformed into a new creation (2 Corinthians 5:17) only then... are we saved. And of course,—It truly is—impossible with Man! But not with God!

Friends, do not be discouraged in trying to live "a good life," or working to be a "good Christian." Instead, rely on Jesus as your Righteousness – your right standing with God. He is The Way!

Dear Master, thank You for making it possible for us to be in complete right standing with You, through our faith in Jesus. You are so kind and merciful to us.

"All Things Are Possible"
Newsboys
https://youtu.be/-OEyZfVNs_c

September 27

Today's Encouragement is Matthew 13:22 ESV *"As for what was sown among thorns, this is the one who hears the word, but the cares of the world and the deceitfulness of riches choke the word, and it proves unfruitful."*

Choke the Word –

The cares of the world and deceitfulness of riches choke the Word! If you've done any gardening at all you know that weeds can choke a good plant, cutting off sunlight, absorbing the nutrients in the soil, and sometimes actually wrapping around a good plant to physically choke it, like a python crushes its prey.

Imagine (forgive me for this graphic example but it's His imagery not mine) putting your hands around the neck of the one bringing you the Word of God and choking Him... Horrifying! But that is what He said that we do... when we allow the cares of life, our worries, our efforts to "make it" financially, to rule our hearts....

Friends, His Word is choked out when we allow worry, cares, pursuit of wealth, or anxiety to dominate our thoughts and hearts, rather than trusting His Word... trusting His Truth, trusting in Him.

Lord, help us turn away from the cares of this world, from the deceitfulness of riches, from fear, worry, anxiety, and instead help us to Trust in You, and depend on Your Word—so that Your Word is fruitful in our lives.

"Trust in You"
Lauren Daigle
https://youtu.be/qv-SXz_exKE

September 28

Today's Encouragement is 2 Chronicles 32:7-8 NLT *"Be strong and courageous! Don't be afraid or discouraged because of the king of Assyria or his mighty army, for there is a power far greater on our side! He may have a great army, but they are merely men. We have the Lord our God to help us and to fight our battles for us!" Hezekiah's words greatly encouraged the people.*

Be strong and courageous –

These words "Be Strong and Courageous" were also said centuries before by Moses to Joshua as he assumed leadership of the nation of Israel (Josh. 1:9) and later by David to Solomon as he became King in David's place (1 Chronicles 22:13).

Hezekiah the King encouraged the people with these same words. And we can be encouraged also by these words—because "there is a power far greater on our side!"

Friends when we see what we're up against, the battle we are facing: illness, financial stress, divorce, loss of a loved one, depression, anxiety, addiction... whatever enemy is looming to destroy us... God's power is far greater! And He is with us! His words to us today, are still—"Be strong and courageous!" "We have the Lord to fight our battles for us!"

Father, we are unable to do anything without You (John 15:5), help us to be strong and courageous, to trust in Your strength and Your power to defeat whatever enemy we may face. Because we belong to You, You love us, and You fight for us!

"My God Fights for Me"

Charity Gayle/Micah Tyler/Kaden Slay

https://youtu.be/t1LagOBYFqQ

September 29

Today's Encouragement is 1 Corinthians 13:13 NLT *Three things will last forever—faith, hope, and love—and the greatest of these is love.*

Will last forever –

Interesting that these three things which last forever–are all dependent upon both God and man. Without Him, faith and hope are meaningless, and love is only selfishness. Yet these three eternal things... lasting forever... (Selah, pause and consider that) are all between God and us; all relationship based. Without Him these are empty thoughts, and without us, God's children, they are useless ideals.

Here are some explanatory verses about each:

Faith— *Faith shows the reality of what we hope for; it is the evidence of things we cannot see.* (Hebrews 11:1 NLT) *And it is impossible to please God without faith.* (Hebrews 11:6 NLT)

Hope— *We were given this hope when we were saved. (If we already have something, we don't need to hope for it.)* (Romans 8:24 NLT)

Love— *This is real love—not that we loved God, but that he loved us and sent his Son as a sacrifice to take away our sins.*(1 John 4:10 NLT)

My friends, these three virtues define the depth of our relationship with God. Of all our possible pursuits, these three have eternal value... our **Faith** in Jesus, the Salvation and Forgiveness He provides us, our **Hope** in the promises He has made to us—His good plans for us, protection, provision, and finally God's **Love** for us, flowing freely into us, living within us, and overflowing out from us to God and to His people.

Father God, please strengthen our faith, our hope, and our love. That we would be filled with these eternal blessings.

"One Thing Remains"
Jesus Culture
https://youtu.be/6_KXsMCJgBQ

September 30

Today's Encouragement is Jeremiah 29:12-14 NLT *"In those days when you pray, I will listen. If you look for me wholeheartedly, you will find me. I will be found by you," says the Lord. "I will end your captivity and restore your fortunes. I will gather you out of the nations where I sent you and will bring you home again to your own land."*

I will be found –

Did you ever notice? So often God's promises to us are dependent on our initial action. "If you look for me..." [Then] "you will find me."

This occurs often in the Word. The "if...then." So, this leads us to a few clear conclusions. One is this: You may've heard the expression, "God is a gentleman, He won't go somewhere He's not invited." He waits on us to initiate.

Like the prodigal son story, God the Father waits for the son to return home...but he's watching for his son... Could God have gone and rescued the son? Of course... but He waited for the son to initiate, to turn from his failed life, and to start to return home... There are numerous other examples of God inviting us, and then awaiting our response.

Is He inviting us today to take some new step of faith? How will we respond? The blessings of responding to His invitation are immeasurable...

"If you look for me, I will be found by you." And His blessings will follow!

Father God, help us to sincerely look for You, to seek You, to pursue You... that we may surely find You! Nothing else matters!

"Jesus at the Center"

Israel Haughton

https://youtu.be/XQspvrTBd6E?t=27

October 1

Today's Encouragement is Luke 15:12-13 NLT *"The younger son told his father, 'I want my share of your estate now before you die.' So his father agreed to divide his wealth between his sons. A few days later this younger son packed all his belongings and moved to a distant land, and there he wasted all his money in wild living."*

I want my share –

This son could not have done more damage! He was IN the Father's household, in HIS family, a beloved SON... but he Rejected God's Love and blessings and went his own way... living in sinful self-will.

But when life got hard, the money ran out; he realized his mistake, and he returned to his Father God!

And when he returned... how did God the Father respond to him? With open arms, celebration, gifts of grace and acceptance and even covered him with a beautiful robe, effectively cleansing him from all the filth of his folly!

Notice the Father did all this: mercy, grace, and cleansing before the son "cleaned up his act"! God does all the cleansing... my friends, all we need to do is turn away from our own way, turn to Him and ask!

We all, at times fall away, sometimes willfully, sometimes gradually drifting... isn't it an amazing blessing to realize: God is always ready to welcome us home with open arms?

Father, help us to come to our senses and decide to return to you, realizing that Your Immeasurable Love and Grace are always available to us, when we turn to you.

"When God Ran"

Philips, Craig and Dean

https://youtu.be/-sApe5XWyRQ

October 2

Today's Encouragement is 1 Peter 4:1 NLT *So then, since Christ suffered physical pain, you must arm yourselves with the same attitude he had, and be ready to suffer, too. For if you have suffered physically for Christ, you have finished with sin.*

Arm yourselves –

With the same attitude which Jesus had... what attitude was that?

Is it—be ready to suffer? Remember Jesus' prayer in the garden? *"Father, if you are willing, please take this cup of suffering away from me. Yet I want your will to be done, not mine."* Luke 22:42 NLT

What is encouraging about this message you may ask? Just this- the last sentence *"For if you have suffered physically for Christ, you have finished with sin."*

Don't we all want to be finished with sin? I certainly do! Let's consider this—we are (now, already) cleansed, perfectly, and eternally from all sin by the blood of Christ. God has no record and no memory of it. He looks at us, His deeply loved children, and sees us just as pure as Jesus. So, what does "finished with sin" mean? Since Christ has suffered for us and borne all our sins, why then are we now being told...we too must suffer in order to be finished with sin?

Is it possible that it means: as believers we are to choose—to be finished with and put an end to our earthly human attraction to sin? That is, we are to choose to end, refuse, sever, all the human desire(s) which—against our better (spiritual) judgment, entice us into sin.

We can, by suffering, finish with sin! It's no fun. The suffering involved is real, but ,my friends, sin loses its luster when suffering is involved.

Father, help us to arm ourselves with the attitude of Christ, recognizing it is better to suffer than to surrender to sin.

"The Breakup Song"
Francesca Battestelli
https://youtu.be/kzI_NpWnaLI

October 3

Today's Encouragement is Mark 11:25 NLT *"But when you are praying, first forgive anyone you are holding a grudge against, so that your Father in heaven will forgive your sins, too."*

First forgive –

Here is another example of God teaching us that we must take a step toward Him, we must respond to Him, then He will act. "If – Then."

We are to forgive others first... and then after we forgive others... God forgives us. This is confirmed in Matthew 6:14-15 NLT *"If you forgive those who sin against you, your heavenly Father will forgive you. But if you refuse to forgive others, your Father will not forgive your sins."*

IF you forgive... Then God will.

If we refuse... God will not.

This is a clear, if uncomfortable, truth of the Word.

It's never easy to forgive, some hurts are truly "unforgivable," yet God's truth isn't limited to the small things, like our occasional hurt feelings. This truth applies to even the greatest injustice, betrayal, and even intentional harm done to us my others.

Remember, my friends, Jesus was betrayed, lied about, beaten, whipped, and tortured to death... And His response? *"Father, forgive them..."* Luke 23:34

My friends, forgiveness, extended from us to another person, is our recognition of the immeasurable forgiveness we have already received from God. And when we forgive others... we are set free ourselves! Free from bitterness, resentment, and painful memories. Forgiveness sets us free!

Father God, thank You for the forgiveness you've provided us through Christ. Help us to completely forgive, to let go of our wounds... because we too have hurt others, and yet, You've completely and mercifully forgiven us.

"Forgiveness"

Matthew West

https://youtu.be/h1Lu5udXEZI

October 4

Today's Encouragement is 2 Chronicles 33:13 NLT *And when he prayed, the Lord listened to him and was moved by his request. So the Lord brought Manasseh back to Jerusalem and to his kingdom. Then Manasseh finally realized that the Lord alone is God!*

And when he prayed –

Manasseh was an evil king! He did terrible things, insulting God, and His Temple! He even burned his own son as a sacrifice to idols! He led the people to worship false gods. Although God warned him and the people, they wouldn't listen to God's warning and then suffered terribly at the hand of a ruthless conquering nation...

But——

During this time of suffering, Manasseh, the evil, hard-hearted king who had committed terrible sins... prayed.

He recognized his sin in his suffering and turned to God for help... *And when he prayed, the Lord listened!* God restored him and his people to their homeland! *Then Manasseh finally realized that the Lord alone is God!*

Father, we thank you humbly for your great mercy, and Your grace that is undeserved, because just like Manasseh, we have sinned greatly, and even turned away from you at times. Help us to continually turn to You in prayer! Thank You Father, for your unlimited, undeserved Grace and Love and Mercy!

"When Momma Prayed"
Randy Travis
https://youtu.be/dnWr07WuMM8

October 5

Today's Encouragement is 1 Peter 4:16 NLT *But it is no shame to suffer for being a Christian. Praise God for the privilege of being called by his name!*

No shame to suffer –

I admit, I don't want to even think about it, write about it or consider it. I'd rather it wasn't there. I've ignored, even denied it most of my Christian life... the idea of suffering because of my faith.

You might conjure up thoughts of an atheist roundup of Christians: "Denounce Christ or Die!" with a gun to our heads, but there are many forms of suffering for our faith. It may be exclusion from the gang at work who go out partying while you go home to spend the evening with your family. It could mean suffering the loss of your job because you stood up for your Christian principles at work. The ways we might suffer are unlimited and in today's society—growing!

So, recognize my friends when suffering of one type or another does come along, "It is no shame!"

Rather, the privilege of suffering for His Name is a blessing! For which we can praise God!

Father, please grant us the privilege of praising you whenever we suffer for being Yours.

"The Cause of Christ"

Kari Jobe

https://youtu.be/byHwKMa6NJY

October 6

Today's Encouragement is 2 Corinthians 1:20a NLT *For all of God's promises have been fulfilled in Christ with a resounding 'Yes!'"*

All of God's promises –

Including these:

"For I know the plans I have for you," says the Lord. "They are plans for good and not for disaster, to give you a future and a hope." (Jeremiah 29:11 NLT)

"Do not be afraid or discouraged, for the Lord will personally go ahead of you. He will be with you; he will neither fail you nor abandon you." (Deuteronomy 31:8 NLT)

"No, I will not abandon you as orphans-I will come to you." (John 14:18 NLT)

"For this is how God loved the world: He gave his one and only Son, so that everyone who believes in him will not perish but have eternal life." (John 3:16 NLT)

And many, many more!

God always keeps His promises to us. We trust Him, by faith, to fulfill those promises... and friends, He already has! All His promises have been fulfilled!!! Already!! And this is how... all His promises are "Yes!" in Christ!

Father, please open our eyes, hearts, and understanding to see what You have already done through Christ, in our lives! Help us believe that You already have, and will continue to, fulfill all of Your kind, generous, wise, and amazing promises to Your beloved children.

"Promises Never Fail"

Bethel Music

https://youtu.be/tw5HDkJTS7I

October 7

Today's Encouragement is 1 Timothy 6:12 NLT *Fight the good fight for the true faith. Hold tightly to the eternal life to which God has called you, which you have declared so well before many witnesses.*

Fight the good fight –

Somehow, we often lose sight of the truth that we are in a spiritual battle, a war. We are told to fight, put on the full armor of God (Eph. 6:10-18), take a stand against the devil's schemes, resist him (James 4:7), wage war (1 Tim. 1:18), and wield the sword of the spirit... which is the Word of God (Eph. 6:17). The weapons of our warfare are spiritual and powerful! (2 Corinthians 10:4) But remember they are weapons—for War!

How often have you, like me, thought, "Why is this happening to me?" "Why is this so difficult?" "Why are there so many troubles, difficulties, and trials?"

My friend, read the verse again. We are in a Fight! And we are told to "Fight the good fight for the true faith"! Though we are often provided with periods of rest and peace, we cannot forget that the battle still rages! We are assured of victory... as we fight!!! — not with our anger, not our human schemes and plans... but in God's way, in God's armor, with His sword of the Word, and with His battle plan!

Father, strengthen us for the battle You have placed us in, advise us of Your plan and assure us, once again Lord – that no weapon formed against us will prevail! Amen, in Jesus' Name!

"Don't Tread on Me"
We the Kingdom
https://youtu.be/9dowS2k2TS4

October 8

Today's Encouragement is Mark 12:2 NLT *At the time of the grape harvest, he sent one of his servants to collect his share of the crop.*

To collect his share –

In this parable, Jesus told of a man who planted a vineyard, fully prepared it–winepress, fence, watchtower–everything; then, he leased it to tenants. When he sent someone to collect His share... the tenants refused and beat the man.

Notice this came about when the crop was ripe, when the vineyard was full of a rich harvest, and the landowner only requested His share... from His own vineyard! But the ungrateful, selfish tenants refused—to give Him—His rightful share.

My friends, all that you and I, or anyone else has... comes from and belongs to God! All of heaven and earth are His! He alone gives us the health, the blessings, the ability to earn and accumulate things. All is His!

Will we give Him His share? Remembering that He is the source of everything, every good and perfect gift (James 1:17). Historically, He has taught us that one-tenth from the first fruits of our work, which is our earnings, that is "His share." Will we refuse to give it?

It didn't go well for the selfish, rebellious, and ungrateful tenants of this vineyard... But—in contrast, the blessings of honoring Him with a tithe, the first fruits... are immeasurable! He has even promised to open the windows of Heaven for us! (Malachi 3:10)

Father God, help us relinquish our selfish control of all that You have given us. Help us to recognize that You alone are the source of everything good!

"With All I Am"

Hillsong

https://youtu.be/qZ_-5JplSVg

October 9

Today's Encouragement is James 1:12 NLT *God blesses those who patiently endure testing and temptation. Afterward they will receive the crown of life that God has promised to those who love him.*

Endure Testing and Temptation –

We all want to be among those that God blesses. We seek Him and long to be close to Him! So, how do we experience His blessings? One way, James provides for us—Patiently endure testing and temptation.

He goes on to explain (v14-15) *Temptation comes from our own desires, which entice us and drag us away. These desires give birth to sinful actions. And when sin is allowed to grow, it gives birth to death.*

It begins within us, our own desires in our hearts and minds... which entice, tempt, and drag us away... away from God, away from right, away from truth. And these desires then give birth to sinful acts... which then give birth to death. It's the process of sin. It can take only milliseconds, or it can take months. Yet the process is the same....

Being close to God, seeking Him, honoring Him is the greatest (only?) defense we have against temptation.

So, how do we endure temptation? Refusal, just say "no": flee from it, turn away, remove all triggers, pray, and confess, there are numerous spiritual tools we can use. But at times my friend, we simply must patiently endure testing and temptation. The only way to do this is with God's help... praying for His mercy, deliverance, and strength which He has promised us He will always provide!

Thank You Father God, for always teaching us Truth. For always providing a way out, a way through, and a way home for us. Help us when tempted, to cry out to You for help, and to patiently endure as we trust in You to help us. Thank You for Your innumerable blessings. We pray in Jesus' Name.

"While I Wait"
Lincoln Brewster
https://youtu.be/NswPPVgMaPE

October 10

Today's Encouragement is Mark 14:38 NLT *"Keep watch and pray, so that you will not give in to temptation. For the spirit is willing, but the body is weak."*

Keep watch and pray –

We don't need much convincing, do we? We've all recognized this truth within ourselves; we have the desire to be faithful, to honor God, to live right, to do as Jesus would do. But we all find this verse to be true... our flesh, the thoughts, and actions of humans, are weak... unable—on their own—to resist temptation... "We all have sinned" (Romans 3:23).

And the answer? Keep watch and pray! So that... In order not to—fall into temptation- we keep watch and pray. We understand prayer fairly well, but what does it mean to "keep watch"?

Consider a watchman in ancient Israel, standing guard for his shift on a tall watchtower, keeping watch for any sign of the enemy approaching. He would scan the horizon for any signs, he would listen for any sounds, all his senses would be heightened while on duty... to any sign of danger. This is keeping watch!

So, for us today, could it mean being aware of the places the enemy is likely to attack...the plans and the tools he uses, our weakest areas, the sound of his tempting voice?

Being aware of his ways makes us better able to keep watch! Being ignorant of his ways, or paying no attention to them, will ultimately make us his victims.

Father God, help us to always pray and also to keep watch, to be good watchmen, aware of the ways of our enemy, his strengths, and our own vulnerabilities.

"Watch and Pray"

Twila Paris

https://youtu.be/qzrapujYRS8

October 11

Today's Encouragement is Mark 12:34 NLT *Realizing how much the man understood, Jesus said to him, "You are not far from the Kingdom of God." And after that, no one dared to ask him any more questions.*

Not far –

The scribe had just said that to love God and your neighbor is more important than obeying the Law. He knew this to be true, yet... as Jesus said, he wasn't quite "there yet"... he was not far, he was close but...

What else is there besides knowing this truth? Love God and love others? These are the two greatest commandments. Isn't knowing this enough?

Well... No. The Kingdom of God is ruled by our King Jesus, and belief in Him as Lord, Savior, Son of God... is The essential final step into the Kingdom.

Knowing about God and Jesus, acknowledging His truths, reading the Bible, going to church, and even doing what He says, all these things can get us close... to this same point of being '"not far";... However, it is only Faith in Him, belief in Who He is, reliance on as him as the One who saves us from our sin...which brings us fully and finally into The Kingdom of God!

Father God, open our eyes to Your Truth that thinking, knowing, and doing are not enough... but only belief in Jesus as our Savior brings us into Your salvation.

"Our God Saves"

Paul Baloche

https://youtu.be/q6um7z4qvY8

October 12

Today's Encouragement is 2 Timothy 2:25 NLT *Gently instruct those who oppose the truth. Perhaps God will change those people's hearts, and they will learn the truth.*

Gently instruct –

Paul writes these words of counsel to the younger Timothy. He's advised him previously in verses 23-24 to avoid arguments, not quarrel, be kind, and be patient... and here he begins with the wisdom of his years and his walk with God... "This is what you are to do instead of fighting with others... gently instruct...."

With patience, calmness, and confidence, gently instruct...

And then, not in arguing or quarreling, but through gentle teaching... perhaps, (there are no guarantees here) it may be that God (God's work, not ours) will change their hearts and they will learn the Truth.

My friends, it is God's work to change hearts, to open eyes to His Truth. Yes, He uses us to gently instruct, so that He may work as He chooses... but He doesn't want us to fight, argue, or quarrel. We fight when we mistakenly believe it is all up to us!

Rather, we are called to calmly plant seeds... and then God determines which seeds take root and grow in faith, and which seeds, even though faithfully planted, even with gentle instruction, do not take root.

Father God, thank You for giving us the clear responsibility to share Your Love, Your Truth, Your Mercy with the people around us. Help us do so with gentle instruction, trusting that You will change hearts as You know best.

"Change My Heart, O God"
Maranatha Music
https://youtu.be/IlSmG-_eJTU

October 13

Today's Encouragement is 2 Timothy 2:24-25 NLT *A servant of the Lord must not quarrel but must be kind to everyone, be able to teach, and be patient with difficult people. Gently instruct those who oppose the truth. Perhaps God will change those people's hearts, and they will learn the truth.*

Servant of the Lord –

Yesterday we considered our responsibility to gently instruct, today let's think about how we are instructed by others.

Paul's instructions can be used to teach us both perspectives... that of a teacher/instructor, and also that of a student/learner. The opportunity here is to recognize how a true servant of the Lord will teach us as students (we are all still learning!).

Friends, a genuine "servant of the Lord" will teach us God's Truth with kindness, patience (for we are all difficult people at times), and with gentle instruction. This servant will recognize that it is God who leads us to the Truth, and not the teacher/preacher, nor their power, nor persuasive arguments.

Is it possible that – we can only become—those hearts whom God changes—when we have such true "servants of the Lord"—kindly, patiently, and gently instructing us in the Truth!

Father God, grant your people the wisdom and discernment, to recognize the gentle instruction of Your servants who teach us. Help us avoid those teachers who are not gentle, patient, kind, or who resort to quarrels and arguments. We need Your Spirit to change our hearts, not man's arguments or persuasive teaching.

"Speak, O Lord"
Keith and Kristyn Getty
https://youtu.be/my90e3a_nlM

October 14

Today's Encouragement is John 1:4-5 NLT *The Word gave life to everything that was created, and his life brought light to everyone. The light shines in the darkness, and the darkness can never extinguish it.*

The Light shines –

These amazing words at the very beginning of John's gospel reveal so much truth. "The Word" as used here describes Jesus; it is He that gave life to everything! And He gave Light to everything also!

He clearly stated this truth in John 8:12 NLT *Jesus spoke to the people once more and said, "I am the light of the world. If you follow me, you won't have to walk in darkness, because you will have the light that leads to life."*

He Is The Light! And by following Him we are free from the darkness!

Darkness is a metaphor for sin; it is the time of day (but not the only time) when crimes and sins are committed, when we think we might get away with it.... But the clear Light of Day exposes the reality! Sin cannot hide very well in the Light.

In His Light, His Presence, the truth is revealed, and our sin, and our need for Someone to save us from ourselves are laid bare. And my friends... (v5) the darkness can never extinguish THE LIGHT! Jesus is always Victorious!

Father God, please help us to choose to walk in the Light, the Light of Jesus.

"In the Light"

DC Talk

https://youtu.be/e2qzxY5a37o

October 15

Today's Encouragement is Romans 2:4 NLT *Don't you see how wonderfully kind, tolerant, and patient God is with you? Does this mean nothing to you? Can't you see that his kindness is intended to turn you from your sin?*

His kindness –

The ESV translates the last sentence as ... *God's kindness is meant to lead you to repentance?*

Our repentance, our recognition of sin, and our resulting desire and decision to turn away from sin and turn To God... this is genuine repentance and only results from God's Kindness!

Friends, our God is not angry, nor vengeful, nor bent on punishing people for sin. He IS Love! Love is His character... it's who He is! And His love is demonstrated (perfectly through Jesus) and through His Kindness! In kindness—He made a way for us to be cleansed and reborn and granted eternal life!

Beware those who focus on fear, wrath, anger, or other attributes of God. Friends, it is His forgiveness we need... His Amazing Grace... His Kindness and His Love. This brings us to repentance, helps us to turn away from our selfish ways and to turn to Him!

Father God, we are grateful for Your amazing kindness for us. Help us to experience Your kindness and love more fully each day, and so, to turn toward You, and turn away from our selfish ways.

"Your Kindness"
Leslie Phillips
https://youtu.be/xeZe1NzjNoQ

October 16

Today's Encouragement is 2 Corinthians 5:21 ESV *For our sake he made him to be sin who knew no sin, so that in him we might become the righteousness of God.*

The righteousness of God –

So that...

In Him (Jesus)... *We might become...*

The righteousness of God...???

Certainly, we are nothing without Him, indistinguishable from the mass of humanity, going nowhere, accomplishing nothing of lasting value, and living a life of meaninglessness. But IN HIM... in Christ, my friends, Everything is different, everything is renewed, and granted significance! We become significant! And that—not slightly, but vastly, beyond even our imagination!

This passage proclaims the unimaginable truth... in Him, we become...

The Righteousness of God!

How is this possible? Only by Jesus, the One who took our place... who became sin! He became our Sin! Took it on Himself...

And the exchange, my friends, the unimaginable exchange...?

When He took our sin, He stepped into our place... then—We stepped into... His Righteousness, into HIS place! ...Into perfect righteousness (right standing with God!)

Because of Jesus becoming our sin, we are... now, already, the Righteousness of God. We represent Him to this world, as just described in v20, we are His ambassadors! His Righteousness!

Father God, honestly this is just too wonderful for us to comprehend... first, that Jesus would take upon Himself All our sin, and second, in this unimaginable divine exchange, He would allow us to become Your Righteousness! Help us to accept this overwhelming, astounding Truth Lord!

"Divine Exchange"

Charity Gayle

https://youtu.be/MTYjklpNlsI

October 17

Today's Encouragement is John 15:4 ESV *"Abide in me, and I in you. As the branch cannot bear fruit by itself, unless it abides in the vine, neither can you, unless you abide in me."*

Abide in me –

He repeats it here and in the following verses... because it is so critically important that we abide In Him so that He will abide in us.

Other translations use the words: dwell, remain, or live in me. The Amplified reads, "being vitally united to"...

Friend, this is an invitation from Jesus to be IN Him, to live IN Him, to be vitally united TO Him, to remain, to dwell... always IN Him! This is what Jesus offers us, what He desires for us... to be in such a real and uninhibited relationship with Him so that He lives in us, and we live in Him!

Father God, help us to desire this closeness with Jesus so that we are only alive with Him, abiding, dwelling IN Him... this is our prayer!

"Abide"

Aaron Williams

https://youtu.be/BLDEt9KP2O0

October 18

Today's Encouragement is Isaiah 30:19-21 NLT *O people of Zion, who live in Jerusalem, you will weep no more. He will be gracious if you ask for help. He will surely respond to the sound of your cries. Though the Lord gave you adversity for food and suffering for drink, he will still be with you to teach you. You will see your teacher with your own eyes. Your own ears will hear him. Right behind you a voice will say, "This is the way you should go," whether to the right or to the left.*

See your teacher –

Notice the process, the progression in this passage...

- Stop weeping, Ask for help, He will be gracious, and He will respond Even though we have adversity and suffering He will still be with us. He will teach us, We will recognize Him as our teacher with our spiritual eyes, We will hear Him with our spiritual ears. He will speak to us and show us the way to go!

So often when we are given "adversity for food and suffering for drink," experiencing the troubles and trials in this life... we ask:

- "Where's God?"
- "Why is this all happening to me?"
- "What did I ever do to deserve this?"
- "What am I doing wrong!"

Remember what Jesus said?... *"Here on earth you will have many trials and sorrows. But take heart because I have overcome the world."* (John 16:33b NLT)

Father God, help us to continue to look to You for our help, for wisdom, for your Healing Hand, even though our troubles linger longer than we want, trials continue to press in on us, and we wonder if You have abandoned us... Help us to pray, Trusting You, and to remember that You have overcome this world and have promised to show us the way to go.

"I Am Not Alone"
Kari Jobe
https://youtu.be/MbbCGqK6uNc

October 19

Today's Encouragement is Hebrews 6:10 NLT *For God is not unjust. He will not forget how hard you have worked for him and how you have shown your love to him by caring for other believers, as you still do.*

He will not forget –

God will not forget or ignore the Love we have shown to Him, by loving His people; by caring for other believers. This is our "hard work" for Him—caring for others!

Now people (all of us) are fickle, we often forget, overlook, miss, even deny the kindnesses of others. And those of us who strive to live the Gospel, caring for other believers, honoring God, and working for Him... we are all going to be very unappreciated by people in this life!

Rarely someone may say a heartfelt "thank you," but generally... because we are all sinners who are saved by Grace alone, we are an ungrateful people. This is just a reality, not a condemnation.

But God!—He will NOT forget! He remembers the work we have done for Him, and still do... the work of loving and caring for others!

In Matthew 6:1-4, Jesus teaches that we are to do our good deeds, acts of kindness, caring for others, not to be seen by them, nor to be recognized by others, but in order to honor God! And He is the One we want to respect, and He is the One who will reward us! Our recognition is not from people!

But God will NOT FORGET the love we have shown Him by caring for others!

Thank You, Lord, that You are Just. You remember the good that we do... and You blot out our sins with the precious blood of Jesus. You are so very Good!

"Build Your Kingdom Here"
Rend Collective
https://youtu.be/Y6iVLeNfl2U

October 20

Today's Encouragement is Luke 7:13 NLT *When the Lord saw her, his heart overflowed with compassion. "Don't cry!" he said.*

With compassion –

There's something beautiful about this word—"Compassion."... Here, it is coming from Jesus' heart... to this grieving woman....

In numerous other passages, the compassion of Jesus is clearly displayed. Matthew 9:36 NLT *When he saw the crowds, he had compassion on them because they were confused and helpless, like sheep without a shepherd.* And Matthew 14:14 NLT *Jesus saw the huge crowd as he stepped from the boat, and he had compassion on them and healed their sick.*

Often Jesus was surrounded by people needing Him, a healing touch, a word of hope, food for their soul... but He never was overwhelmed by this, nor exasperated by the needy crowd.

No, instead, He was repeatedly... Moved to Compassion!

What a beautiful and clear description of the perfect Heart of Jesus. He was, and He still is Compassionate!

Friends, when we are pleading on our knees—whether in brokenness, sorrow, or desperation—Jesus hears, He sees... and He has Compassion for you and me!

Thank You, Jesus, for the beautiful compassion You have for us! Help us, Lord, to trust in, and rest in... Your Kindness, Compassion, and Grace.

"The Lord is Gracious and Compassionate"
Vineyard Worship
https://youtu.be/7Xzk9qtlvuo

October 21

Today's Encouragement is John 14:13 ESV *"Whatever you ask in my name, this I will do, that the Father may be glorified in the Son."*

In my Name –

His Name is not "magic"—it's far greater... It is Holy!

It is the Name above all names!

At His Name every life will submit to His majesty, power, glory...

Even those who denied Him recognized the mysterious power of His Name and prohibited His disciples from speaking or teaching—in His Name (Acts 4:17-18)!

Powerful doesn't adequately describe His Name. Nor does Majestic, nor Glorious, every word or phrase, every book, or even an entire library—all are woefully inadequate to describe His Name! Mere human words, thoughts, and understanding are all futile attempts, but fail to adequately describe Him and His great Name!

This Holy Name is—Jesus...

The greatest Name in the Universe...

Father God, thank You for introducing us to the Wonderful, Beautiful Name of Jesus! Thank You that, because of the Power of than Name of Jesus, in His Name, nothing is impossible! Father God, thank You that as we merely speak His Name in faith, His Grace rules over every situation. Help us to Speak His Name over all our needs.

(please don't miss this song!)

"I Speak Jesus"

Charity Gayle

https://youtu.be/SV4sYN173HY

October 22

Today's Encouragement is Lamentations 3:21-23 NLT Yet I still dare to hope when I remember this: The faithful love of the Lord never ends! His mercies never cease. Great is his faithfulness; his mercies begin afresh each morning.

Hope when I remember –

Jeremiah wrote the sorrow-filled book of Lamentations to express his grief and the sorrow of the nation when they were suffering greatly at the hands of their enemies. The book is hard to read because of this great sorrow. But!– In the midst of this heavy grey fog of grief...emerges this brilliant jewel of God's Truth!

This is my Hope-

He is faithful to us!

His faithful Love never ends! His mercies never stop!

His faithfulness to us is Great! Far beyond our ability to understand! His mercy for us is renewed every morning, it is inexhaustible!

In the darkest time of his life, as his homeland, the nation he loved, plunged into a death spiral. There was no food, no worship, no wealth, no joy, no health, no kindness, nor compassion... when all around him, all hope, seemed lost...

Then he remembered...

The faithful love of the Lord never ends...

Then he had - Hope!

Father God, only You can spark the fire of Hope in the hearts of those who have lost all hope. We all face dark times; some are unimaginable in their despair... Speak to us Your words of Hope! Thank You Father for Your Faithfulness, Mercy, and Love for us!

"Great Is His Faithfulness"

Charity Gayle

https://youtu.be/MINFdzCqGrU

October 23

Today's Encouragement is Luke 11:9-10 NLT *"And so I tell you, keep on asking, and you will receive what you ask for. Keep on seeking, and you will find. Keep on knocking, and the door will be opened to you. For everyone who asks, receives. Everyone who seeks, finds. And to everyone who knocks, the door will be opened."*

Keep on –

His disciples asked him (v1) "Lord, teach us to pray..."' And he taught them the Lord's Prayer... then immediately He relates a parable about being persistent, consistent, determined, dedicated... in asking, praying for what you need. And then in v9-10, *"Keep On!"*

It seems almost impudent, almost rude, almost demanding, the way the parable reads... and yet He then clearly instructs us—"Keep on! Keep on Asking God for what you need!"

Friends, Jesus is telling us that God responds - when we Keep On... Jesus told us to "Keep On"!

We too often give our prayers one shot and then we move on– in the next breath to another prayer need, then another. Now, of course, God does NOT get tired of hearing our prayers! He is not a man who has a short fuse or limited patience... He IS Love; He is Our Loving, Kind, Patient, Perfect, Almighty Heavenly Father (there aren't enough words to describe Him!)

So, we are wise to pray with persistence, with consistency, with diligence, with intention, with focus and confidence... because He told us to!

The "when" is up to Him, it may be Moments, Days, Years, Decades, a lifetime... but all time is the same to our God... so we just trust Him, He knows the absolute best way and best time to answer!

So, my Friends,—Pray! And Keep On Praying!

Father, Thank You that you never tire of hearing us pray. Thank You that You are attuned to our prayers, grant us strength and faith to persist in prayer.

"Keep Praying"
Maverick City Music
https://youtu.be/fGaAIDKhGmw

October 24

Today's Encouragement is Luke 12:35 NLT *"Be dressed for service and keep your lamps burning,"*

Keep your lamps burning –

Jesus taught us eternal truths, using common examples and parables as tools—so that we might understand. Not everyone did or does understand what He taught, but for those who have the ears to hear and eyes to see, His truths were, and are still, very clear.

Luke 12:37a *"The servants who are ready and waiting for his return will be rewarded."* This counsel to, "Be Ready"! follows His teachings on these truths:

- Seek God's Kingdom
- Do not be afraid
- Give to the needy
- Provide treasures for yourself in Heaven.

Following these messages, He then advises us... Be Ready!

How do we keep our lamps burning? Through worship, through relationship with Him, through Bible study, through honest spiritual conversations with other believers, listening to biblical teaching that inspires your faith... there are many ways to keep the spiritual fire within stoked. But friends, it is not automatic; it is a decision, a choice we make... to continue to believe, to keep on believing, trusting in Him and in His mercy and His immeasurable love for us. Keep your lamp burning strong in faith. And remember to ask Him for His perfect help with this or any other spiritual need, because He loves you....

Father God, help us to be ready, to be doing what You have taught us, to be faithful, so that whenever You call upon us for service, and finally, when Jesus returns, we are ready, dressed for service with our lamps burning!

"Ghost"
Crowder
https://youtu.be/g5QcXlfa44s

October 25

Today's Encouragement is Psalm 11:7 ESV *For the Lord is righteous; he loves righteous deeds; the upright shall behold his face.*

He loves righteous deeds –

Of course, we know that our good deeds do not earn us a ticket to heaven, we can never "do enough" to be saved - for salvation is by faith. (Eph. 2:8)

And of course, we know not to do our good deeds to be seen by people, because there is no real lasting value in that. (Matt 6:1)

But, my friends, consider this verse for a moment... *The Lord is righteous ... and He loves righteous deeds....*

Because we belong to Him, and because we love Him (the greatest commandment) we want to bring a smile to His face, we want to please Him... and here is one way to do so... by doing things which are right and good... not to be seen by others, not so that we earn our salvation... but simply to please our Loving, Perfect, Father God!

Righteous deeds can take many forms, here are just a few examples from the Bible:

- The woman who anointed Jesus' feet
- A cup of cold water
- An offering of a few coins (all she had) Forgiving others
- Any kindness done for others
- The possibilities of good, right, and loving deeds are endless!

And when we do anything in this way... God is pleased! Because He loves righteous deeds!

Loving Father, help us to Love You well. Work in our hearts, renew them, so that kindness, generosity, and Your Perfect Love for others flows through us! We ask that such righteous deeds become second nature to us. Because we Love You—we want to please you, our Wonderful Father.

"For the One"
Jenn Johnson
https://youtu.be/2Y1ROPUdUNU

October 26

Today's Encouragement is John 14:6a NLT *Jesus told him, "I am the way, the truth, and the life."*

The Truth –

Jesus spoke the truth, always! And here He explains... that He, Himself, IS the Truth! He doesn't say, as some may think, "I know the Truth," nor "I can teach you some true things," nor "I've become enlightened, so I have many truths to teach you," No! He clearly and simply made this amazingly bold proclamation of... Who He Is!—I AM!

As God described Himself to Moses at the burning bush... I AM! So also, Jesus proclaims... I AM! Jesus IS The Truth!

It's challenging to describe this concept... because it is God we're thinking about, after all, and who are we to try to understand Him! Yet we have this wonderful gift... the Book He gave us...; so that we are given the gift of being able to understand some things about Him!

And Jesus is The Truth!

His nature as God and Man,— His words... every single word... is Truth!

His works... every single deed... is Truth!

His emotions... compassion, sympathy, even His anger... is Truth!

Everything about Him is Truth!

Father God, so many are seeking truth, in so many ways... help us to know! And help us to show others, that Jesus IS The Truth, and He is the Way and the Life!

"Christ Our Hope in Life and Death"

Keith and Kristyn Getty

https://youtu.be/OibIi1rz7mw

October 27

Today's Encouragement is Mark 4:17 NLT ...*"But since they don't have deep roots, they don't last long. They fall away as soon as they have problems or are persecuted for believing God's word."*

Fall away –

Sometimes in this spiritual battle between God and evil, we will see casualties of war. Some choose to follow Christ, enduring the challenges and battles of the Christian Life, and are victorious! Sadly, there are those who choose one of many "other ways" and are lost to the enemy. The road of Faith in Christ is narrow, but the way is broad that leads to destruction. (Matt.7:13-14)

Sometimes these casualties are folks who attend our churches. Those who run into problems in life and come to church looking for answers... but when troubles come (Mark 4:17) they fall away.

Sometimes it's members of our family: a child who chooses to turn away from parents and never returns, a spouse who chooses themselves and their own way and leaves. They fall away.

Friends, we all have choices in this life, and we are constantly making choices, some minor and some major. But always we 1) have the ability to choose, and 2) will deal with the consequences of those choices.

Finally, please notice the missing element for these who fall away... they do not have deep roots! We can deepen our roots, my friends—by choosing to trust, to pray, to absorb His

Word, to worship, to praise, to allow God to rule our lives, hearts, and minds... by asking Him!

Father God, may we all be among the faithful, who do not fall away when trouble or persecution for believing You comes our way. Help us Lord, to sink our roots—deep in You—to stand firm in Faith in Jesus!

"For Your Splendor"
Christy Nockels
https://youtu.be/DC_QCKCuAM8

October 28

Today's Encouragement is Luke 4:1 NLT *Then Jesus, full of the Holy Spirit, returned from the Jordan River. He was led by the Spirit in the wilderness.*

The wilderness –

- Moses herded sheep for 40 years, (Acts 7:30)
- Israel spent 40 years in the wilderness, (Acts 7:36)
- Jesus spent 40 days in the wilderness (Luke 4)
- Paul stayed 3 years in the wilderness (Galatians. 1:17-18)

The time spent in the wilderness is symbolic of a spiritually dry, difficult, challenging, sometimes life threatening—and for believers— life-transforming experience. It may be days, months, or —years. The length of time and the circumstances differ, the degree of isolation (human and/or spiritual), confusion, temptation, suffering and even more... will differ.

Is it possible that we all will spend some time there... in our own spiritual wilderness? Time spent waiting on God to do His work within our hearts and minds. A time of waiting, learning to trust Him, learning to hear Him—dealing with doubts, sin, fears, loneliness—the list is unlimited. Even Jesus spent 40 days there....

Some of us have been through such "wilderness" times, some of us may have more ahead of us, and some may be there now. Wherever we are in our spiritual journey, He is With you! He has promised to be!

Deuteronomy 31:8 NLT *"Do not be afraid or discouraged, for the Lord will personally go ahead of you. He will be with you; he will neither fail you nor abandon you."*

Help us, Father, to trust You even when,—especially when—we are in a wilderness of sorrow, grief, confusion, isolation, questioning or pain. You have promised never to abandon us. Thank You!

"In the Wilderness"
The Isaacs
https://youtu.be/2tRb1-g1xKA

October 29

Today's Encouragement is Luke 19:48b NLT ...*all the people hung on every word he said.*

Every word He said –

This verse describes the people who followed Jesus, they heard Him speak... and "hung on every word"! Today's song describes "standing on every promise of Your Word."

What are we hanging on? Standing on?

Is it God's Word, His Truth, His promises? Jesus Himself is The Word!

We each choose what we stand on or cling to... Is it the Truth of God's Perfect Love for us, revealed through Jesus?... Or is it something else? A philosophy of some person? A religion which requires us to do things to earn Gods favor? Maybe a belief system we've created for ourselves, picking the best pieces of other options to create a patchwork concept of our own? The possibilities are endless. And every other option fails!

Yet there is only One Way. The God-Man Jesus said in John 14:6 NLT *"I am the way, the truth, and the life. No one can come to the Father except through me."*

He has made many wonderful promises to us and given us The Word and His Words of Life.

Father God, help us to daily "hang on" Your Word, and to "stand on" Your every promise! Thank You, Lord, for Your Word!

"Every Promise of Your Word"
Keith and Kristyn Getty
https://youtu.be/0DpSIIiWkEM

October 30

Today's Encouragement is Isaiah 26:3 NLT *You will keep in perfect peace all who trust in you, all whose thoughts are fixed on you!*

Perfect Peace –

1 Peter 5:7 NLT *Give all your worries and cares to God, for he cares about you.*

Philippians 4:6-7 NLT *Don't worry about anything; instead, pray about everything. Tell God what you need and thank him for all he has done. Then you will experience God's peace, which exceeds anything we can understand. His peace will guard your hearts and minds as you live in Christ Jesus.*

Do you see it? God's Peace, His Perfect Peace... is available to us!

It isn't automatic, it isn't normal for us—harried, fretting, obsessing humans— but it is available to those who trust God! How?

Review these verses (and there are many others) which reveal to us the key choices we must make in order to experience (Philippians. 4:7) God's Perfect Peace *which exceeds anything we can understand* !

Some excerpts from these verses:

Trust Him, Fix your thoughts on Him, Give Him (release to Him) all your worries and cares. Don't worry—instead Pray! Tell Him your needs and Be grateful, thanking Him for everything He has done!

We've been given complete forgiveness and eternal life, for this alone we can be eternally grateful!

Notice the result of these choices... Then—after we have done these things, made these choices... then—we will experience God's Peace!

Father, Your kindness and blessings for us are truly wonderful, and far beyond our understanding! Help us to choose to live in Your Peace!

"Peace"

We The Kingdom

https://youtu.be/uW6xcmqfiY4

October 31

Today's Encouragement is Philippians 4:11 NLT *Not that I was ever in need, for I have learned how to be content with whatever I have.*

How to be content –

Notice that Paul writes, "I have learned.... This contentment then, isn't really a natural outlook, or an attitude, nor is it the modern term "worldview... rather, it is a learned trait, a skill, a developed perspective of a healthy mind and spirit.

Contentment is a wonderful blessing! To be at peace with who you are, what you have, who you are around, with every circumstance about you... how wonderful would that be?

This Contentment isn't giddy optimism, blinded to the needs around us or to our own need to change, adapt, and improve. It isn't complacency, lazily refusing to better ourselves or our situation. This is Personal Peace— Accepting everyone and everything as it is... recognizing God is in full control, and that He provides for our every need.

Even in our most dire circumstances, in pain, sorrow, illness, loneliness... even then... Contentment can be ours!

Read the gracious wisdom of Philippians 4:4-13 (especially 6-7) and you will clearly see the process of—Learning How to be Content!

Thank You, Father God, that You desire Your children to live in Peace, and to be Content with the blessings You have granted us in recognizing that You know exactly what we need, and that You are our Source!

"It Is Well"

Bethel Music

https://youtu.be/8Wb_WD1emFQ

November 1

Today's Encouragement is Psalm 14:2 NLT *The Lord looks down from heaven on the entire human race; he looks to see if anyone is truly wise, if anyone seeks God.*

If anyone seeks God –

The Lord, Himself, looks down... He Is looking for us!! You and I are among those who seek God... we read His Word, we praise and worship Him, we pray and Hope in His every promise... We are among His chosen, adopted, children! We are immeasurably blessed! And as this passage reveals... He looks to see if we are seeking Him, if we are truly wise! He's actively checking in on us to see how we're doing!

Now, my friends, this is not some harsh schoolmaster, a legalistic tyrant watching for some infraction of their own laws... No! This is our Kind, Loving Father!

He looks to see who is wisely seeking Him!... And His response? When He sees us seeking Him, in any number of valid ways.... His response?

Is it possible... that His response... Is Joy?

Could it be? Could we be a source of Joy to our Heavenly Father?

Luke 15:20 NLT *"So he returned home to his father. And while he was still a long way off, his father saw him coming. Filled with love and compassion, he ran to his son, embraced him, and kissed him."*

Father God, Your Love for us is far beyond our understanding! That You would seek out those people who seek You, that You would watch for us, see us turning to You, in prayer, in worship, in studying Your Word, with searching hearts. That you would embrace us so warmly... it is too wonderful for us to understand. Help us, Lord, to accept... to trust... to believe... that You Love us that much!

"How He Loves Us"

Crowder

https://youtu.be/aCBOF21Xx44

November 2

Today's Encouragement is Luke 21:37-38 NLT *Every day Jesus went to the Temple to teach, and each evening he returned to spend the night on the Mount of Olives. The crowds gathered at the Temple early each morning to hear him.*

Early each morning –

Notice the specific elements of this passage:

Every day Jesus taught - Every night he rested

Early each morning - the people gathered To hear Him - the words of life

My friends, when we choose to hear His words... every day... early each morning... we join this great cloud of witnesses (Hebrews 12:1) who over the centuries have sought to hear His words, every day, early each morning.

There is something about -

Early morning—it's quiet, uninterrupted, it sets the pace, atmosphere, perspective of the upcoming day, starts us off right, strengthens and encourages us for the challenges we will have this day.

And something about -

Every day—our consistency is an indication of the priority we place upon our relationship with Him.

There's a biblical concept called, The first fruits. All the acceptable offerings, which God asked us to surrender to Him, are the best, the first of everything. The first and best fruit from the orchard, the first and best animals born, the first and best of our lives... are His! We don't really "give" anything to God... He already has it all... but by our choice, as we acknowledge His ownership, and surrender our control, our "perceived ownership," possession of our lives, time, money, family, career - everything - In doing this, we are telling Him, "We recognize Your complete authority over this... over all things!"

Early (First)— **Each day** (Consistently)

Father God, may we place You First each day. May our song—and our hearts, minds, and spirits—rise to You early in the morning. As we listen to You through Your Word.

"Holy, Holy, Holy"

Selah

https://youtu.be/SL8p7NtjSK4

November 3

Today's Encouragement is Psalm 46:10 NLT *"Be still, and know that I am God! I will be honored by every nation. I will be honored throughout the world."*

Be Still –

These are God's words to us... of course... yet please listen carefully to hear His Heart in this.

Be Still! Quiet Yourself! Calm Down! Stop!

And Know... and Recognize... that I AM God!—Creator, Master, All-Knowing, All-Present, All-Powerful— I am In Complete Control!

Friends, we get so caught up in our minds... our busy-ness... our tiny worlds... we must learn to Be Still!

To quiet our souls— *I have calmed and quieted myself, like a weaned child....* (Psalm 131:2a NLT) Because God IS!

God created us for times of Rest... we are designed by Him to rest for a third of each day and instructed to rest one day a week... too often, we ignore this reality, and we wear ourselves out in frantic busy-ness.

God's Love for us, draws us, invites us, to come before Him and to Rest in His presence, to be Still and Trust Him. We choose: Rest in Him... or Work ourselves to death.

Father God, we are helpless without Your power at work within us— Help us to Rest in You, to Be Still, to quiet ourselves in Your Presence. To Trust You and to Worship You!

"Still"

Hillary Scott

https://youtu.be/APAgH2gfNHU

November 4

Today's Encouragement is Luke 20:26 NLT *So they failed to trap him by what he said in front of the people. Instead, they were amazed by his answer, and they became silent.*

Amazed by his answer –

The entire chapter of Luke 20 describes the desperate attempts of the religious leaders to trap Jesus in His words. They failed!

Even in their brilliant plotting and obsessive diligence, they failed! Jesus always pointed out their errors and misunderstandings in their questions and accusations. So much so that they weren't just silenced by His answer... they were Amazed!

We know that a few of these religious leaders began to trust Him, but most chose to protect their own power, to not risk the loss of their "control," to continue to attack this man who was teaching love, kindness, and compassion and healing all who came to Him— claiming to be God's Son....

Yet even they, these blinded, self-righteous, murderous people... were still... Amazed!

Amazed is the right response to Jesus. He is Amazing! His Love, His Mercy, His Grace, His Presence, His Power... everything about Him truly is Astounding! He is truly Amazing!

Father God, may we always recognize Who You are, Who Jesus is, and may we also stay amazed by You!

"Stay Amazed"
Gateway Worship
https://youtu.be/hB8sXDLs8nM

November 5

Today's Encouragement is Genesis 4:26b NLT *...At that time people first began to worship the Lord by name.*

First began to worship –

When Adam and Eve walked with God in the Garden, there was complete, open communication. No secrets, no unasked questions, and no unanswered question. They had unlimited access to God Himself.

Just as the entire creation was perfect, the garden was perfect, the man and woman were perfect, so also God's relationship with His Creation, His favorite creation, man, and woman... was... perfect!

Yet, we sinned! We chose to doubt God, to think for ourselves, to listen to the seductive questioning of God's Goodness, to disobey Him... clearly and intentionally, and to choose Sin.

Humanity lost its perfect relationship with God in that moment... time went on, and a few generations later, we see this amazing statement... "At that time people first began to worship the Lord by name."

The intimacy of the Garden was gone, by our sinful choice... But!... Because we have an innate need to be in relationship with God... we began to worship Him, to call upon Him by Name!

Father God, help us to understand the depth of our need to be in right relationship with You. Because You alone are worthy of being Worshipped. We choose to honor You with our Worship, now and always.

"When I Look into Your Holiness"
Integrity Music
https://youtu.be/jfIT3rooJWQ

November 6

Today's Encouragement is 2 Corinthians 12:8-9 NLT *Three different times I begged the Lord to take it away. Each time he said, "My grace is all you need. My power works best in weakness." So now I am glad to boast about my weaknesses, so that the power of Christ can work through me.*

My power works best –

In weakness? Really Lord? Aren't we supposed to always be ... Victorious? Conquering everything? Having everything figured out? Having all the answers?... Through prayer and Your presence in our lives... free from all weaknesses? Evidently Not!

Paul's deeply personal confession of this thorn in his flesh is tremendously vulnerable. He's admitting to God and believers through the ages, that ... try as he might... presumably through prayer, fasting, pleading, begging God "to take it away...."

And God said "No." This painful weakness, which was possibly a sin or an illness, allowed him to realize—He was not God. God knows more than we do; God is strong and in complete control, and we are weak!

My friends, when we struggle in prayer, begging God to take it away, as Jesus did in the garden on the night he was arrested... remember the end of His prayer... "nevertheless, not my will but Yours be done."

At some time, perhaps each of us will come to a point in our journey of faith, where we come to accept that the weaknesses, which we have fought so hard to overcome. This point is intentionally designated to keep our spiritual pride under control... and our need for God's grace, clearly prevalent in our hearts and minds.

Father God, You can do anything, including allowing our weaknesses to demonstrate Your strength. Thank You for Your Grace, cleansing us from all sin and weakness, that we may come to You in our honest weakness and be embraced by Your Power, Grace, Forgiveness, and Love.

"Your Grace Is Enough"
Matt Maher
https://youtu.be/LISbMRp0Y64

November 7

Today's Encouragement is John 2:7a NLT *Jesus told the servants, "Fill the jars with water."*

Jesus told the servants –

In this passage Jesus is attending a big wedding. The bride and groom are about to be very embarrassed because there isn't enough wine for the party. A wedding feast was the greatest party ever held in that culture, the same is true to an extent today for most people, and this would be very devastating for everyone... especially the bride and groom.

But—everything changed—when Jesus spoke....

He said, "Fill the jars with water." And everything changed! There was more than enough, more than a hundred gallons! of the very best wine! The embarrassing situation was averted... because Jesus spoke!

Remember how God formed all of creation? He Spoke! ... and God saw that it was Good!

And "The Best" is the result! Jesus speaks, everything changes and—the Best is the result!

Father, Thank You for speaking words of life to us, help us to listen to Your Words, and then to obey, so that we too may see the blessings of more than enough...of the very best...

"Everything Changed"
Zach Williams
https://youtu.be/QsVV6bYenFY

November 8

Today's Encouragement is Romans 12:2a ESV *Do not be conformed to this world, but be transformed by the renewal of your mind....*

Renewal of your mind –

As always, it is our choice: To continue our lives unchanged, even though saved by His Grace, and to merely "cohabitate" as many relationships do these days, or to grow deeper in relationship with Him. Unlike marriage, we are second and He is first, and life with Him means we can become transformed to be more like Him.

Did you notice How are we transformed?

It happens when our mind is renewed, reborn, re-created, cleaned out and rebuilt... the NLT reads, "*changing the way you think,*" the Amplified reads, "*the* [entire] *renewal of your mind* [by its new ideals and its new attitude]."

My friends, do you see it? We are transformed—as God changes our minds—completely, entirely. This means our minds can become free from fear, doubt, and negative questioning of God's faithfulness—to become renewed—full of Faith, Hope, and Love, confidence in His Grace and Mercy, His provision and protection of us!

It is our minds which direct our lives. And our thoughts determine which direction our lives will go, toward Christ or away from Him. Sure, there are many other directions to select from... but only this choice matters....

Father, we admit we cannot change, we cannot become like You, without Your power transforming us, changing our thinking, renewing our minds. Give us the strength to turn away from conforming to this world and its ways and to choose to surrender to Your transforming work in our lives. We want to be Yours, Lord. Transformed into Your children.

"Child of God"
Kathryn Scott
https://youtu.be/cNeNGN2q-r8

November 9

Today's Encouragement is Deuteronomy 8:3b NLT *He did it to teach you that people do not live by bread alone; rather, we live by every word that comes from the mouth of the Lord.*

We live by every word –

Too often in the daily busyness of this life, we find ourselves tossed around, discouraged, depressed, doubting, and generally hopeless. It seems inevitable, we have times of strength and then times of weakness. Is it possible that our nourishment might be a contributing factor to this situation?

When I eat healthy, I am stronger, more alert, and more optimistic and even more hopeful. When I eat poorly, not enough healthy food, or too much junk food... I begin to slide downhill physically. Our spiritual lives are similar... we need healthy spiritual food to stay spiritually healthy.

So, my friends, what is the source of your spiritual food, your daily bread?

Is this devotional, as spiritually nutritious as it might be, the sole source of your "soul- food" intake?

May I suggest you can personally go to His table and feed your soul from the many truths there... and going yourself allows you to take in as much as you need!

Now a little bit of God's Word, like this daily encouragement, is a very good thing, a good spiritual meal to begin your day. Hopefully it is enough to sustain you all day long. However, there are often times when we need more! Friends, we always can go to His Word directly to receive exactly the spiritual nourishment that our souls may require.

Father God, help us to come to You alone... every day ... and whenever we need strength and encouragement... for "You alone have the words of eternal life." (John 6:68)

"Hungry"

Vineyard Worship

https://youtu.be/erQku5-O0Y0

November 10

Today's Encouragement is Psalm 27:13 ESV *I believe that I shall look upon the goodness of the Lord in the land of the living!*

I believe –

It may seem obvious, but we are controlled by, guided by, influenced by... what we choose to believe.

And we each choose what it is that we believe. We choose to believe the Bible is God's Word for us... or to believe it is a dusty old book of tales and confusing stories which have no relevance to our lives today.

We choose to believe Jesus is Lord and Savior... or that He was a fable...or just a wise man who had some interesting things to say.

We choose. And what we choose to believe my friends, determines the direction of our lives.

We choose to believe that things are going to be okay, and we have a positive outlook on life, or we choose to believe things are going downhill fast, and our outlook grows dark, and we see only the decay around us.

All based on what we choose... to believe...!

David was a realist, and in this Psalm, he acknowledged that his enemies were all around him, that they were lying about him... that God had not yet answered his prayer—but he closes the psalm with these word, and he states boldly, in faith and confidence and hope... I believe!

In Faith...

he chooses... to believe...

that He will see the goodness of God in this life!

Father, help us continue to choose to believe—in Your Love for us... the salvation we have in Jesus...Your goodness—and that You will show Yourself strong in our lives... that we too, will see Your goodness in this life!

"Goodness of God"

Bethel Music

https://youtu.be/-f4MUUMWMV4

November 11

Today's Encouragement is John 4:28-29 NLT *The woman left her water jar beside the well and ran back to the village, telling everyone, "Come and see a man who told me everything I ever did! Could he possibly be the Messiah?"*

Left her water jar –

When she met Jesus, talked with Him, heard Him say, (v26) *"I am He...."* she left her water jar and RAN back to her friends and told Everyone! About Jesus!

Like Mary, who sat in rapt attention at His feet, ignoring the many hostess duties over which her sister Martha obsessed (Luke 10:38-42)... this Samaritan woman, after spending time with Jesus, talking with Him, and listening to Him... left her water jar (her duties and responsibilities), and she RAN to tell others to come... to Jesus!

My friends, too often we obsess over our daily duties... I do at least. And in doing so, I overlook or neglect what matters most! Here it is sharing about Jesus! In Mary's case it was "sitting at His feet." In both situations... Jesus is the focus! And the chores and cares of this world are set aside—neglected even— for the higher, greater, eternal purpose of knowing Him and after spending time with Him... making Him known!

Father God, help us to choose the highest purpose this day- to sit at your feet, learn from You, and share with others the Joy of knowing You!

"Find Me at the Feet of Jesus"
Christy Nockels
https://youtu.be/5wUJVt7U1L0

November 12

Today's Encouragement is Psalm 27:1 NLT *The Lord is my light and my salvation- so why should I be afraid? The Lord is my fortress, protecting me from danger, so why should I tremble?*

My salvation –

At times we just need to have a little talk with ourselves.

Hear David as he speaks God's wisdom, protection, and blessing to... himself! As if he was saying "Why am I afraid, why am I trembling? ...The Lord is MY light, MY salvation, and My fortress... I have nothing to fear!"

We all sometimes get overrun by emotions, external circumstances, dangers, and well, just life... and we lose sight of The Eternal Truth. Life happens, bad things, good things, accidents, blessings... all are a part of this earthly life. The Eternal Truth is God IS! God Loves YOU! And We can be forgiven and restored to a right relationship with God, by faith in Jesus Christ as the One who Saves us! That's Truth, and Forever Truth!

And it is Jesus who is the Light, our Salvation, our Fortress, our help!

So why should we be afraid or tremble? Well, we have no other option when we take our eyes off Him - we're stumbling, bumbling, flopping around like a just landed fish on the deck of the boat - without Him... we are nothing!

But my friends - He is our Salvation!

Lord Jesus, help us to return to Your Truth daily, to remember that You are For us! And You alone are all we need!

"The Lord is My Salvation"
Keith and Kristyn Getty
https://youtu.be/kyLL04p0ms8

November 13

Today's Encouragement is Genesis 22:8 ESV *Abraham said, "God will provide for himself the lamb for a burnt offering, my son." So, they went both of them together.*

God will provide –

Abraham had been asked by God in v2, to give up his son as an offering to the Lord. At no other time before or since, has God asked for a human sacrifice! It's unthinkable that He ever would... yet He did! And Abraham in broken-hearted obedience... did so....

But God! At just the right moment, v12, *He* [God] *said, "Do not lay your hand on the boy or do anything to him, for now I know that you fear God, seeing you have not withheld your son, your only son, from me."*

Don't miss the wonderful messages here—

God called

Abraham obeyed

He offered his son... his only son...

God provided a Sacrifice

Abraham rejoiced and took his son home.

When we obey God's call— however small or great it may seem— God provides! We don't know the outcome... it is by Faith that we obey... but we choose to trust His heart! And we trust that He will always provide!

Father, we choose to trust You, that You will provide everything we need. Help us to surrender to You everything... everything we love, all we hope in... just as Abraham did.

(This beautiful song reveals the amazing similarities between Abraham's sacrifice of his son, and the Father God offering Jesus for you and me.)

"God Will Provide a Lamb"

Michael Card

https://youtu.be/7IM71Fh1Q_c

November 14

Today's Encouragement is Psalm 32:5 ESV *I acknowledged my sin to you, and I did not cover my iniquity; I said, "I will confess my transgressions to the Lord," and you forgave the iniquity of my sin. Selah*

I will confess –

Notice the process he describes:

- Acknowledgment of sin

- Decision to confess – "I will confess"

- Confession (to the Lord) pouring out all our sin, in honesty, withholding nothing

- Forgiveness – God's Mercy and Grace is given to those who Love Him and confess their sinfulness and their need for Him.

It seems that the concept of confessing sin is often neglected in our modern faith. Some Churches have established confession as a requirement, a ritual; yet the confession is too often to a person rather than to the Lord. This verse teaches clearly that confession is between the sinner and God, alone.

What happens when we confess and acknowledge our sin? We admit to God that we know it is wrong, we have done this wrong, and we are asking God to forgive us... And we become free of our sin! Forgiven by God, Himself!

Now notice what happens when we do not confess- (v3) *"For when I kept silent, my bones wasted away through my groaning all day long."* Refusing to confess keeps our sin rotting within us, eating away at our lives like a cancer...

Father God, help us to honestly confess our sin to You, and to become free from its destructive power, eating away at our lives. Thank You for offering perfect Forgiveness to us when we recognize, acknowledge, and confess our need for Your Mercy and Grace.

"Amazing Love"
Newsboys
https://youtu.be/nwjTT2bqKk0

November 15

Today's Encouragement is John 6:48-50 ESV *"I am the bread of life. Your fathers ate the manna in the wilderness, and they died. This is the bread that comes down from heaven, so that one may eat of it and not die."*

The bread of life –

Jesus taught us by using physical examples to reveal spiritual truths. For example, He said, "You must be born again," (John 3:3), "I will give you living water so you will never thirst again. (John 4:14). His challenging teaching was intended to separate those who believed in Him completely and those who were merely curious about Him. In fact, *After this many of his disciples turned back and no longer walked with him.* (John 6: 66 ESV)

My friend, following Christ is not for the crowd, not for the thrill-seeker, not for those who just want to get something. Following Christ means giving up everything we have and that everything we are... for Him! Because – He is the Bread of Life!

We take him into ourselves, symbolically, spiritually, by faith, and by taking communion, the Lord's Supper - We become part of Him in doing so. Many turned away before they could come to understand His truth.

Father God, help us to continue to learn from You, to remain open to what You have to teach us; for, You are never finished teaching, guiding, feeding us in this life. Thank You Father for the Bread of Life, the Living Water, and all that Jesus is!

"I Am the Bread of Life"

John Michael Talbot

https://youtu.be/Uhk42nq1jwE

November 16

Today's Encouragement is Joel 2:12-13 NLT *That is why the Lord says, "Turn to me now, while there is time. Give me your hearts. Come with fasting, weeping, and mourning. Don't tear your clothing in your grief but tear your hearts instead." Return to the Lord your God, for he is merciful and compassionate, slow to get angry and filled with unfailing love. He is eager to relent and not punish.*

Turn to Me –

At times, we all are in grief. It may be the tragic loss of a loved one, or of a marriage, a dream, a hope, a career... these can cause very deep grieving and sorrow. We may also grieve over own sin as in this passage, when we recognize that we have turned away from Him, gradually and unconsciously, or suddenly and intentionally... we have turned from Him to ourselves, or someone or something.

In either type of grief – an unimaginable loss – or our unimaginable sin...

God expresses to us in this passage that we can Turn to Him; Return to Him, and Now is the time! We can give our hearts to Him (a decision we make). Tearing our hearts inwardly...away from our grief, away from our sin and sorry... and returning to Him

He invites us to Turn and Return to Him... because He is Merciful and Compassionate, slow to anger and FILLED with UNFAILING LOVE!

Thank You Father, that You are always ready to accept us, when we turn from ourselves, our sin, our sorrow... and return to You!

"The Lord is Gracious and Compassionate"
Vineyard Worship
https://youtu.be/7Xzk9qtlvuo

November 17

Today's Encouragement is John 8:12-13 NLT *Jesus spoke to the people once more and said, "I am the light of the world. If you follow me, you won't have to walk in darkness, because you will have the light that leads to life." The Pharisees replied, "You are making those claims about yourself! Such testimony is not valid."*

The Light of the world –

Jesus clearly told the world who He is! He spoke repeatedly of His relationship with God, and His kingdom, among other truths about Himself. Notice the response of those without ears to hear... they ignored His statement! They focused instead on the fact that He was speaking this about Himself... *"such testimony is not valid,"* which by their Law meant there needed to be a second witness.

Jesus proclaims Himself as the light of the world... and they critically evaluate His statement by their laws....

My friends, we can take Jesus at His word! We need no measure, no outside evaluation, no logical confirmation of Who He Is! He has told us! We need to "deal with it," responding to His truth... just as He said... without man's evaluation, or logical examination, or critical dissection!

He IS! The Light! The Way! The Truth! The Life! The King of kings! The Lord of lords! The Son of God!

Father, help us, fallible, weak, confused, sheep-like human beings... to accept as Truth... Your Word!

"Great Light of the World"
Bebo Norman
https://youtu.be/XMDoyMsE2fc

November 18

Today's Encouragement is Psalm 23:1 NLT *The Lord is my shepherd; I have all that I need.*

My Shepherd –

We often lose the power of words which we've heard too many times, sadly. The words haven't lost their power and meaning; yet we lose the ability to hear that power and meaning.

As with this beautiful familiar Psalm, the power and meaning remain: He is our shepherd, guide, leader, protector, provider, the Source of all we need and all we could ever want!

"I have all that I need"—do we? Do we recognize that all we need...is found in Him, provided by Him.

My friends, recognize this truth, and then rest in this truth—God, Himself, is your guide, protector, and provider. And because of this... we can recognize and rest in all that He provides; He is all we need.

(From this song) *"Father, You're all I need, my sole sufficiency, my strength when I am weak, the love that carries me. Your arms enfold me, till I am only, a child of God."*

"Child of God"

Katheryn Scott

https://youtu.be/cNeNGN2q-r8

November 19

Today's Encouragement is Romans 7:18 NLT *And I know that nothing good lives in me, that is, in my sinful nature. I want to do what is right, but I can't.*

Nothing good –

In much of Romans 7, Paul lays bare the ugly truth of sin. He admits to God and to us, that he does the sin which he hates. He wants to do what is right, but...

How is this encouraging? Because this is just the introduction, not the conclusion... in chapter 7 Paul confesses this great frustration, the struggle with the sinful nature... which we all have! But then, in v24-25, he reveals that we are completely and perfectly saved from ourselves—and from our sin—by Jesus!

And that's not all! (Although Jesus is always enough!) in the next amazing chapter 8, we learn, we are not condemned (v1), we are no longer slaves (v15), but we are His adopted children (v16), He helps us in our weakness (v26), and He works in all things for our good (v28)! We are more than conquerors (v37)! And there are many other wonderful examples of God's Grace—His unmerited favor—in this beautiful chapter 8!

Friends, the reality of our sinful nature is a harsh and ugly truth; nothing good lives in us!

But recognizing this indicates so clearly our need to be saved... by Someone other than ourselves! Jesus is the only One!

Father, help us confess our sin, accept Your Grace, and then live as Your grateful, forgiven, victorious, and freed sons and daughters.

"Redeemed"

Big Daddy Weave

https://youtu.be/_p31gY0t4pA

November 20

Today's Encouragement is John 10:37-38 NLT *"Don't believe me unless I carry out my Father's work. But if I do his work, believe in the evidence of the miraculous works I have done, even if you don't believe me. Then you will know and understand that the Father is in me, and I am in the Father."*

Know and understand –

Jesus understood how difficult it would be for people to grasp the truth that He was God's Son, that He and the Father are one (v30). So here He makes an allowance, a simpler pathway to acceptance, "Even though you don't believe me, believe the works"!

Amazing, isn't it? That by believing the works Jesus has done, we can *"know and understand that the Father is in me and I am in the Father."*

Jesus' many miracles (and He did far more than those recorded in our Bible), were clear evidence that He was Lord over all! Lord over health and illness, demons, and plants, and even Lord over death itself. And all this was before His own miraculous resurrection!

We are blessed today to have the biblical record of both, His deeds, and His words... '"that we may know and understand" that Jesus and the Father are One!

Our Father, please help us to accept and believe, even to "know and understand" this truth of Your Oneness—Father, Son, and Spirit.

"I Know"
Kim Walker-Smith
https://youtu.be/mAq-74wRSFQ

November 21

Today's Encouragement is John 10:27-30 ESV *"My sheep hear my voice, and I know them, and they follow me. I give them eternal life, and they will never perish, and no one will snatch them out of my hand. My Father, who has given them to me, is greater than all, and no one is able to snatch them out of the Father's hand. I and the Father are one."*

No one –

Do you hear that my friends? No One can snatch you or me from Jesus' Hand, which is the same as the Father's Hand!

At times, we must confess, Isaiah 53:6a ESV *All we like sheep have gone astray; we have turned—every one—to his own way.* We wander, we doubt, we question, we sin, we fear... all this is our going "astray," leaving the path of Faith and Trust. Yet my friends, reread today's verse... No one can snatch us! We're un-snatchable!

Not only this!!! Read the rest of Isaiah's proclamation... even though we wander, we stray from faith... this doesn't change the truth of who we are, or *Whose* we are!

Because *the Lord has laid on him [Jesus] the iniquity of us all.* (Isaiah 53:6b)

Father God, help us to know that...You hold us in Your Hand—Jesus holds us in His nail-scarred Hand—and nothing can change this Truth!

"The Unseen Hand"

Marty Stuart

https://youtu.be/1_UPfvYwcmQ

November 22

Today's Encouragement is John 11:21 NLT *Martha said to Jesus, "Lord, if only you had been here, my brother would not have died."*

If only –

How often have we said, or thought, or prayed... we called for You, Lord!... If only You had come when we asked You for help! We needed You to... save us from... heal us... rescue us... to help... us!

Martha was Lazarus' sister, she had sent Jesus a message days before that Lazarus was sick, hoping that Jesus would come and heal him. Jesus got the message, fully understood the gravity of the Illness and had complete knowledge of what would happen... But He didn't come!

Jesus didn't come and heal Lazarus... as He had done before. All He had to do was think or speak a word, and healing would be complete, no matter where He was.

But my friends... He didn't come! He didn't heal!

We know the rest of the story, but Mary and Martha, Lazarus' broken-hearted, grieving sisters did not! Not only had Lazarus died... but Jesus did not help! He did not answer their prayers! He ignored their plea, their prayer!

...Or so it seemed to these women, believers in Him, followers of Jesus... His dear friends. For several days, maybe weeks, Lazarus lay ill, then he died. And yet, nothing from Jesus. Jesus seemed to abandon them; He had failed them; He wasn't the loving, all powerful, true friend who they believed Him to be!

But the story wasn't over yet!

My friends, when we are in this place spiritually— our prayers unanswered, our fears realized— our loss, our grief, our betrayal, our own failures... all are real! The loss is real! Jesus did not do what we asked! He broke His promise to do whatever we ask in His name! ...or so it may seem.

Father God, thank You for opening our eyes to see that You are never finished with us. Even death does not end the story of Your relationship with us! You are always working for us!!! When we cannot see it, or even imagine how You could be "in this situation"... You are still Lord! You have a plan! You make a way!

"It's Not Over Yet"
For King and Country
https://youtu.be/XmTmTMcdxOs

November 23

Today's Encouragement is Job 28:1 ESV *"Surely there is a mine for silver, and a place for gold that they refine."*

A place for gold –

In this chapter Job talks about wisdom, that it cannot be found on this earth; even looking into the depths of the earth, where gold and silver are mined, will not lead you to wisdom. And he ends this chapter with a true "nugget" of golden wisdom ... Job 28:28 *"And he said to man, 'Behold, the fear of the Lord, that is wisdom, and to turn away from evil is understanding.'"*

The Wisdom of God is available to you and me today, more than to any other generation on this earth—ever... The Bible contains God's Wisdom, just as the earth contains gold and silver. Just as precious metals and jewels are mined from the earth, so also is wisdom "mined" from God's Word. Just as gold mines are found all over the earth, so too is Wisdom found throughout God's Word.

We must look for it! We must know what to look for... and then diligently search! it is available to us, and it is far more precious than the metal and gemstones which men seek with all their efforts!

Open the Word, Ask God to speak to you through His Holy Spirit and His Word. He will!

Because He loves you and He desires for you to know Him more! Allow His Word to teach you His Wisdom, His Way, His Love, His Power, His Grace.

This treasure is readily available, my friends, it only requires a little effort, a little time, a little intentional seeking... to "mine the gold and silver," to discover Infinite Truth, Measureless Love, Amazing Grace, and so much more.

Father God, we thank You for the Gift of Eternal Life through Jesus! We thank You for Your Word that leads us to Him, that draws us to You, that guides us in wisdom and love. You are so very good to us!

"Perfect Wisdom of Our God"
Keith and Kristyn Getty
https://youtu.be/hSnzYnOe6kI

November 24

Today's Encouragement is Proverbs 12:25 NLT *Worry weighs a person down; an encouraging word cheers a person up.*

An encouraging word –

There's plenty in this world to worry about! Plenty of discouraging things! The economy, wars, cultural upheaval, pandemics, ... this list is endless! The information about these situations is also limitless; everywhere we turn... there's plenty to worry about! Plenty of fuel for the consuming fire of anxiety and fear!

This devotional is intended to help you overcome the fear, worry, anxiety of this world, with the very encouraging Word of God. His love, protection, provision, —His plans for us, what He has already given us, and also what He has planned for us!

What we choose to focus on is our own individual decision:

The dis-couraging or

The en-couraging...

My friends, we can choose to focus on His encouraging words! To Trust and Hope in Him and His Word!

Here are just a few:

And we know that God causes everything to work together for the good of those who love God and are called according to his purpose for them. (Romans 8:28 NLT)

For I know the plans I have for you," says the Lord. "They are plans for good and not for disaster, to give you a future and a hope." (Jeremiah 29:11 NLT)

"I have told you all this so that you may have peace in me. Here on earth, you will have many trials and sorrows. But take heart, because I have overcome the world." (John 16:33 NLT)

Father, we thank You for Jesus our Savior, and for Your Word which encourages us to trust and hope in Him!

"I Look to You"

Selah

https://youtu.be/MvlgG9Uqa6g

November 25

Today's Encouragement is Psalm 37:5-7a ESV *Commit your way to the Lord; trust in him, and he will act. He will bring forth your righteousness as the light, and your justice as the noonday. Be still before the Lord and wait patiently for him....*

He will act –

Think about that first verse for just a moment with me please: *"Commit your way to the Lord; trust in him, and He will act."* Too often we fire off a quick prayer and then charge ahead with our own plans!

Recognize that His actions are often not what we would expect because... "He is God and we ain't!"

Isaiah 55:8-9 *"For my thoughts are not your thoughts, neither are your ways my ways, declares the Lord. For as the heavens are higher than the earth, so are my ways higher than your ways and my thoughts than your thoughts."*

It's God doing these actions not us! Our part is to

- Commit our way Trust in Him
- Be still before Him Wait patiently for Him.

And, my friends, He will Act! He will do for us—our good!

Father, please help us to trust You, to rest in You, and to wait for You.

"My God Fights for Me"

Charity Gayle

https://youtu.be/t1LagOBYFqQ

November 26

Today's Encouragement is John 1:5 ESV *The light shines in the darkness, and the darkness has not overcome it.*

The light shines –

This verse, at the introduction of John's book, is an ancient statement of both current and eternal Truth. Jesus IS the Light of the world! (John 8:12)

Jesus, the Light, shines in the darkness. The darkness is real, it is always present (until He ends all darkness forever). And yet, even in this terrible darkness—The Light, Jesus, —shines... and the darkness is powerless to overcome His Light!

My friends this world is truly dark... our current circumstances can seem overwhelming. Death, depression, decay, addiction, confusion of identity, illnesses and suffering seem to surround us... and this is true! Even around us believers, there is much darkness! This is the reality, the darkness which we live in....

But, there is The Light! And no darkness, no matter how black or bleak, within or without us, can overcome His Light!

Imagine with me for a moment, the darkness of Calvary. Jesus had been crucified and the daylight became darkness— all the hopes of his disciples were crushed; they hung their heads in sorrow. The greatest man they'd ever known... the hope for everyone, the one who they thought would save everyone... had been cruelly tortured and mercilessly killed by the evil darkness. And for three long dark days... all hope was trampled into the dust... or so it seemed.

Yet, three days later, and every moment since...

The light shines in the darkness, and the darkness has not overcome it.

Thank You, Jesus, for continuing to shine, to illuminate the darkness of this world!

"Shine, Jesus, Shine"

Maranatha Music

https://youtu.be/nTIGVIcHsFE

November 27

Today's Encouragement is Psalm 46:1-2 ESV *God is our refuge and strength, a very present help in trouble. Therefore we will not fear though the earth gives way, though the mountains be moved into the heart of the sea.*

A very present help –

Ever known someone who never seems to have any troubles? It seems to us they live a rather "charmed" life— No illnesses, no work problems, a blissful marriage, making lots of money— always posting happy pictures on Facebook... you know the type...

Is it possible my friends...?

That God has,—in His immeasurable mercy and kindness to us—allowed us the privilege of having some troubles in this life...?

Consider.

God is Omnipresent— everywhere without any limitation. So, He is always "very present," always near, always available. So why... "in trouble"? Because that's when we Need Him, Seek Him, Cry out to Him, Pray to Him...

Those people who seem to have it all together, don't see any need for God's intervention in their lives... often don't even want it... "life is pretty good just as it is, thank you very much!"

Yet, as the Psalm reads... in our troubles... God is Very Present!

Now I don't believe God "sends" or "gives" us troubles, Jesus simply stated that we would have them, (Matthew 16:33) it's just a part of life here in this broken world.

A line from this song reads, "For if I'd never had a problem, how would I know that God could solve them. How would I know what faith in His Word could do."

Father God, thank You for problems and troubles that bring us to You... so that we may know that You are Near! Keep us near to You, Lord, whatever that takes.

"Through It All"

The Isaacs

https://youtu.be/lughm2Os0ew

November 28

Today's Encouragement is John 13:12 ESV *When he had washed their feet and put on his outer garments and resumed his place, he said to them, "Do you understand what I have done to you?"*

Do you understand –

What a question! From Jesus to his disciples... from Jesus to you and me.

We can name (though we may not fully understand) some of the wonderful things that Jesus has done for us:

- Made us righteous, restored a right relationship between man and God
- Reversed, erased, corrected our every sin
- Made us completely new, reborn
- Granted us Eternal Life
- Adopted us into His own family
- Made us His friends

...and so very much more!!!

Yet, it is true isn't it, we often really don't understand what He is doing... and so we ask....

"Why does it have to be this way?"

"Why are You silent God?"

"Why didn't you do what I asked for and prayed for?"

Remember that His ways are not our ways. (Isaiah 55:8) We often do not understand what He is doing or has done, but! (v7) Jesus answered him, "What I am doing you do not understand now, but afterward you will understand."

Friends, we live by Faith. We Trust Jesus even when we don't understand the What, Why, or How of His ways. Because we believe Him! Because we choose to Trust Him! And He has told us... we will understand at some future time!

Father God, help us to trust You when we don't understand, and when we do. You are our True Hope.

"Trust His Heart"

Babbie Mason

https://youtu.be/XWk8DRwDYDc

November 29

Today's Encouragement is John 15:4 ESV *"Abide in me, and I in you. As the branch cannot bear fruit by itself, unless it abides in the vine, neither can you, unless you abide in me."*

Abide in me –

The Greek word *meno*—here translated as "Abide," also means remain, "dwell, stay, continue..." We would probably use the word "live."

Friends, Jesus here tells us to Stay in Him, make our home, our dwelling place... "in" Him, continuously be with, and in Him as our home, the place we live...

This home is not just a place to eat and sleep at night... it is a place where we always are—not only a physical location but a state of mind, a dwelling place, a continuous residence.

Friends we are at home in this life, as we abide with, dwell in, remain continually with Jesus. He's our Fortress, our Help, our Peace.

This home is Now! And it is Forever! We don't just begin to "dwell in Jesus" after we leave this life, but as we believe in Him and He lives within us, we are Now! dwelling with, abiding in Him.

One day we will be with Him eternally, and yet, that eternity has already begun... we can abide, live, make our home with Jesus, now!

Lord Jesus, help us to abide in You. Teach us, guide us, lead us to dwell in, abide in, continue in You. You are our home.

"I Will Bring You Home"
Michael Card
https://youtu.be/6O5Es0etqTM

November 30

Today's Encouragement is John 15:9 ESV *"As the Father has loved me, so have I loved you. Abide in my love."*

Abide in my Love -

Abide—to dwell, stay, remain, to always consistently be present-

In—surrounded by, not beside or on, or under, but deep inside... in relationship, covered with, embraced by...

My—the source is Jesus, the Son of God, no other source, not your family, not a pastor, not you or me or the church or the Bible... none but Jesus!

Love—It isn't our love... which is too often selfishly motivated, even self-focused... but His Love that we can abide in. The Love of Jesus is the greatest Love ever known. No other love comes close, we aren't even adequate to generate love for another person, much less for Him... but when His Love fills us, we can do all things through Christ, including Loving Him and loving others... when we remain, dwell, abide in His Love!

Father God, help us to abide in the Love of Jesus.

"The Faithful Love of Jesus"

Hillary Scott

https://youtu.be/oxL6WyAmMZ8

December 1

Today's Encouragement is 1 Corinthians 2:2,5 ESV *For I decided to know nothing among you except Jesus Christ and him crucified... so that your faith might not rest in the wisdom of men but in the power of God.*

Nothing except –

There are so many things we can "know" and learn about, so much wisdom to explore, so many different options we can seek after.

Externally focused—history, hobbies, politics, culture wars, technology...

Self-focused—social standing, social media, careers, image, health, fitness, families, church activities...

We have numerous options, but what really matters? What remains? What has lasting value for us as individuals, and for others? What has significance?

We may explore some of the many possible answers to this question, yet the Truth is: only one thing matters... only one thing transforms, only one thing holds hope for us and mankind...

Jesus Christ and Him crucified-

Father, Help us to focus our lives, our learning, our hearts, and our minds on knowing You, Lord God, our Savior Jesus Christ, and the Holy Spirit—ever present within us! Thank you for saving us!

"All I Have Is Christ"

Sovereign Grace Music

https://youtu.be/pA5mMBtWKeg

December 2

Today's Encouragement is Ezekiel 37:14 NLT *"I will put my Spirit in you, and you will live again and return home to your own land. Then you will know that I, the Lord, have spoken, and I have done what I said. Yes, the Lord has spoken!"*

You will live again –

In chapter 37, Ezekiel recounts his amazing experience with God. God brings him to a valley filled with dry bones, symbolic of the spiritual deadness of the nation, they despaired *"All hope is gone."* (v 11)

But God...

Friends, what can be more devoid of hope than dry bones? No one would ever give the slightest thought to dry bones ever coming to life... But God...

Ezekiel 37:10 NLT *So I spoke the message as he commanded me, and breath came into their bodies. They all came to life and stood up on their feet—a great army.*

They came to life! God caused the flesh to be restored (v8) and breath to restore their spirits (v9) and DRY BONES began to LIVE AGAIN!

One can argue that this was "just a vision," that's it's only symbolic, that it was ancient history... yet, my friends, isn't this what God does in us when we accept Jesus as Savior? Romans 6:11 NLT *So you also should consider yourselves to be dead to the power of sin and alive to God through Christ Jesus.*

No matter how hopeless our situation may appear at this moment, God isn't finished with us! Our Hope is Eternal, for both this life, and the next! We will LIVE AGAIN!

Father, strengthen our Hope, our confidence in Jesus, so that we do not despair, regardless of our circumstances... for we place our trust in You above all else.

"Christ Our Hope in Life and Death"

Keith and Kristyn Getty

https://youtu.be/OibIi1rz7mw

December 3

Today's Encouragement is Genesis 39:21 ESV *But the Lord was with Joseph and showed him steadfast love and gave him favor in the sight of the keeper of the prison.*

But the Lord –

Joseph was righteous! He refused the advances of his master's wife, although she tempted him day after day (v10). So, she falsely accused him, and Joseph went to prison.

This man of God who had been sold into slavery by his brothers (without cause) now was in prison (without cause).

Friends, Joseph had "every right" to be bitter, angry even! He was honoring God, refusing sin, and yet—still punished!

But the Lord...! As some say today, "But God!"... God isn't finished, the story isn't over yet!

Joseph was rescued from prison miraculously and became the second most powerful ruler of Egypt,...

But Joseph had been in prison, still innocent, for two years (Genesis 41:1)! During those two long years in prison, Joseph could easily have chosen bitterness, doubted God cared or even existed..., and he could have decided it was useless to follow God's ways. He had twice suffered greatly for his faithfulness... but he didn't doubt or get angry at God! The Word says nothing about his own internal struggles, all we see is his faithfulness... even when that very faithfulness led to suffering.

But the Lord...! God was with him,— in prison, and before prison, and after prison... the Lord was with him!

Father, we thank you that just as You were with Joseph in good and bad times, You are also with us! Help each of us, Father, to continue to choose to abide in You, in Your Love, to choose to trust You regardless of our circumstances or the cost!

"The Cause of Christ"

Kari Jobe

https://youtu.be/byHwKMa6NJY

December 4

Today's Encouragement is John 15:11 ESV *"These things I have spoken to you, that my joy may be in you, and that your joy may be full."*

Your joy may be full –

When I read something like this from God's word, a promise that seems... too good to be true... I try to remember to ask myself: "Did Jesus fail?" Did He fail to do what He said He would? Did He fail to be who and what He claimed He was and would be? Did He make idle promises? Was He just kidding with us? Leading us on? Maybe, as some believe, such promises were only to those who were physically present at that moment in history.

Here He was speaking to the disciples at this moment. Was it only for them? He had just said "Abide in me and you will bear much fruit," and He went on to tell them to love one another... Is any of that limited to "just" the disciples?

Friends, His promises are True! And for all of those who follow Him, we are all His disciples! (Remember, the "originals' weren't the most devoted at first either!)

We can have His Joy in us... Fullness of Joy! Because of the things He has spoken to us!

Is it possible? Is He working in us, re-creating, refining, and rebirthing us as His own brothers and sisters, adopted children of the Living God? You bet your life He IS! We are His workmanship! And He's not yet finished! What more do we need to have His Joy within us? And complete Joy!!!

Father God, please help your children to choose Your Joy over all other things. Thank You for offering us Your Joy!

"Joy of the Lord"
Rend Collective
https://youtu.be/fcG9HApTC_Q

December 5

Today's Encouragement is John 17:26b NLT [Jesus prayed,] *"Then your love for me will be in them, and I will be in them."*

Will be in them –

Let's pause and consider (selah) this closing statement of Jesus' final prayer before he was arrested.

"Your Love for me will be in them"—can you imagine how great, deep, immeasurable, is God's Love for Jesus? God's Love is perfect, complete, pure, unselfish; it fills and strengthens and heals and upholds! It is so far beyond our understanding of Love, that it should be named something different!

"I will be in them"—still more amazing, unimaginable... Jesus in us! Words fail...

Friends, I confess, sometimes I don't "feel like" either God's Love or Jesus Himself is in me... in fact, rarely have I ever felt or sensed such an amazing realization! Yet, my friends, reread this verse.... Jesus asked the Father in prayer for exactly that! Did God say "No"? Or "Later"? Or is it just possible that... whether we recognize, acknowledge, or "feel" it... this is Truth!?

God's Love and Jesus Himself— these are IN you and me! Astounding!

... the riches of the glory of this mystery, which is Christ in you, the hope of glory. (Colossians 1:27b ESV)

Lord God, please open our hearts, minds, souls to the Truth You have for us: not what we feel, think, nor logically conclude... but Your Truth alone! You choose to live in us!

"Christ in Me"

Bright City

https://youtu.be/gOTy81waxIA

December 6

Today's Encouragement is Luke 21:17-18 NLT *"And everyone will hate you because you are my followers. But not a hair of your head will perish!"*

Because you are my followers –

Are you, like me, shocked at the spiral into decadence of our world today? It seems to move faster and faster, to become darker and darker, people sinking to ever deeper levels of what was once unimaginable depravity.

Now, I don't want to play the "ain't it awful" game!... But we must acknowledge the rapidly changing world we face today.

As followers of Jesus, we now face the times which He spoke of in this passage... and we are truly hated by much of the world, for our beliefs, for our faith in Jesus.

Here's the encouragement, my friends! Jesus knew this was coming! He warned us and He prepared us, and He promised us... *"not a hair..."!*

We live in a decaying society. But God! We are hated for following Jesus. But God! He will keep us safe! Sheltered in His arms!

Father God, strengthen us for today's challenges, our struggle with sin, and the hatred we might encounter. Help us to Love others—still —just as You have loved us.

"Sheltered in the Arms of God"

Hillary Scott

https://youtu.be/GVEM_cc5uFo

December 7

Today's Encouragement is John 13:7 NLT *Jesus replied, "You don't understand now what I am doing, but someday you will."*

But someday –

We've experienced this ourselves, but sometimes it's hard to remember the concept... we don't understand what is happening!

This is why we must live by Faith! We don't know everything! We must walk in faith, not only by what we see or understand or feel... God is Spirit, we are His Spiritual children... John 3:8 NLT *"The wind blows wherever it wants. Just as you can hear the wind but can't tell where it comes from or where it is going, so you can't explain how people are born of the Spirit."*

But in our earthly minds we want a clear picture of what the plan is!

"What are the next steps?"

"Where exactly is this leading us!"

"Why God?"... We want to know; we want control!

My friends, God is in Control! We, as sheep, as children, as followers, as disciples (students), are following Him, His Will, His plans, His ways! We only see our next steps!

Consider Psalm 119:105 NLT: *Your word is a lamp to guide my feet and a light for my path.* The lamp of Jesus' day wasn't a flashlight! It illuminated only a small circle and at that, dimly! Only enough light for the next few steps! The rest of the pathway is only visible after—we take the next step of faith!

"But someday you will"! Someday we will understand! His promise! Till then, we walk by Faith that He is in control!

God asks us to trust Him, rely on Him, depend on Him... this is the essence of surrender. As we do so... He leads, we follow. And someday we will understand!

Father God, at times this walk of faith is so difficult, we long to see Your hand at work, we long to know what You are doing, and yet, we understand, that we will someday understand, and that is good enough for us. Strengthen our faith while we walk this life.

"God Is in Control"

Twila Paris

https://youtu.be/STX2NYuhvfM

December 8

Today's Encouragement is Ecclesiastes 3:1 NLT *For everything there is a season, a time for every activity under heaven.*

There is a season –

Have you recognized that we live in seasons of time? Childhood, youth, adulthood, and maturity (being gentle with us older folks!) and spiritually as well:

There are low times and high points, valleys, and mountains.

Sometimes we're up, and sometimes down.

Strong or weak, hopeful or despairing.

For everything there is a season. And for every season there is a beginning, a duration, and an end! Things change; relationships begin and end, and in this same way, even our faith has its ups and downs–highs and lows, strengths, and weaknesses.

Our Bible is full of Truth, and it records of the varied seasons of life for the men and women of our spiritual ancestry, like David, Joseph, Ruth, Peter, and Paul... This record is provided to strengthen our faith—especially during those valleys.

And when we are strong in our faith, we can lift up those around who are struggling. When we have encouragement to share... we strengthen others by doing so. When we are discouraged, we can seek encouragement from the Bible, from brothers and sisters in faith, and from God directly! Just remember—this season will end; we only need to trust and wait on Him.

He's still God! His presence and His power are not dependent upon our feelings, attitudes, nor even our faith!

Father God, please strengthen us for the valleys of our lives, and help us remember the mountains and that You are Present,— still the only All-powerful God whatever the season!

"God on the Mountain"
Lynda Randle
https://youtu.be/HUBY9TxnAMw

December 9

Today's Encouragement is Psalm 42:11 NLT *Why am I discouraged? Why is my heart so sad? I will put my hope in God! I will praise him again- my Savior and my God!*

I will –

This Psalmist recognizes/reveals an important truth...

He asks himself: Why am I discouraged? Why is my heart so sad?

What's wrong with me? My attitude stinks, I have lost hope! I feel like giving up...

He's discouraged, depressed, down, and giving up.

But in asking himself, he suddenly realizes what he needs to do! And makes the decision (his circumstances and feelings haven't changed!) to do it!

"I know what I need to do!—I will put my hope in God!—I will praise him again- He is my Savior and my God!"

The answer to our discouragement, sadness, grief, depression, sorrow, doubts, fears... every malady known to man... Is it possible...this is the answer? —Choose/Decide to put your Hope in God! And Praise Him... again and again... and proclaim Him as your own Savior and your God!

So, my friends, when you find yourself (as we all do at times) at the bottom, in the fog, depressed, sorrowful, doubting, hopeless... consider that there is a better way. Raise your eyes to Heaven; choose to believe again; choose to have hope in Him and praise Him for who He is!

Father God, please help your children to surrender our emotions and feelings to Your Love and Your Hope. Help us to praise you and so be lifted out of sadness, discouragement, or despair... You are our Hope!

"My Hope"

Paul Baloche

https://youtu.be/KojhRGDr6rA

December 10

Today's Encouragement is John 21:4-6 NLT *At dawn Jesus was standing on the beach, but the disciples couldn't see who he was. He called out, "Fellows, have you caught any fish?" "No," they replied. Then he said, "Throw out your net on the right-hand side of the boat, and you'll get some!" So, they did, and they couldn't haul in the net because there were so many fish in it.*

So, they did --

Remember Jesus had just been crucified, buried, and resurrected. Although He had already appeared to them, He was no longer physically with them.

So, Peter and the guys went fishing! Is it possible they had given up on Him, returned to their old lives? And yet had caught nothing all night! Till Jesus came into the picture!

So, they did! They heard what He said, didn't even realize it was Jesus, and so they did... and so—they caught a huge catch of 153 fish, that they couldn't even pull the net into the boat! (There were 7 fishermen!).

This isn't about fish, nor about the miracle especially... but obedience! They DID what Jesus said. They were tired, exhausted from fishing all night; they were sad because their friend and hero who had been killed (but then appeared to them behind locked doors) wasn't around any longer. These guys were close to giving up all hope!

But – They DID! They obeyed Jesus, they listened to His advice, they followed His instruction. And the result, wasn't only a miracle... they encountered Him! Even had breakfast with him!

Father God, please help us to hear Your voice, Your wisdom, Your instructions... and to simply obey! Your way is always best for us!

"Speak, O Lord"

Keith and Kristyn Getty

https://youtu.be/ubRlJj8xkds

December 11

Today's Encouragement is Acts 2:46 NIV *Every day they continued to meet together in the temple courts. They broke bread in their homes and ate together with glad and sincere hearts.*

Meet together –

"Church'" as we know it today can take many different forms. And the form is only a matter of your personal preference and comfort level. Still there are a few essentials.

First, that we gather in Jesus' Name. He is the purpose.

Second, that we share ourselves... extend God's grace, acceptance, and love to the family of believers.

Finally, that the Word is present, both the Biblical truth and the Spirit of Christ.

With these essentials, we are bound together in a family relationship with brothers and sisters in Christ. It can be messy, even painful, but it can also be joyous.

This is where we learn and grow, where relationships are born and cared for, where the family of God gathers regularly to learn of Him and be with Him.

Lord God, help us to seek and nurture a church home. And to go there regularly to be fed Your Word; to share Your love. For there is no substitute.

"Church [Take Me Back]"

Cochran & Co

https://youtu.be/ss4zs1DJLjU

December 12

Today's Encouragement is 1 John 2:14 NLT *I have written to you who are God's children because you know the Father. I have written to you who are mature in the faith because you know Christ, who existed from the beginning. I have written to you who are young in the faith because you are strong. God's word lives in your hearts, and you have won your battle with the evil one.*

Lives in your hearts –

John writes to us, God's children, both to those who are mature and who are young in the faith... These amazing words... God's word lives in your hearts... and You have won (already) your battle with the evil one.

Did you hear it? See it? Believe it?

- To the young in the faith: God's Word—living and alive within our hearts!
- Our battle with the evil one—Already won!?
- And to the mature in the faith: You know Christ!

My friends, these truths belong to us and are eternal! They cannot be disputed! These are not for "some special believers"... but for all of us! All of God's Children have these blessings! While we may not feel like it, we may not see evidence of it, we might even be skeptical... our attitudes don't have any effect on God's promises! His Truth is inviolable!

God's Word lives in our hearts—like seeds growing in the soil, unseen, so God's Word takes root within us, and grows deep roots, and produces fruit in time... and remains.

Father, help us recognize the power of Your Word within our hearts, living and alive... and to draw upon Your Word for strength and hope and courage for the struggles of the day... for we have already won the battle!

"Word of God Speak"

MercyMe

https://youtu.be/JTY-UKgLlXs

December 13

Today's Encouragement is Matthew 11:28 NLT *Then Jesus said, "Come to me, all of you who are weary and carry heavy burdens, and I will give you rest."*

Come to me –

Recently I've spoken to several people; all are sincere believers, but all were dealing with significant frustration and anxiety. These are praying followers of Jesus, there's nothing "wrong with" their faith, no lack of strength nor devotion. Yet, their current challenges threaten to overwhelm their faith...

And frankly, to the extent that we believers experience anxiety, fears, frustrations, and worries... these in essence have overcome our faith!—Not finally, not permanently, but practically so! We are, at that time, yielded to fear and turned away from faith!

Our Bible is full of truth about believers who lived before us, and who lived through such trials, failures and in most cases, restoration! Remember Jesus came to save sinners (1 Tim. 1:15)!

My friends, the answer, whenever we come to such a place, "to the end of ourselves"... is to "Come to Me," come to Jesus again... to turn to Him... Here and Now! It is always time to turn to Him for help... always Here, always Now.

Help us, Lord, to recognize our continuous need to Come To You, to bring our burdens to You and let go of them, and then, to Rest in Your strength, grace, and perfect peace.

As you worship with this song, release all your fears, anxiety, cares, stresses, frustrations, anger, self-pity, shame, grief, sorrow... all of "IT," whatever is frustrating you, tormenting you, clawing away your peace, threatening your contentment in Him... release that to Him. He can handle it, we cannot. And He promises, 'I will give you Rest'!

"Here and Now"

Paul and Rita Baloche

https://youtu.be/cFYdLTwhh_A

December 14

Today's Encouragement is Exodus 5:22-23 NLT *Then Moses went back to the Lord and protested, "Why have you brought all this trouble on your own people, Lord? Why did you send me? Ever since I came to Pharaoh as your spokesman, he has been even more brutal to your people. And you have done nothing to rescue them!"*

You have done nothing –

Moses was frustrated! He was embarrassed, doubting God; he was just fed up! He had obeyed God, gone to Egypt, convinced the leaders of his people, Israel, that God had sent him to deliver them from Pharaoh, and he had told Pharaoh what God had instructed him to say. But in response, Pharaoh only made things much worse for them! So, it's as if Moses was saying, "God, I'm doing everything right! But Pharaoh isn't cooperating! The people of Israel are mad at me, too! Why did You do this to me?!" "You have done nothing..."

Sometimes we get this way too! We ask, "God, why aren't You answering my prayers? Why is all this bad stuff happening to me?"

Friends, God is very patient! But we are very *impatient*! God knows the beginning and end; we're focused on the past and present, but we have no clue about tomorrow. God sees all of time far more clearly than we see the present! He's not finished! The story's not over yet! There's more to come!

What if we add three letters to Moses' complaint... just 3 letters that change everything!

Y.E.T. – God hasn't done anything... YET! But He will!... The story isn't over!

Father, help us to trust You, to ask You for help, guidance, deliverance–whatever our need,– and then to wait...in trust... for You.

"The Story's Not Over"

Jeremy Camp

https://youtu.be/0WNhsajTmFs

December 15

Today's Encouragement is Revelation 1:17a NLT *When I saw him, I fell at his feet as if I were dead.*

When I saw Him –

The Bible is full of descriptions of encounters with Jesus. This final description in Revelation 1:12-16 is one of the most detailed and most powerful, probably because this encounter is with the resurrected Jesus in all His Glory!

Another encounter example is when Jesus was arrested; the soldiers, battle-hardened and fearless, fell back and cowered in His Presence... John 18:6 NLT *As Jesus said, "I AM he," they all drew back and fell to the ground!*

Friends, as we encounter Jesus in our day, He is the Glorified One of Revelation 1. Yet, His Power is the same which caused the soldiers to fall back. His Loving Heart for us is still the beautiful love that caused Peter to jump overboard and swim to Him in excitement! (John 21:7)

Will you dare to encounter Him in your heart, and mind, and soul for just a moment? Now?

Pause your hurried mind and life. Play this worship song and... Behold Him...

Father God, please help us to encounter Jesus in this moment.

"Behold Him"

Paul Baloche & Kim Walker-Smith

https://youtu.be/_izK4kI_wm

December 16

Today's Encouragement is Exodus 6:8-9 NLT *"I will bring you into the land I swore to give to Abraham, Isaac, and Jacob. I will give it to you as your very own possession. I am the Lord!" So Moses told the people of Israel what the Lord had said, but they refused to listen anymore. They had become too discouraged by the brutality of their slavery.*

I will –

God promised… but Israel refused to listen. And the reason they refused? They were too discouraged by their current circumstances…

Aren't we just like that? My situation is too dire! My problems too big! The giant Goliath is too powerful for anyone to defeat! The economy is collapsing! No one loves me!

Friends, there are terrible trials in this life. Some which cause us to think, "No one should have to endure this!" Such difficulties are real and tragic! In this time, we can cling, with every ounce of faith we can muster, to His promises…. We can desperately cling to Him—Seek Him, pray, read His word, listen to hopeful preaching, sing, praise, and worship Him, just spend time in His presence. He is there, available, listening, and always loving us!

Remember Jesus acknowledged to us… "in this world, you WILL have trouble," but then He added, "But take heart because I have overcome this world!" (John 16:33)

Whether our circumstances are terrible or trivial; our faith a tiny mustard seed or a giant oak… we must remember and return to God's many promises. And we must choose to trust Him and Stand on His every promise!

Father God, thank You for Your unlimited patience with us. Help us to trust that You Will! When You choose. And help us to stand on every promise of Your Word.

"Every Promise of Your Word"

Keith and Kristyn Getty

https://youtu.be/ffvYSWDErYE

December 17

Today's Encouragement is 2 Corinthians 5:17 ESV *Therefore, if anyone is in Christ, he is a new creation. The old has passed away; behold, the new has come.*

A new creation –

In Romans 8:18-25 Paul speaks of a time when all of creation will be made new. The idyllic creation of Eden, of Genesis, is now stained, corrupted by the Sin of mankind...But Scripture tells us that God isn't finished yet! Not YET! And one day—"all creation will be set free from its visage to corruption." (Romans 8:21)

Likewise, my friends, we too, as believers in Christ, are set free from our bondage to corruption! We are already–now! New Creations!

And in the same manner, as the physical re-creation of the entire world, we, the children of God, who were once under the curse of Eden's sin, are now set free, and now are new creations (2 Corinthians 5:17) and YET... God's still not finished with us! Not YET! ...

Consider 1 John 3:2a NLT, Dear friends, we are already God's children, but he has not yet shown us what we will be like when Christ appears.

He has not yet shown us! Not YET!

What we will be like!!! When Christ appears....

Friends... there is still YET... more to come!!!

Father, we know so little now, and yet you've already revealed so much... help us to continue to Trust You today, for every tomorrow, to Trust that you aren't finished, that our story isn't over YET, and that You are still re-creating us!

"The Story's Not Over"

Jeremy Camp

https://youtu.be/0WNhsajTmFs

December 18

Today's Encouragement is Psalm 63:3-5 NIV *Because your love is better than life, my lips will glorify you. I will praise you as long as I live, and in your name I will lift up my hands. I will be fully satisfied as with the richest of foods; with singing lips my mouth will praise you.*

Better than Life –

Imagine... His Love is Better than Life! When our life seems pretty good... His Love is even better, and when our life is very, very, hard... His Love is Better! Certainly, He deserves all the honor and praise we can give him for His Immeasurable Love for us!

I always first think of praise as singing to Him. It's rather awkward to do this walking around Walmart! ... BUT... what if praising Him, "as long as I live"... meant that I also spoke about Him, His goodness to me, His love for me and all people, wherever I went... as long as I live?

What if my first and last response—to every problem I encounter—was a decision of faith, trust, and hope in His unlimited love and grace for me, and for all people? What if... as v5 states, I would then be fully satisfied, as if I'd just eaten a wonderful meal?... What if... singing His praises, and honoring him with my thoughts and words... was fully satisfying? Is it possible it would be satisfying to our Father God also?—Is it possible?

Lord God, please help me to keep Your love first in my heart and mind so that I can walk a life of praise, honor, and gratitude for who You are, for the grace You've granted me, and for Your Immeasurable Love for me.

(take a deep breath, calm your mind, and then experience this blessing)
"My Lips Will Praise You"
Twila Paris
https://youtu.be/CIwjX0SN8-k

December 19

Today's Encouragement is Exodus 14:14 NIV *"The Lord will fight for you; you need only to be still."*

The Lord will fight for you –

These were Moses' words to the people of Israel. They had just been miraculously freed from the cruel grip of Egypt by God's powerful hand through 10 devastating plagues. Each plague affected only the Egyptians... but not God's chosen people, the Egyptians' Hebrew slaves!

Now Israel was trapped, with the vast Red Sea before them and the furious and powerful Egyptian army behind. Untrained, unwilling, and unprepared for battle they cried out, "We were better off as slaves!" Read this beautiful story of God's deliverance in Exodus 14.

Lord, please help us remember how You have miraculously stepped in and rescued Your people in the past, and help us to trust that You will do so again... for each of us! Help us to rest in the peace that—You will fight for us!

"Red Sea Road"
Ellie Holcomb
https://youtu.be/pvDmrsqTdjg

December 20

Today's Encouragement is Ezekiel 3:11 NLT *"Then go to your people in exile and say to them, 'This is what the Sovereign Lord says!' Do this whether they listen to you or not."*

Say to them –

This world is a fallen place. People generally have no ears to hear, no eyes to see—the Love of God as revealed through Jesus Christ.

The encouragement today is—to share God's Love anyway! Speak to them anyway! Whether they listen or not!

I admit this goes against my nature. I want to say, that if someone asks me, I'll be happy to tell them... but as God told Ezekiel... it is not only the open ears who need to hear the Gospel!

We can't all stand on streetcorners and preach, but in our workplace, our homes, the places we shop, and with neighbors... we can share God's Love for them and for us, in any number of ways.

We don't know, my friends, what is in their hearts, what they need, what pain or stress they may be experiencing... but God knows! And He will give you the words to say! (Exodus 4:12). Our part is to be faithful. God does the real work; we just cast the seeds. And trust Him.

Father God, please give us the boldness to share with others, the greatest gift ever given... Your Love through Christ! We ask in Jesus' Name.

"When You Speak"
VOUS Worship
https://youtu.be/dXgpUyt6KoQ

December 21

Today's Encouragement is Acts 4:12 NLT *There is salvation in no one else! God has given no other name under heaven by which we must be saved.*

No other name –

The "Name" is the manner or mechanism of salvation... we have life in His Name. (John 20:31)

The Name was determined by God, revealed to Joseph; (Matt. 1:21) ...it wasn't randomly chosen.

His Name holds the power! *"Yes, ask me for anything in my name, and I will do it!"* (John 14:14 NLT)

His Name is above every other! *...Therefore, God elevated him to the place of highest honor and gave him the name above all other names.* (Philippians 2:9 NLT)

At His name, everyone and every living creature should bow... *that at the name of Jesus, every knee should bow, in heaven and on earth and under the earth,* (Philippians 2:10 NLT)

What a gift! What a treasure! What a privilege we have! We know His Name!!! We are His brothers and sisters! We are His friends!

And, my friends, there is no other Name!!!

Father God, open our eyes and hearts to the wonder, glory, and power of The Name of Jesus.

"There's No Other Name"
Francesca Battistelli
https://youtu.be/PYin2dCzVKg

December 22

Today's Encouragement is Isaiah 9:6 ESV *For to us a child is born, to us a son is given; and the government shall be upon his shoulder, and his name shall be called Wonderful Counselor, Mighty God, Everlasting Father, Prince of Peace.*

A Child is Born –

Ever think about why are there so many names used for Jesus? Because no one name can describe Him.

There is one name, which is special to me, though each one carries such depth... and that is Immanuel. It means, God-with-Us. The perfect name for the Son of God, who was born, lived, died, and returned to life on this earth 2000 years ago. He's just as present today, living within His Children–you, and me–as He was then. His comforting presence and His unlimited Grace are just as abundant and clear.

Father God, thank You for Jesus, ...for Your beautiful plan, Your indescribable gift, —Your undeserved mercy, grace, and Your perfect Love—extended freely to all who accept it, through our Savior, Your Son, Jesus—Immanuel—God with us.

"Immanuel"
Michael Card
https://youtu.be/mrmMQdkBPwY

December 23

Today's Encouragement is John 1:4-5 ESV *In him was life, and the life was the light of men. The light shines in the darkness, and the darkness has not overcome it.*

The Light Shines –

In this monumental introduction to the book written by John... We see the amazing revelation of Jesus.

Too rich for a brief description, but notice... He Was in the beginning, (v1) both with God and God. He created all things (v2). Repeated for clarity(v3) ... all things!

In Him was Life (v4) and the life was the Light of men. And today's focus...The Light Shines.

Notice carefully, friends, the change in tense, John changed from the past tense describing Jesus as the Word... to the Present tense! Even Now...

The light shines and the darkness is defeated... It's Him, not our light, but His...

Yet we bear His likeness, He even said that we are the Light of the world (Matthew 5:14). And this Light of Christ within us is all-powerful, my friends! No darkness can overcome His Light within us or without us, His Light overcomes all of the darkness of this world.

We need no convincing of the darkness within us and without us... it's so painfully clear. Yet His power, His Light, His Spirit dwelling within us... is invincible! No darkness shall overcome His Light!

Encouragement, Reassurance, Confidence, Affirmation, Faith, Hope, Courage, Boldness, and Strength are all maximized when we behold Him as He is! The Light! Of men, Of the World, of the Universe, of all Time, of all Life!

Father God, Your gift to us, to this world, is so vast, far beyond our full comprehension... and what we do comprehend, we often fail to live up to. Yet, You have grace for our frailty... Help us to "live as people of light"! (Ephesians 5:8b)

"Adore"

Graham Kendrick

https://youtu.be/faI0XCnSUO8

December 24

Today's Encouragement is Luke 2:8-11 NLT *That night there were shepherds staying in the fields nearby, guarding their flocks of sheep. Suddenly, an angel of the Lord appeared among them, and the radiance of the Lord's glory surrounded them. They were terrified, but the angel reassured them. "Don't be afraid!" he said. "I bring you good news that will bring great joy to all people. The Savior—yes, the Messiah, the Lord—has been born today in Bethlehem, the city of David.*

Good News of Great Joy –

These men were just minding their own business, watching over their sheep, as they had always done.

But one night, one life-transforming, unbelievable night, An angel...!

An angel appears with a message about a baby being born... and suddenly –

- the still darkness of night
- was transformed into brilliant day
- as innumerable angels appeared and
- proclaimed in deafening awe...

"Glory to God in the Highest!"

Luke 2:13-14 (NLT) *Suddenly, the angel was joined by a vast host of others—the armies of heaven—praising God and saying, "Glory to God in highest heaven, and peace on earth to those with whom God is pleased."*

Did you see it? The armies of heaven! Just imagine this for a moment! Selah.

Such is the impact of this one life upon all humanity, upon all eternity. Our routine existence – interrupted by the Divine – and transformed – into Glorious Light!

Can you imagine?

Wonderful Father, help us to see, with fresh eyes, as these shepherds did... the armies of heaven, in glorious song, in brilliant light, rejoicing without reservation, the birth of our Savior Jesus. May we be filled with awe, as they were... at the life-transforming arrival of God in flesh, Immanuel – God-with-us!

"Noel"

Lauren Daigle

https://youtu.be/jGg7KdN19rs

December 25

Today's Encouragement is Luke 2:13-14 NLT *"Suddenly, the angel was joined by a vast host of others-the armies of heaven-praising God and saying, 'Glory to God in highest heaven, and peace on earth to those with whom God is pleased.'"*

A Vast Host –

Imagine with me, the still of a desert night, watching your sheep, as you've done for countless nights... complete silence except maybe a few bleating sheep,

Then—Suddenly —

An angel appears in brilliance! And announces (v10) *"I bring you Good news of Great Joy... The Savior, The Messiah is born!"*

And that's not all...

Suddenly—as if heaven cannot contain its Joy!!! The armies of Heaven also appear in Glorious, unimaginable Praise to God!!!

You ask Why? Why such unique rejoicing from Heaven to Earth?

Because, my friends, with this moment, the Gift of Jesus begins! Now, God changed everything!

Now, a new Era of time, of hope, of human relationship with God is born!

Now, all of humanity has the opportunity for eternal salvation! ...simply by faith in Him! As if Creation was reborn... Everything Changed.

Never before my friends; never since.

As if Heaven could not contain...

... its Joy!

Just consider for a moment, as you watch and listen and become swept up in this wonderful "heavenly music"... If humans can voice such beautiful glory to God... what must the Vast Host of the Armies of Heaven sound like?

Father, no words or music from this life can do You justice! Yet we do our best and praise You as best we can. May our worship bring You joy.

"Hallelujah Chorus"

A 'Flash mob'

https://youtu.be/SXh7JR9oKVE

December 26

Today's Encouragement is Luke 2:28-30 NLT *Simeon was there. He took the child in his arms and praised God, saying, "Sovereign Lord, now let your servant die in peace, as you have promised. I have seen your salvation."*

As You have promised –

God had promised Simeon (v26) that he wouldn't die before he saw the Messiah. So, on the day of his dedication, 8 days after the birth, the infant Jesus is brought to the temple, and the Holy Spirit brought Simeon (v27)!

Simeon (v28) took the child in his arms and praised God... "Now, Lord, I can die a happy, peaceful man because... just like you promised me... my eyes have seen Your salvation!"

Can you imagine... this aged gentleman, who for years had held on to this promise of God... Now holds the completion of that promise!

And we today, hold in our hearts, the completion of all God's promises... Jesus.

Our Messiah, the Lord of lords, King of kings... the final Word! We need nothing else! Just like Simeon, we are completed by His presence.

Father God, You are always faithful to Your promises, You are always faithful to us! Grant us also this gift... that we will remain faithful to You, for all our days. We ask in Jesus' Name!

"Faithful to the End"
Bethel Music
https://youtu.be/5YP_5gjdxGY

December 27

Today's Encouragement is 1 Corinthians 1:27 ESV *But God chose what is foolish in the world to shame the wise; God chose what is weak in the world to shame the strong.*

But God chose –

You and I may be, or feel like, "a nobody" in this world, my friends. Foolish and weak "in the world."

But look at this list of "nobodies" that God chose to use to announce the arrival of the Savior of the World!

- Mary, an unwed teenage girl from a tiny town, visited by an angel.

- Unnamed shepherds who witnessed the utmost Heavenly angelic concert!

- Aged Simeon (and Anna next) whose life was fulfilled at God's promise fulfilled... simply by holding this infant Jesus...

Just as He had done many times before:

- God used a donkey to speak to Balaam (Numbers 22:28)

- He used a stammering reluctant sheepherder to deliver an entire nation from slavery. (Exodus 4:10)

- He used a shepherd boy to destroy the ruthless giant (1 Sam 17:49)

The examples are everywhere in our book...
God uses ordinary, foolish, weak, people and things... For His purposes!
To shame, to silence, to shut the mouths of the strong and powerful!
Ordinary... like you and me!
This is whom God chooses—whom He uses!
Father God, thank You for coming to us, ordinary people, with the Good News of Your Love and Mercy and Grace for all who will believe in You!
"Who Am I"
Casting Crowns
https://youtu.be/3rT8Re1EIQc

December 28

Today's Encouragement is Acts 4:13 NLT *The members of the council were amazed when they saw the boldness of Peter and John, for they could see that they were ordinary men with no special training in the Scriptures. They also recognized them as men who had been with Jesus.*

They were ordinary men –

Wait, aren't we talking about the great disciples of Christ, Peter, and John? They lived with Him for years, heard and saw Him preach with their own eyes, and witnessed miracle after miracle! Weren't they holy? Perfect? Floating-on-a-cloud-Apostles-of-Jesus?

Uh,... No! My friends, they were still—ordinary. Except in this way: They had ... Been with Jesus!

When we have "been with Jesus"... all bets are off! Everything is different! We cannot help but be transformed as we spend time in His presence!

Today, as we open His Word and hear His voice in the Word, He will speak to us through His Word, as we are able to hear. We spend time with Him in prayer, (listening more than speaking please!)

Do you want to be like Peter and John... an ordinary person who has been with Jesus?

Thank You, our Wonderful Father, for giving us the opportunity to Be With Jesus today. Help us to determine to make the time, and to take full advantage of every opportunity to ...Be With Jesus.

"Nobody"
Casting Crowns
https://youtu.be/rOooelyA9Ws

December 29

Today's Encouragement is Hosea 6:6 ESV *For I desire steadfast love and not sacrifice, the knowledge of God rather than burnt offerings.*

For I desire –

Ever ask yourself?... Or if you're really bold, ...ever ask God...? What does God want? What is God's desire?

Like me, you probably will not. And why? Because we aren't giving any (or very little) thought to Him!—To His perspective; To His desires. We are totally focused on our own wants, desires, and needs. To be fair, some of us focus on the wants of others, also. We then set about striving to achieve and accomplish these things, our desires, with all our might.

My friends, it's good to have goals and desires. It's good to strive to meet these. But if we've placed our efforts on anything counter to, or instead of, the desire of our God and Father... it is ultimately futile.

For God tells us clearly what He desires: "steadfast love... and the knowledge of God" and "not sacrifice..."

Wouldn't it be a good idea to focus on what God desires?

Father, help us to consider Your heart, Your desires, Your plans, and purposes and not exclusively operate from our own desires!

(This beautiful worship song focuses on our desire, not God's. Sadly, I couldn't find one which is focused on what God desires!)

"One Desire"

Hillsong

https://youtu.be/tG3HDRKK2Vc

December 30

Today's Encouragement is Galatians 5:22-23a NLT *But the Holy Spirit produces this kind of fruit in our lives: love, joy, peace, patience, kindness, goodness, faithfulness, gentleness, and self-control.*

This kind of fruit –

Notice it is the work of the Holy Spirit, to produce fruit, over time, (fruit takes time to develop) and in the lives of mature believers (fruit does not come from immature trees!)

This is a process, my friends:

Gods Spirit...

Works within us to produce...

The mature ripened fruit of these attributes of God...

His Love, His joy, His peace, His patience, His kindness, His goodness, His faithfulness, His gentleness, and His self-control.

From the presence of His Holy Spirit living within us, working within us, to produce... Evidence of His Presence... The Fruits of His Spirit!

Don't see this fruit in your life? There are two possible reasons:

1. It just hasn't been enough time. Fruit comes from mature trees, it takes time.
2. Another possibility is that the Holy Spirit (the Tree in this analogy) within you isn't properly acknowledged and nurtured. Trees need sunlight, water, and nutrients from the soil. These are spiritual—our devotion, listening to God, worship, our relationship with Him. Relationships between people (including us and God) can be weak or strong, based on the attention we give that relationship.

It's God's work! Yet, we must do our part, which is nurturing our relationship with His Spirit.

Father, as You work within us, by Your Holy Spirit, help us to nurture our relationship with You, to accept, to remain willing to be transformed by Your work within us!

"Fruits of the Spirit "
Hillsong Young and Free
https://youtu.be/bOaN1NXJsXY?t=57

December 31

Today's Encouragement is Genesis 6:9b NLT *Noah was a righteous man, the only blameless person living on earth at the time, and he walked in close fellowship with God.*

Fellowship With God –

Several people in the Bible were described as having a close relationship with God.

Adam, Enoch, Noah, Moses, David, and many others in the Old Testament. But, in the New Testament, when Jesus lived on earth, a new type of relationship with God was revealed! And all His disciples had the opportunity to walk in close fellowship with Him... Yet, James, Peter, and John are most often mentioned as the closest to Him.

And today, after His death and resurrection, we now have a perpetual relationship with God, the Father, Jesus the Son, and the Holy Spirit. 2 Corinthians 13:14 NLT *May the grace of the Lord Jesus Christ, the love of God, and the fellowship of the Holy Spirit be with you all.* The Fellowship...

Friends, we all have a variety of relationships, our families, spouses, friends, and co-workers... some relationships are close and precious to us, and some, not so much. Some end and some new relationships emerge. For relationships to grow, there are a few essentials: time together, communication, patience, forgiveness, understanding... and these cause relationships to become close, important, and even precious...

Why? Because God created humankind to need relationships! With others, but most importantly... with Him!

And we all have access to Him... and it is up to us to determine the degree of closeness of this all-important relationship. We are saved by His Grace, and He now lives within us... the depth of this relationship (and nothing else really matters my friend...) is up to us!

Father God, we long for a close and growing relationship with You! First, because You are God, Creator and King, Lord of all and the most excellent, beautiful, powerful, and glorious One of all... and You are our perfect, loving Father! And because we have this need within us to be in fellowship with You! As You designed us... to walk with You in the Garden... Now through Jesus' Grace, we are restored to the sinlessness of Adam and we long to walk with You.

"Walk with You"
Zach Williams
https://youtu.be/rM9u9y5OHuw

I'd love to hear from you! Feel free to contact me at rdefoore@gmail.com to discuss, question, debate, or clarify any of these devotional messages or other matters of faith. I will also be honored to support your prayers with mine, praying with you (not only for you) as you ask God to direct your paths.

9 798223 700654